Gay Fandom and Crossover Stardom

Gay Fandom and

Duke University Press Durham & London 2001

Crossover Stardom

James Dean, Mel Gibson, and Keanu Reeves

MICHAEL DeANGELIS

© 2001 Duke University Press
All rights reserved
Printed in the United States of
America on acid-free paper ∞
Typeset in Janson by Tseng
Information Systems, Inc.
Library of Congress Cataloging-
in-Publication Data appear on the
last printed page of this book.

FOR ANDREW

Contents

Acknowledgments

$\mathscr{W}$riting the history of the reception practices of a subculture that remained largely invisible until recent decades is a challenging assignment, especially considering that most of the documents that appear in gay publications remain unindexed. I am therefore grateful for the services and cooperation of outstanding research facilities at the University of Texas at Austin and Northwestern University. The knowledgeable archivists at The Margaret Herrick Library and the Warner Bros. Archives made my all too brief research visit to Los Angeles enormously productive. The librarians at the Canadian Lesbian and Gay Archives in Toronto and Chicago's Gerber Hart Library were welcoming, accommodating, and supportive. I also thank the Fairmount Historical Society, whose proprietors were kind enough to open the doors of its museum on a snowy December morning.

Portions of chapter 4 have appeared in an anthology on youth culture published by Toronto's Media Studies Working Group and edited by Murray Pomerance. In addition to being a discerning editor and accomplished scholar, Murray has also become a good friend whose enthusiasm has carried me through many difficult times.

Several friends and colleagues devoted considerable time in reading draft versions of this book. Janet Staiger offered invaluable commentary throughout this project, and I consider myself very fortunate to have been given the opportunity to work with a scholar of such distinction. My interest in this study began in 1994, when I was enrolled in Mary Desjardins' stimulating and challenging seminars in Theory of Melodrama and Stars and Fan Culture at the University of Texas. Mary continues to be an inspiration to me. Sabrina Barton, Tom Schatz, and Gigi Durham offered attentive readings, and the commentary of Alex Doty, Margaret Goscilo, and Milena Banks on the Mel Gibson chapter was immensely useful. Constance Penley remained close to my heart throughout this project. My DePaul colleagues Susan McGury, Marisa Alicea, and Susanne Dumbleton offered both emotional and intellectual support. I am deeply indebted to Ken Wissoker, Katie Courtland, and the anonymous readers at Duke University Press for their insightful commentary, guidance, integrity, and patience.

Stimulating discussions with my friends and colleagues Walter Metz, Antonio LaPastina, Adriana Olivarez, Christina Lane, Susan Murray, Alison Macor, Megan Mullen, and Anne Morey were invaluable in helping me to maintain focus and momentum. Conversations with students in my film classes at the University of Texas and DePaul University proved to be enlightening in unpredicted ways, and I thank especially Laura Jones, Michael Cimo, Steven Wilson, and Eugenia Williams. I am also grateful for the encouragement of Carol Coopersmith, John Westby, and Peter Forster. Special thanks to my family and especially to my sister Patty, who never doubted my abilities, even when I was not so sure. My dear friend Patrick Savage helped me to imagine this book before I started writing it. I wish he were here now to see the finished product.

Finally, and most emphatically, I thank Andrew Ramos, without whose love and support I might never have developed the courage to pursue my dreams. For more than fifteen years, this warm, caring, and wonderful man has shown me what it means to know a place called home, and I have held this place in my heart even when hundreds of miles have separated us. I look forward to the years ahead with my partner for life.

*A*lone one night in the summer of 1982, at a local multiplex in Urbana, Illinois, I saw *The Road Warrior* for the first time, not out of any interest in its postapocalyptic setting or its themes, but because I was so drawn to the man in torn, black leather featured prominently in the newspaper ads. I didn't really know or care that he was Mel Gibson — he wasn't yet a household word in America — but with his strong and solid frame, his grave and intense features, and his tender, piercing eyes, this towering figure embodied an ideal version of the man who had dominated my attention for the past two years — a man (let's call him George) with whom I had developed an almost eerily subtle, acute, intuitive form of communication, first at the local gay bar where he would dance alone (by choice), and later just about everywhere (the place never mattered). Many friends commented upon the powerful "energy" that George and I generated whenever we were together, which was just about all the time. I couldn't deny this. The dynamic was so intense that at times, for me, it verged on obsession. For months, I went to bed thinking about George, and I woke up with the same person in mind.

In mind *only*. We never spent the night together. Of course I was very much open to the possibility, and for days on end I would think of little else. I wasn't diverted even after acknowledging that more and more of our conversations were centering upon his attraction to women. After weeks of rehearsing and agonizing over a confession scene, one night I forced myself to "bring the moment to its crisis" and reveal to George my attraction. The joy of this instant release was immediately disrupted by a pause that felt interminable, followed by three cutting words: "I can't reciprocate."

As strong as my desire had been, my elaborate fantasies of George had never featured any scenes in which the "correct" response to my confession was his "coming out" and realizing that I, and only I, had finally enlightened him to the joys of a same-sex sexual relationship. While I was certainly hurt, I wasn't very surprised by George's response. My feelings ran much deeper than rejection, and in the days that followed my confession, I felt overcome by a profound sense of loss. George was still there, and from his perspective, at least, nothing had changed in our interactions. I, however, had changed: I found myself less "present" in our conversations, less excited about the next time I would see him. Soon enough, I caught myself making up excuses to avoid him, not out of anger or spite, but because in a very real and inescapable way, something felt dead in me.

What had I wanted from George? What exactly had I lost? It wasn't until that night at the multiplex, with no more than three or four others in the audience, that I began to consider these questions. Disguised as Mel Gibson, the screen version of George revealed very little about himself, his pain, or his joy in the course of this one-hundred-minute narrative. His attraction resonated in what he did not say, through what he disclosed only through subtle facial expressions and his limping gait, in what he allowed me to *imagine* that he was feeling as he roamed the desolate landscape of a barren, cruel world with his Dog. Mad Max appeared to me as the most erotic of human creatures, not least because his sexuality appeared boundless and undefined by any specific acts meant to confirm that he was ultimately "straight" or "gay." The film not only allowed my desire to remain active and creative, it encouraged it, even after the closing sequence, in which the Feral Kid admits his own continued fascination before the image of the receding hero who "lives on, only in my dreams."

I left the theater that night feeling inspired, affirmed, and aware that what I had just felt through Max corresponded to what I had lost with George: the "energy" that my friends had noticed, the beacon of energy signaling the presence of desire—a sexual attraction certainly, but also a sense of connection that was indifferent to limits. So intoxicating when I had hovered on the brink of erotic prospect, my thoughts of George were now plagued by the barrier of the resonant and definitive "no," but Max had become a wholly accepting and receptive entity, confined though he was to the realm of fantasy, accessible yet entirely freed from the burden of attainability.

Certainly this was a peculiar admission, and while I was initially tempted to frame it in pathological terms, it didn't strike me as some ultimate sign that fictional characters had become more interesting to me than real people, or that I would now dedicate myself exclusively to impossible relationships (whether with people or fictional constructs). Contrasting with my troubled perception of George, rather, my connection with Max was very much about *possibility*, empowerment, intimacy, and the potential to permit my feelings to emerge and reveal themselves unchecked—a potential that was (and often still is) easier for me to maintain through the "spectator/character" dynamic of cinema than in interpersonal relations.

Since 1982, my experience in that theater with Mad Max has frequently recurred with other male actors, but its familiarity does not prevent it from feeling like a new and exciting encounter each time it happens. It is quite "personal" in the way that any intense emotional response must be, yet it also involves complex psychological, social, and political dynamics that have remained unexplored in most discussions of the relationship between gay viewers and Hollywood stars—discussions that almost inevitably center upon the concept of *camp*. Clearly, the full range of potential and actual practices that gay men have used to inspire and empower themselves through star reception cannot be solely attributed to the camp phenomenon. First, unlike the immediacy of the emotional dynamic I have just described, the empowering aspects of camp, as Andrew Ross clarifies, are based on a temporal disjunction, in which "the products . . . of a much earlier mode of production, which has lost its power to dominate cultural meanings, become available, in the present, for redefinition according to contemporary modes of taste."[1] Second—in gay male audience studies, at least—camp traces an investment of affect across gender lines, articulating how and why gay men respond in specific ways to

Hollywood *actresses*. Third, camp operates primarily as a phenomenon of identification. Accordingly, Richard Dyer and Janet Staiger explain the importance of Judy Garland's persona to gay men in the 1950s and 1960s on the basis of a perceived likeness: the actress and the gay subculture shared an outsider status to which they mutually responded with resilience and perseverance.[2] Even camp's interrogation of boundaries between socially defined gender roles has been conducted within the realm of "an identification with women as emotional subjects in a world in which men 'acted' and women 'felt.'"[3]

Moving star-audience relations beyond the realm of camp, this work examines the historical production of three *male* Hollywood star personas—James Dean, Mel Gibson, and Keanu Reeves—and the reception strategies that gay men have used to structure their relations with these stars. Examination of the components of Hollywood star discourse (promotional, publicity, critical, and narrative) in the context of psychological, medical, legal, and academic discourse from the early 1950s to the present further allows for an exploration of the operations of "crossover" appeal, in which a star's popularity with "straight" audiences also accommodates a strong gay male following. This crossover appeal is sometimes, though not always, the result of a gay subculture's subversive practices. Certainly, gay male audiences have engaged in what Stuart Hall describes as "resistant" and "oppositional" readings in appropriating these popular cultural icons.[4] Quite often in the last fifty years of American film history, however, studios, public relations firms, and even the stars themselves have promoted crossover appeal—often, paradoxically, at the same time that they maintain an interest in keeping star images strictly heterosexual. As will be seen, the potential for such crossover appeal arises from historical moments of crisis in dominant constructions of American masculinity; in response to these crises, ever conscious of profit margins, the Hollywood film industry has often been quite strategic in allowing for star appeal across the often blurry lines of sexual orientation. Not only do such moments of crisis invite us to rethink the relationship between the "mainstream" and the "marginal" in American culture, but they also provide gay men and emerging gay subcultures with a means of empowering themselves.

The greater network of star texts functions as a fantasy scenario, one that permits spectators and fans to access the star persona emotionally and sexually, on the requisite condition that certain ambiguities in the star's textual and discursive constructions are maintained. Ambiguity enables both self-defined straight and gay spectators to access and negotiate star personas through texts and discourses that operate as fantasy. As Elizabeth Cowie explains, fantasy allows spectators to participate in scenes of desire. The pleasure of fantasy does not depend on actually attaining the desired object; instead, it involves a "happening and continuing to happen" that sustains pleasure by keeping the viewer *engaged* in a scene of desire.[5] Ambiguous star texts accommodate such fantasy engagement, yielding pleasure not only by permitting spectators to stage scenes tailored to their own specific needs, but also by promoting the drama of overcoming obstacles to fulfillment, which Cowie describes as "the making visible, present, of what isn't there, of what can never *directly* be seen" (127–28, emphasis in the original). Certainly, the star's own sexual orientation presents one obstacle that gay male audiences must confront in fantasy relations, yet fantasy does not require the viewer to determine the star's ultimate sexual orientation; it requires only that the viewer remain engaged in the *process* of negotiating identities and overcoming obstacles.

The structure and operations of melodrama can help us to understand how such fantasies empower disenfranchised subcultures to "claim" popular cultural icons. Christine Gledhill makes a crucial connection between melodrama and the cultural function of stars, arguing that the "star" becomes an important figure in the classic moral struggle between good and evil. Strategically eliciting the "truth" and "meaning" central to melodrama since its earliest manifestations, stars carry the burden of representing "clearly articulated personal identities," yet this burden requires audiences to struggle to negotiate, and to attempt to resolve, the ambiguities and contradictions presented in the various texts that construct stars.[6] Extending this notion of burden, Richard Dyer suggests that stars "represent what are taken to be people typical of this society; yet the types of people we assume characterise our society may be singularly absent from our actual day-to-day experience of society."[7]

What forms do these negotiations and struggles take in the dynamic relationship between audiences and stars? To answer this question, it is important to emphasize—as Linda Williams does in her fascinating work on the "body" genres—that melodrama is a highly *participatory* genre structured around the concept of loss, and motivated by a desire to avoid or overcome such loss.[8] Williams argues that melodrama enacts a "fantasy of the origin of self" in which the subject attempts to gain back the loss of her/his origin, to reclaim a state of wholeness, through an impossible return to "an earlier state most fundamentally represented by the body of the mother." This return to origin may involve the audience's desire to witness the union of two protagonists separated through the course of fate, a "utopian desire that it not be too late to remerge with the other who was once part of the self."[9] Steve Neale describes this struggle for a return to origin as "a fantasy of oneness, therefore total and effortless communication and mutual understanding," thus marking a desire for connectedness.[10] Melodramatic narratives present protagonists with a series of obstacles that frustrate these attempts to reconnect and reunite. The genre's narrative strategy involves a hierarchy of knowledge and point-of-view, in which audiences are provided with crucial narrative information that remains withheld from the characters. Neale notes that this hierarchy causes the audience to feel helpless — "if only they knew what I know" — and to fear that the imbalance will remain unresolved or that it will be corrected too late for the characters to intervene in their own fate.

Both because and in spite of such feelings of helplessness, the audience of melodrama plays a crucial role in discovering truth, meaning, and order within the narrative, and the dynamic between protagonist(s) and audience is centered upon notions of emergence and redemption. In the struggle to reconnect, the protagonist is always in the process of either emerging as an emblem of truth and meaning, or redeeming herself/himself by rectifying past mistakes; correlatively, the audience's investment of emotion requires that it maintain the ability to participate in these processes of emergence and redemption. As we will discover, reconnection and reunion may operate between characters within a given narrative, and between the protagonist and the audience, since the audience's affective investment in the protagonist's struggle is also an attempt to forge and maintain a connection with this protagonist.

The fact that an ultimate return is impossible (for the protagonist or the witnessing audience) poses no definitive obstacle in the realm of fantasy. What remains crucial is the continuous dynamic — offered by melodrama and the notion of genre itself, with its emphasis on formulas and repetitions—that allows the audience to keep experiencing the pleasure of working through a problem. In fact, the impossibility of ultimate resolution helps to explain how the melodramatic mode can be extended, as Gledhill and Mary Desjardins suggest, from a structure that operates within a single narrative to a dynamic that engages the audience's emotions over time—one that involves individual films as well as the intertextual star discourse that promotion, publicity, and critical documents offer.[11] Also, as a structuring principle of narrative and narration, melodrama exceeds the boundaries of any specific genre. Indeed, as we will see, narratives that center upon the threat of loss, that invite their protagonists to emerge and redeem themselves, and that dramatize reconnection and return to origin, replay the structure of the melodramatic fantasy not only in the classic "family melodrama," but also in such diverse genres as the detective thriller, the action-adventure film, and the buddy film.

In all cases, if an audience's interest in fantasy remains pleasurable only to the extent that ultimate resolutions are deferred, film studios and public relations agencies maintain a significant economic investment in extending the star's process of emergence and redemption by withholding and disclosing information over the course of a career. Within and across film narratives, the audience's continued emotional investment in the star figure, and the star's continued accessibility to the desires of spectators across the lines of sexual orientation, depend on maintaining the star's ambiguity by perpetually deferring the disclosure of an emerging "truth" that ultimately centers on the star's sexuality.

By focusing this examination of melodramatic emergence and redemption on James Dean, Mel Gibson, and Keanu Reeves, we can begin to appreciate several aspects of the complex dynamic between gay male audiences and Hollywood stars across history. First, it allows us to trace the historical shifts in agency and control over the construction of male sexuality. Despite the fact that James Dean worked in an era when studios purported to hold close control over the construction and circulation of accessibly heterosexual star images, his premature death paradoxically secures his ability to emerge perpetually, for decades to come, as a figure whose ambiguity and rebellion extend to the realm of sexuality. In the absence of additional film roles, the postmortem Dean becomes yet more susceptible to multiple readings of what, and who, he was and might have been had there been no fatal car crash. Agency and control over the star image shift from the realm of production to reception, and with the increasing empowerment of a gay community that becomes more visible and vocal after the 1950s, Dean is transformed into a "gay icon" by the early 1970s.

Mel Gibson's career traces a reverse trajectory of emergence. He attains popularity in the United States in the late 1970s and early 1980s, a time when sexual ambiguity of celebrity figures was being exploited (both ostensibly and overtly) for its potential to reach a wide variety of target markets, including gay consumers. Gibson initially did little to controvert the wide accessibility that the press attributed to him, yet over the next ten years, through his increasingly vocalized antigay conservatism in an era that supported his political beliefs, the process of his sexual emergence stabilized into the most unambiguous identity of the quintessentially heterosexual family man — one which a yet more politically active gay subculture largely began to perceive as hypocritical. Certainly, other Hollywood stars of the 1990s besides Keanu Reeves have benefited from a social and political climate in which undefined and ambiguous sexuality is tolerated, and indeed nurtured, as a sign of sincerity and authenticity, yet Reeves remains not only one of the most active participants in the construction of his own ambiguity, but also a figure whose perpetually emerging sexuality is most extensively deliberated and celebrated in public forums and new technologies that the gay subculture has used to speak its own diverse desires.

The melodramatic mode also demonstrates how, across time, a star's potential to be read as gay or "gay-receptive" remains a function of gay culture's historical preferences for representing itself and for responding to these representations. James Dean's image is associated with the same rebellion and disdain for social conformity that gay discourses of the 1950s were using to describe the homosexual's position in relation to mainstream culture. For many gay men, rebellion constituted the requisite step in developing an identity resistant to the pathological definitions that social agents of control imposed on it. To rebel meant to embrace one's outsider status in order to locate others who shared this status, instead of internalizing social alienation as a personal, psychological illness. In the late 1970s and early 1980s, the most prominent version of masculinity marketed to an emerging, post-Stonewall gay community was initially the working-class "hunk" figure who was also one of the primary figures of desire in the visual discourse of physique magazines that had found a wide gay male audience before Stonewall. Although the appeal of Mel Gibson's image was tempered to reveal a physical and emotional vulnerability, his embodiment of the working-class hunk made him a most appealing figure for a sector of the gay community at that historical moment. In the 1990s, when many gay men became more outspoken and politically active in their resistance to mainstream culture's stereotypical representations of homosexual identity, Keanu Reeves's "panaccessible" image responded to the many ways in which individuals construct their own sexual identities. Transcending any definitive formulation of what a gay man "is," how he "looks," or what he "wants," Reeves embodies multiple identities that have been and continue to be appealing within and outside gay culture. He is sometimes a rebel or outsider, he can be hard and muscular, but he is never exclusively either, and he remains always capable of exceeding the constraints that any single image imposes on him.

Finally, this study uses the melodramatic mode to respond to an ongoing critical debate about the connections and distinctions between "identification" and "desire" in star/audience interactions. The debate dates back to Freud, who describes "what one would like to *be*" as "identification," and "what one would like to *have*" as "object-choice" (emphasis in the original).[12] In her discussion of lesbian identification and desire in avant-garde cinema, Teresa deLauretis argues convincingly that any mixing of these two categories confuses ego-libido and object-libido.[13] Focusing on homoerotic photography and film, Thomas Waugh is equally convincing in asserting that the power dynamic between men-as-observers and women-as-observed-objects does not necessarily apply to male-male visual exchange: "we (often) want to be, we often are the same as the man we love."[14]

Unlike the avant-garde cinema that deLauretis considers, the consumerist nature of Hollywood cinema, and of promotional and publicity-oriented star texts, *requires* an exploitation of the marketing potential inherent in this confusion of identification and object-choice, of "being" and "having" an object. As we will see, the crossover between these two psychological phenomena is strongest at those historical moments when the dominant culture acknowledges the gay subculture as a trendsetting force capable of influencing mainstream tastes, as was the case in the late 1970s and early 1980s, when the working-class hunk image became popular, or in the most recent historical period, in which sexual ambiguity has become fashionable. Equally important, we witness the most striking mixture of the two phenomena as audiences exert more control over the meaning of the star image, and when self-identified gay men empower themselves by reshaping star images through their own creative, written expressions. Accordingly, if gay men's emotional investment in rebel star figures during the 1950s seems to have been confined to the practice of identification and a recognition of likeness, this appearance is a by-product of a specific political and cultural climate, in which gay men had little access to forms of circulated written discourse where they might speak their own desires. By the early 1970s, however, a more visible and empowered gay subculture gains access to forms of expression that more clearly relate its own desires to those of the rebellious star whom they admire and emulate.

The melodramatic mode has accommodated fantasy scenarios that require identification while enabling the "scene" of same-sex desire to be imagined and visualized, even at those moments when history has not authorized the circulation of this desire in verbal or written discourse. Within the fantasies of origin that these star personas organize, identification and desire emerge from a complex dynamic involving the place of a subject in relation to an object, and the movement of the subject toward and away from this object. This psychological dynamic also has a distinct political dimension, since it involves the individual's search for a sense of place in the world, and an attempt to construct one's identity in social terms. By tracing the historical evolution of these subject/object relationships in terms of a dynamic between self and other, one can begin to turn critical debates about identification and desire in a new direction.

If gay men in the 1950s were borrowing terms from other contemporary discourses to construct a model of the social outcast that addressed their position within 1950s culture, chapter 1 shows how the narrowly circulated texts that these men produced also indicated the importance of piecemeal reassembly of prominent historical figures whose homosexuality was disavowed by the mainstream. The gay appropriation of James Dean's persona involved a negotiation of the boundaries between self and other that have informed gay identity politics throughout the postwar period. This negotiation occurs within the texts of the star's melodramatic narratives—both the family melodramas of Dean's three major films, and the noncinematic texts that accentuate the star persona's accessibility by strategically withholding and disclosing information about the actor's offscreen life. Each of these texts traces the star's progression from a state of unanchoredness toward a state of connectedness. By dramatizing the possibility of bridging the distance between the self and other, Dean is consistently placed in scenarios in which he is moving toward or away from designated fixed points. The goal or destination of the movement takes many forms, yet the movement always functions as a return to origin, to a place where the groundless hero will find redemption. The fact that the source of this redemption often becomes the body of the maternal figure, and that the journey is also a movement toward the moment of death, emphasizes the impossibility of the desired return. Indeed, death is something approached, but also avoided and deferred, to sustain pleasure, yet the rapidity of the hero's approach accentuates its urgency and the poignancy of these scenarios of motion.

This motivated movement without the promise of reaching the desired destination is enhanced by structured textual ambiguities that anticipate a moment of resolution and reconnection while suspending this moment indefinitely. There always remain details to be revealed about the star in these narratives, and especially after Dean's death, the desires of narrators who author their own stories, and of the fans who read them, continue to determine and control the "truth" and "meaning" of his life. It is through the narratives' openness to a wide range of such desires that the scenarios can accommodate multiple readings within the fantasy of traversing spaces and regulating and transcending boundaries between self and other. Such negotiations of space and time between agent and object of desire apply not only to the dynamics between Dean and the object of his search within the narrative, but also to the dynamics between the spectator and Dean. The narrative replays or "stands in" for the spectator's search, positioning Dean as the pivotal point within two dynamics that curiously transpose identification and desire. The spectator is invited to identify with Dean as he searches for his desired object; indeed, the gay spectator's choice of Dean as a figure of self-representation is often based on a likeness, a perception that Dean's unanchored rebel status mirrors the spectator's own unanchored sense of place in the world.

At the same time, within the dynamic between spectator and star, Dean becomes the desired object of the search, with the spectator regulating and negotiating the distance between himself and this object of his own desire. In fact, similar principles govern the operations of each dynamic: both rely on a difference and distance between the subject and the object of the search. While ultimate access to the object may be unattainable, the ability to *imagine* this access is what produces pleasure and sustains desire. By elaborating these scenarios, we see how a fantasy of connectedness and reunion often described as "universal" relies on a specific set of historical conditions to activate its dynamics of identification and desire. The fantasy does not equate identification with desire, but rather, it organizes a subject position within two correlated dynamics in which the locus of identification in one scenario is also the locus of desire in the other, with the spectator participating in both relations *simultaneously*.

In chapter 2, I explore how the social, political, institutional, and historical developments of the 1960s and 1970s require revisions to narrative scenarios of the melodramatic fantasy of origin. The ambiguously constructed relationship between Jim Stark (Dean) and Plato (Sal Mineo) in *Rebel Without a Cause* (1955), for example, now becomes part of a more overtly sexual scenario that plays out the master-slave dynamic. If in earlier versions the actor sought out objects of desire to substitute for his lost mother, the object of desire is now a *father* figure who replaces the biological father who "abandoned" Dean after his mother's death. These developments reposition self and other within the narratives themselves, and between the author/spectator and the star, to secure the actor's homosexuality. The distance between self and other changes: if earlier narratives configured the return to origin as ultimately unattainable, Dean now *finds* his father figure replacement, and accordingly, the star retains accessibility to the spectator. Yet even here the distance between self and other within the narrative is never fully bridged. Instead, this trajectory of the Dean figure approaching the object of desire is repeated and retraced. No single substitute for the father figure is ever sufficient to fulfill the actor's desire. He must always find others. In some cases, the subjectivity and "authoredness" of the scenarios are foregrounded, through narrators who stage scenes of desire in which they position themselves as both desiring subject and object desired, intermingling socially assigned roles of filiation in utopic reconfigurations of desire at once reciprocal and reciprocated, extending pleasure by always delaying, deferring the moment of sexual climax.

Later in the 1970s, the polarization of sameness and difference that bolstered readings of James Dean as exclusively and incontestably homosexual was replaced by a crossover relationship between the categories of "straight" and "gay" identity and culture. In chapter 3, I demonstrate how Mel Gibson's emergence as a gay or gay-receptive star is exemplary in this regard, correlated with the Hollywood film industry's recognition of the advantages of repackaging the "hypermasculine" body as an object of accessible desire. Aligned with these crossover strategies, the Gibson persona became enmeshed in a complex regulation of self and other occurring in the relationships between protagonist and desired object, as well as between spectator and star, within the melodramatic narrative. As was the case with Dean, Gibson's accessibility to gay audiences involved spatial and temporal negotiations afforded by ambiguities of the star persona. In film narratives as well as star intertexts, Gibson both advances and retreats from an object in relation to which he desires reunion or reconnection, yet the distance between self and other is never fully bridged.

Once again, these movements of advance and retreat are replayed in star/spectator relations: if the star cannot ultimately be connected to any fixed object, *as* an object he becomes susceptible to the multiple appropriations of viewing subjects. As a hero worthy of the spectator's emulation, he accommodates a position of identification based on a mutual unanchoredness. He can also assume the identity of the object for which the subject strives or yearns—an object that needs to be comforted and needs to be loved, in the world of the subject's "if only." The ambiguous construction of the star persona ensures that, for the spectator, Gibson may retain the status of other to enable the spectator's fantasy of reconnecting with this other as an object of desire. The desiring subject can be either male or female, yet for many desiring male spectators of the early 1980s, Gibson's positioning as subject and object of the search correlated with, and responded to, a historically specific manifestation of the cultural-economic phenomenon of being and having the desired object.

The increasingly conservative political climate and the repathologization of the gay male body through the AIDS crisis were to bring an era of reciprocity and crossover to an end, however, and boundaries between gay and straight became resolidified. Urged along by Gibson's own increasingly vocalized conservatism, the dynamics between identification and desire were reconfigured, and deferrals yielded to resolutions. Within film narratives and star intertexts, Gibson's persona resolved its ambiguities of movement and place, ending his search for reunion and reconnection by identifying its object as the heterosexually based nuclear family, positioned as attainable and already attained. For many gay men, this now-resolved narrative scenario offered no position of access to Gibson as a figure with which to identify. Indeed, Gibson himself reinforced the notion that gay readings of his persona were erroneous readings. At the same time, the resolution closed off his access as an object of desire, since this desire had always relied on the possibility that the distance between self and other could be traversed. The identities of (gay) self and (straight) other became more firmly fixed in their own separate domains. With this fixity — the dynamics of approach and retreat stabilized in a relationship of temporal stasis — the subject was now alienated from the removed, distanced object.

The recent crossover strategies of the 1990s have certainly been sparked by the emerging discourse of "inbetweenness" in American culture, in which definitional categories of human identity are perceived as a restrictive and false form of labeling. The discounting of such restrictions is also played out in the theories of social constructionism, which extend "inbetween" discourse for the political purpose of demonstrating the interpenetrability of exclusionary categories of human identity as a form of empowerment to disenfranchised sectors of American society who have been assembled together as the collective Other.

Chapter 4 explores the ways in which Keanu Reeves's persona reflects these developments in the history of border crossings and boundary transgressions. His appropriation by many gay men in the 1990s demonstrates an elaborate connection between the spectator's construction of the star persona and the self-imagining of human identity in same-sex relations. With Reeves, the melodramatic mode organizes a dynamic relationship between two seemingly incompatible aspects of human identity coexisting in gay culture: his persona constantly and laboriously emerges toward an "essence" and the revelation of a "true self" at the same time that any single embodiment of this essence is revealed as an artificial construction insufficient to define him.

This paradox becomes crucial to many gay men's strategies of making Reeves receptive to homosexual desire in fantasy. James Dean's struggle to attain coherence and meaning in an abruptly curtailed life echoed a similar propensity for coherence and wholeness for homosexuals in the 1950s. Mel Gibson successfully recovered the lost object of his search in the mid 1980s by reintegrating with a nuclear family construct that alienated many gay men. The progressive melodramatic narrative of Keanu Reeves, however, develops a figure whose essence is described in terms of instability and incoherence of identity. The instability itself becomes the sign of depth, prompted by the actor's ability to exceed the limitations of any single constitution of identity that individual character performances impose on him.

This malleability of the star's image bears on the relationships of self/other between protagonists within narratives, as well as between the spectator and the star. If the image of Keanu Reeves is always changing and shifting, these self/other relationships momentarily stabilize his position as both attainable and unattainable, yet always accessible, object in fantasy scenarios that organize the spectator's desire within individual texts.

Through the example of Keanu Reeves one also sees how gay spectators' creation of scenes that stabilize the morphing star persona in fantasy exceeds the boundaries established by the content of cinematic and other textual narratives in which the star appears, foregrounding the interpenetrability of fantasy and reality. New "unauthorized" fantasy scenarios are generated through rumor and gossip discourses that the subculture has used to sustain and stabilize the possibility of the "if only" of fantasy. Both mainstream tabloids and gay "dish" columns introduce these rumors as potential truths about the star's offscreen activities, yet for the subculture, whether or not such truths can be verified becomes less important than the fact that they create a place for the fan/spectator to express his own desire. Recent media forums of World Wide Web pages and on-line newsgroups permit the fan to stabilize the dynamic between self and other in fantasy scenarios of one's own design. In these scenarios, Reeves takes the position of an object of the spectator's desire, even as he becomes both a subject and object of desire within the domain of the self-tailored fantasy narrative.

While identification is based on likeness or similarity between subject and object, and desire is based on a perceived difference, the subject often participates in both operations simultaneously. The perception of likeness helps to construct a subject position for both the viewer and the narrative protagonist's entry into the fantasy scenario, offering a necessary first step for placement within a scene. At the same time, the perception of difference between self and other provides a required distance between subject and object that activates the dynamic of desire, spurring the fantasy of contracting distance and overcoming spatial boundaries. In the scenarios I will discuss, the two operations are interdependent, but this connection does not suggest that identification and desire merge at any point.[15]

While fantasy constructs may not be universal, the melodramatic fantasy of origin accommodates a wide variety of subject positions of access to identification and desire, and this helps to explain how, at various moments in history, texts and narratives address disenfranchised spectators without forfeiting their address to mainstream audiences, however these might be constituted. As will be seen, it is largely through the operations of the melodramatic mode that *Gallipoli* becomes a male love story while simultaneously serving as a more universal testament to the sorrow of human loss. The melodramatic fantasy also helps to explain how the reconfiguration of assigned roles of gender, sexuality, and filiation in *Rebel Without a Cause* can be read as both a plea for the transcendence of socially imposed differences between individuals and as an expression of homosexual desire. Finally, melodrama and fantasy make the campfire scene of *My Own Private Idaho* poignant for both self-identified gay and straight spectators who have experienced the pains of rejection in unrequited love.

This seeming universality does not suggest, however, that narrative modes and fantasy constructs erase distinctions between the variable factors of human subjecthood. Regarding the variables of gender and sexuality, Dean's persona accommodates gay, straight, male, and female subject positions because many individuals within each of these categories perceived social pressures of conforming to assigned roles as undue constraints on human individuality in the 1950s. Similarly, in the 1990s the victims of social labeling and definitional categorization have included gay men, but are not limited to any single gender or sexual orientation. For reasons that I will examine, in the late 1970s and early 1980s many straight spectators, both male and female, began to embrace the social and sexual freedoms represented by a gay subculture that responded to their own needs. Additionally, many female spectators have responded to Dean, Gibson, and Reeves because they embody a version of masculinity that is accommodating in its vulnerability rather than overly imposing or threatening. This same vulnerability also accommodates the identification of many self-defined straight males.

Despite these confluences, however, what follows will suggest the specificity of gay male subject positions. This specificity does not imply allegiance to an essentialist notion of human sexual identity that would require all gay men to find a place in the fantasies described. Clearly they do not. I mean, instead, a historically activated specificity. Without it, one could not account for the fact that at a certain historical moment, a star such as Mel Gibson addresses and accommodates the identification and/or desire of both gay and straight spectators, while later in his career this same star closes off access to sectors of his audience on the basis of their sexual orientation. This specificity arises from interdependent operations of legal, medical, social, and cultural factors at specific historical moments and across time—operations that define relationships between self and other. The specificity also emerges from the strategies that the gay subculture continues to develop to intervene in these relationships.

At the outset, it is important to delineate the parameters of the term "gay" throughout this study. The applicability of the term is necessarily limited not only by my own constitution as a self-defined gay, white, and American academic, but by the fact that two of the three stars I focus on are also white, and the intertextual star discourse of publicity, promotional, and critical documents make little attempt to move outside of white racial parameters in their modes of audience address. Even with these qualifications, frequent reference to the not very well-defined gay, white, urban "community" or "subculture" does not assume any uniformity of social practices or political beliefs. I embrace these terms for the sake of convenience to indicate potential social or cultural formations based on an element common to the members of a group, without forgetting the very real diversity of perspectives that such a group maintains.

This qualification is especially important in chapter 3, where I risk being misunderstood to suggest that gay men have been univocally opposed to Gibson's antigay stance, or that his accessibility as a fantasy figure is wholly compromised by his political pronouncements. Colleagues have pointed out that many gay men (some of them self-defined conservatives) continue to hold Gibson in high regard, despite his condemnation of homosexual practices or lifestyles. I know this to be the case as well, yet after extensively examining online newsgroups, gay publications, and dish columns, I have found virtually no written or publicly circulated examples of such a disavowal of the actor's politics. Perhaps one reason for this imbalance is that, in the newsgroups at least, gays have invested much more energy in responding defensively to self-avowed straight Gibson fans, many of whom are quite outspoken in protecting the star's sexual and political identity. I do, however, acknowledge that the choice to limit discussion of these three stars to expressions in written discourse necessarily limits its applicability, and that the transmission of oral culture among gay men warrants much further study.

Finally, by demonstrating how certain male crossover stars accommodate identification and desire within fantasy and the melodramatic mode, I hope to problematize the notion of queer readings of mainstream Hollywood films as "alternative" readings. Queerness is not something to be created or discovered in the realm of connotation, but is rather, as Alexander Doty asserts, "the result of acts of production and reception."[16] Especially in recent American popular film culture, the boundary between mainstream and alternative is wholly unstable. The star personas of Dean, Gibson, and Reeves have broadened the range of what constitutes dominant constructions of socially acceptable masculinity at specific historical moments, responding to the needs of spectators who find authorized definitions of masculinity to be either inaccessible, unattractive, or constraining, whether these spectators are men or women, straight or gay.

CHAPTER ONE

James Dean and the
Fantasy of Rebellion

*F*our book-length biographies of James Dean were published in 1974 and 1975, along with a rash of articles commemorating the twentieth anniversary of the star's death. By this time, the life story of the deceased star had already been extensively recirculated in various other forms: "one-shot" publications, series of articles in popular fan magazines, exposés in scandal magazines, biopics, and at least two other book-length biographical studies. What is particularly distinctive about this mid-1970s work is that it centered on the matter of how to determine the "truth" of the star's sexuality. Grappling with "evidence" that ranged from Dean's sexual involvement with a noted network television producer to his reputed appearance in a porno film to the pleasure of having cigarettes extinguished on his flesh in S&M bars, the 1970s biographers repeatedly asked: Was James Dean gay?

Their answers conflicted. Conceding that Dean had had sex with gay men, some argued that he did so only for survival early in his career; others posited that the star's acts marked him as bisexual. A third group asserted that Dean was incontestably and exclusively gay. A salient feature of this debate was the extent to which evidence of the star's homosexual acts necessarily constituted a homosexual identity.

The debate took place in the first public forum about male sexuality in a Hollywood star in which the voices of self-identified gay men (as well as men who openly acknowledged that they had engaged in homosexual acts, but refrained from identifying themselves as gay) provided themselves with an opportunity to speak and be heard.

Conducted approximately five years after the Stonewall incident in 1969, this public negotiation of a deceased star's sexuality drew its rhetoric from a gay liberation movement in which, as John d'Emilio suggests, "coming out" had begun to be considered as an act of personal affirmation as well as political responsibility.[1] The emergence of the "homosexual Dean" thus coincided historically with the public emergence of a subculture that had become eminently more visible and vocal by the mid-1970s than it had been twenty years earlier during Dean's brief career as a film actor. Yet the potential for gay male spectators to affiliate this star with homosexual practice or identity had existed since the mid-1950s. The fact that such an affiliation was not widely documented in the 1950s, but became prevalent by the 1970s attests to a set of shifting power relations in the public discourse of homosexuality during this span of more than twenty years. In examining the historical reception of a popular male actor working in the Hollywood studio system, the power relations of homosexual discourse are inextricably linked to another shifting set of differential power relations in star discourse. In this set of relations, the ways that audiences receive, interpret, and appropriate the sexuality of star images—in narrative and non-narrative forms—involves the ways in which various agencies authorize the representation of sexuality.

The present chapter elucidates the ways in which social, legal, and political agencies regulated the discourse of homosexuality in the 1950s, the Hollywood film industry's response to this system of regulation, and the strategies that gay men used to intervene in the constructions of personal, social, and sexual identity that were imposed on them. By relating the extratextual discourse of rebellion to the fantasy operations that became accessible to gay men in their relations to Hollywood stars, and evaluating James Dean's three primary film roles in terms of these fantasy operations, I show how queer readings of Dean emerge as imaginable reception strategies as early as the 1950s, while the star persona continued to resonate as an accessible and highly popular figure for self-defined heterosexual audiences. Chapter 2 then proceeds to examine the development of these reception strategies over time, tracing the complex historical emergence of the homosexual Dean.

In a 1957 article for *New Republic*, Sam Astrachan analyzes the appeal of two of the most prominent members of "The New Lost Generation," Marlon Brando and James Dean. Whereas Astrachan reveals a certain scorn and disdain for the aimlessness of both figures, he concedes that he is willing to "sympathize" with Brando, because of both the actor's considerable talents and the moral capacities he demonstrates through his character portrayals. In reference to Brando's role of the alienated, leather-clad, motorcycle gang leader in *The Wild One* (1954), the author observes that "there is a right and a wrong, and it is only when Brando sees that he has been wrong that there is any hope for him." [2] The widespread appeal of Dean's onscreen and offscreen personas is more disconcerting for Astrachan: "In each of the Dean roles, the distinguishing elements are the absence of his knowing who he is, and what is right and wrong. Dean is always mixed-up and it is this that has made him so susceptible to teen-age adulation. . . . In James Dean, his movie roles, his life and death, there is a general lack of identity."

The observation that Dean embodies the alienated rebel hero with whom confused adolescents could readily identify is typical of critical evaluations of his persona in the mid-1950s. The more curious and unique aspect of Astrachan's analysis occurs later in the article, when he suggests that Dean's directionlessness is symptomatic of a larger trend of alienated figures in contemporary fiction who demonstrate a similar lack of personal or social commitment. Citing the recent examples of Saul Bellow's *Seize the Day*, Herbert Gold's *The Man Who Was Not With It*, and James Baldwin's *Giovanni's Room*, Astrachan observes that "without any change in expression, James Dean could have played Gold's carnival peace-time enlistee, and Baldwin's quasi-homosexual (we will leave Bellow's Tommy Wilhelm for the more mature talents of Marlon Brando). . . . The lack of identity that exists in James Dean also exists in the characters of these three authors. Baldwin, unable to finally commit his character to homosexuality, leaves him on a foreign shore unsure even of his sexual nature" (17). The actor's ability to portray these roles convincingly is thus figured not as a sign of the range of his acting talents, but rather as evidence of a homology between Dean the biographical figure and the characters of the novels: in both cases, there is a troubling indeterminacy of character and the lack of a core identity. Moreover, committing oneself to a distinctive social and sexual identity becomes a personal and social responsibility well within the range of Dean's capacities, and the social malaise that Astrachan attempts to derive from the case study stems from the star's active refusal to assume this responsibility—a refusal that the author perceives as all too convenient and prevalent in contemporary culture.

Certainly, Astrachan's comments here fall short of suggesting or attempting to confirm James Dean's homosexual tendencies. Such overt deliberations of the star's sexuality would not be conducted for several years after his death. Astrachan's comments are nonetheless revealing since they show that even in the years shortly after Dean's death, his star persona already harbors an indeterminacy that extends to the realm of sexual orientation. Astrachan also establishes a connection between social and cultural discourses regarding two prominent social "problems" of the 1950s—homosexuality and the alienation and rebellion of youth, configured as "juvenile delinquency"—through recourse to the concept of identity. This connection becomes crucial in the representation of the star's sexuality, in light of contemporary discourses of rebellion and delinquency informing each of Dean's three major film roles, most evidently in *Rebel Without a Cause* (1955), but also in *East of Eden* (1955) and *Giant* (1956).

Homosexuality and Juvenile Delinquency

Although many of the 1970s biographers considered it incontestable and self-evident that James Dean was homosexual, it is difficult to find documented evidence of the star's homosexual orientation in texts of the 1950s, and even more difficult to locate evidence that men who perceived themselves as homosexual in the 1950s also perceived Dean as homosexual. This difficulty does not, however, suggest that the conjectures and assertions of the 1970s biographers were ill-founded or fabricated, nor does the lack of evidence of Dean's historical reception as gay in the 1950s prove conclusively that spectators at this time did not perceive him as gay. Rather, these difficulties point to significant differences in the discursive tools available in American culture in two distinct historical periods—tools that impose limitations upon how a historically specific culture imagines itself, and how individuals are invited to imagine and define themselves within that culture. As Janet Staiger suggests, these limitations manifest themselves as power struggles, cultural contestations over the meaning of the "sign" of homosexuality, how this sign may be circulated in public discourse, and who may appropriate this sign for what purposes.[3]

An examination of the public circulation of the sign of homosexuality in the 1950s demonstrates the workings of this struggle and identifies the agents who assumed the power to regulate how homosexuality could be imagined by individuals in culture. To a significant extent, it reveals a consensus perspective of homosexuality as a pathology that posed a threat to the integrity of the nuclear family as well as the nation as a whole. At the same time, however, the examination demonstrates one manifestation of Foucault's assertion that, in discursive operations, "where there is power, there is resistance, and yet, or rather consequently, this resistance is never in a position of exteriority in relation to power."[4] In the context of the 1950s, this resistance stems from a curious overlapping of discourses: homosexuality shared common discursive features with juvenile delinquency, a social problem that arose from public concern over the presence of a teen culture that had been emerging since World War II. While the dominant ideology used this discursive similarity in an effort to contain the proliferation of both social problems, the overlapping of discourses also provided seemingly disempowered homosexuals with the means to imagine themselves and to construct their own identities in nonpathological terms. They did so by adopting and appropriating a term that was widely used to describe the activity of juvenile delinquents, "rebellion," and adapting this term to the particular circumstances of their own social oppression.

The emergence of homosexuality and juvenile delinquency as prominent issues in the 1950s can be traced to social and cultural changes brought about by World War II. Psychiatric explanations of homosexuality had been prevalent in the United States since the 1920s, as Freudian psychoanalytic discourse progressively infiltrated mainstream American culture. In the war years, however, the military actively sought to detect aberrant and deviant behavior through screening procedures for inductees.[5] At the same time, the enforced isolation and segregation of the population by gender "created substantially new erotic opportunities that promoted the articulation of a gay identity and the rapid growth of a gay subculture."[6] Released in 1948, Alfred Kinsey's *Sexual Behavior in the Human Male* also profoundly affected subsequent efforts of gay subcultural communities to be socially recognized and tolerated. On the basis of interviews conducted with thousands of Americans of varying socioeconomic status, age, vocation, and religious affiliation, the report concluded that one of eight American males had experienced sustained homosexual erotic tendencies for at least three years, and among males he "found that 50 percent admitted erotic responses to their own sex."[7] Likewise, Kinsey found that many individuals with past homosexual experiences later led exclusively heterosexual lifestyles; thus, homosexuality became not only a more common phenomenon but also a fluid rather than a stable identity. The report both confounded and exacerbated attempts to appeal to medical discourse in defining the homosexual as pathological, especially since it suggested that homosexuality was undetectable by human physiognomy. Paradoxically, as Robert Corber suggests, conservative ideologies had substantial interests in restabilizing homosexuality as a category of identity, and by continuing to maintain that homosexuality was an identifiable psychological aberrance, the root of the "problem" continued to be the individual who failed to adjust to sexual norms, and not the culture or society who oppressed the individual.[8]

These conservative efforts justified the State Department's actions in 1950 when it declared that homosexuals were unsuitable for government employment because of potential susceptibility to blackmail threats. Investigations resulted in hundreds of suspected homosexuals losing their jobs.[9] Moreover, in the context of the Cold War hysteria of the late 1940s and 1950s, the homosexual was determined to be further unfit for government service not just because of his lack of emotional stability, but also because his behavior revealed a weakness of character at a time when it was deemed crucial to maintain a "moral fiber" strong enough to ward off corrupting external political influences. The inherent problem of developing a reliable method for detecting homosexuality was resolved by a curious displacement of personal onto political behavior: "If an individual's sexual orientation could no longer be determined by her/his lack of conformity to the norms of male and female behavior, then it could be by her/his politics."[10] The homosexual was conveniently labeled as dangerous in the face of communism, desperate as he was to conceal a sexual identity that carried with it a damaging social stigma and an inherent weakness of character.[11]

As is the case with homosexuality, increased national attention to the problem of juvenile delinquency is traceable to the war experience. If enforced gender segregation of adult men and women fostered the establishment of homosexual communities during the war, it also resulted in more adolescents entering the workforce while attending high school. As James Gilbert suggests, this phenomenon initiated a trend of "adolescent consumerism" in which teenagers began to constitute a targetable market sector for the advertising industry. Premature consumers also threatened the structure of the nuclear family because of their emerging financial independence from their parents.[12] From the late 1940s through the 1950s, rising discretionary income among adolescents helped to generate teenage subcultures shaped according to discrete gender divisions: hot rods for boys, and teen magazines for girls.[13]

If the crisis over homosexuality in the late 1940s in large part resulted from a report that made homosexual behavior and identity more opaque (and thus more threatening), the increase in juvenile delinquency was ostensibly easier to detect through crime statistics. The delinquency phenomenon also resulted in increased government jobs, through the formation in 1947 of two governmental committees assembled to manage and contain the problem: the Continuing Committee on the Prevention and Control of Delinquency (CCPCD), which stressed the importance of action at the local level; and the Children's Bureau, which relied on the testimony of "experts" and centered on social work services. Both new committees spurred national attention to the issue. Gilbert explains that while statistical reports failed to establish sufficient reliability to indicate a progressive increase in delinquency in the postwar period, what certainly did increase both through the trend of quantification and the committee activities was the degree of discourse surrounding the problem. This increase resulted in new classifications of adolescent behavior by experts, redefinitions of juvenile delinquency, attempts to contain and redirect youthful energy toward more productive activities, and anxiety regarding the inability to isolate causes or effects of the problem.[14]

In the 1950s, then, the problem of isolating, containing, and defining

the still ambiguous categories of homosexuality and juvenile delinquency resulted in more widespread concern over the proliferation of
both phenomena, and the dispersal of descriptions within each of these
categories parallels the fear that the phenomena would themselves
proliferate among individuals. Pathological discourse thus became an
appropriate vehicle for the expression of this proliferation, and both
homosexuality and juvenile delinquency were described through metaphors of infection and contagion—metaphors that were used similarly
to incite public concern over the spreading of the communist menace.
The Kinsey Report induced paranoia by demonstrating the ubiquity of
the homosexual: if anyone in the crowd could now be gay (or might become gay later in life), then it followed that homosexuality might proliferate by recruitment: "Homosexuality became an epidemic infect-
ing the nation, actively spread by communists to sap the strength of the
next generation." [15] The Senate Committee on Expenditures in Executive Departments warned that "these perverts will frequently attempt
to entice normal individuals to engage in perverted practices. This is
particularly true in the case of young and impressionable people who
might come under the influence of a pervert. . . . One homosexual
can pollute a Government office." [16] In the discourse of juvenile delinquency, "the predominant metaphor was one of contagion, contami-
nation, and infection," similar to descriptions of other phenomena in
the 1950s that were characterized by an "invasion from the outside."
National attention was focused on the potential corruptibility of impressionable adolescents, whose sense of morality was still under development, and who were thus thought to be more susceptible to suggestion and conversion.[17]

If uncertainties regarding the indeterminate causes and effects of
homosexuality and juvenile delinquency resulted in descriptions of the
phenomena as diseases propagated by communism, the public concern over matters of causality also located the domestic environment
as the origin of a cure for both problems. According to Elaine Tyler
May, "Many contemporaries believed that the Russians could destroy
the United States not only by atomic attack but through internal subversion. In either case, the nation had to be on moral alert . . . [and]
many postwar experts . . . prescribed family stability as an antidote
to these related dangers." [18] The stable family capable of providing a
haven and source of protection required the persistent moral influ-

ence of both parents in the home, as well as a strict division of gender roles between parents. Both of these prerequisites to stability had been threatened since the war years, when fathers were away overseas while mothers worked in factories and offices. The ideal parental role models of the postwar era appeared to be the father who functioned as breadwinner and the mother who resumed her role as family caregiver. While the father's return to a position of control in the family was a necessary demonstration of his own masculinity, a 1958 article in *Look* warned that fathers who worked too much or too hard would necessarily fail to provide their male children sufficient exposure to the ideal male role model: "A boy growing up . . . has little chance to observe his father in strictly masculine pursuits."[19] And the mother's failure to observe the distinction between giving too much and too little attention to her children could have disastrous consequences. As May explains, "Mothers who neglected their children bred criminals, mothers who overindulged their sons turned them into passive, weak, effeminite [*sic*] 'perverts.' Sons bred in such homes, according to psychologists and psychoanalysts, would find it difficult to form 'normal' relationships with women."[20] Clearly, the 1950s mother assumed the more crucial parental role for ensuring that the child would avoid the deviant paths of juvenile delinquency or homosexuality. In the often blatantly mysogynist discourse of gender roles of husband and wife, the female was also held responsible for the pressures that her spouse was forced to endure in order to maintain an ideal masculinity associated with earning power and sexual potency.[21]

In the monogamous heterosexual relationship, both the male and female were expected to conform to their respective gender roles. By emphasizing both the adult male's greater susceptibility to the demands of his female partner and the son's dependence on his mother to ensure stable masculinity, however, dominant cultural discourses empathized more strongly with the male's plight. Early marriage was a requirement for the proper containment and expression of the sexual impulse, and the requisite demonstration of masculine maturity, according to Barbara Ehrenreich, was to marry by the average age of twenty-three: "If adult masculinity was indistinguishable from the breadwinner role, then it followed that the man who failed to achieve this role was either not fully adult or not fully masculine. In the schema of male pathology developed by mid-century psychologists, immaturity shaded into infantilism, which was, in turn, a manifestation of unnatural fixation on the mother, and the entire complex of symptomatology reached its clinical climax in the diagnosis of homosexuality." [22] Reinforcing the equation of maturity with an acceptance of the role of responsible husband, the fear of being tainted homosexual presented the greatest incentive for husbands not to leave their wives: "Homosexuality . . . was the ultimate escapism." [23] Still, it remained the responsibility of the wife not to become so "dominating" or sexually demanding that the husband might find cause to consider such an escape. [24]

It is through a system of categorical oppositions and equations that juvenile delinquency was ultimately associated with homosexuality in the failed domestic environment. Males developed their maturity through the appropriate childrearing practices of their mothers, so that they could eventually integrate socially and assume their proper roles in the domestic sphere as breadwinner husbands. Children who were either overindulged or undersupervised by their mothers would fail to perform this requisite social integration. They might become homosexual, but even if they did not, they remained isolated and socially alienated figures, "loners" who rebelled against the commitments expected of them. Even if they committed no crimes, their antisocial behavior provided sufficient cause to label them delinquents, until they grew older and could assume other social stigmas.

The tensions and contradictions between conformity and individuality, and between rebellion and social integration, are already evident in nationalist public discourse in the postwar era. As James Gilbert explains, in the late 1940s the National Delinquency Prevention Society emphasized the message that, provided with sufficient means of organization, antisocial juvenile delinquents could rapidly evolve into a threatening totalitarian force in the United States. [25] In *The Vital Center*, a 1949 study of communist conspiracy, Arthur Schlesinger blames the individual's social isolation and alienation for his/her decision to join the Communist party; by suggesting that those who have no sense of place in the prevailing social structure are the most susceptible converts to totalitarianism, Schlesinger conflates political affiliation with human psychology and identity. [26]

An article in *Look* magazine in 1958 on the American male's pressures to conform to social expectations associates the loss of individuality with communism and totalitarianism. The article traces a day in the life of a well-adjusted, mature heterosexual breadwinner, who faces the critical realization that his existence has become routinized and mechanical. Societal norms have dictated how he must structure his day in terms of work, where he must live, how he must interact with his neighbors, and whom he must consult for expert advice on how to structure his marriage as well as his leisure time ("One word lay beyond all the advice: it was 'adjust.'"). As his son is engaged in "supervised play" with other children in the playground of his fashionable, high-rise apartment complex, the father watches him being socially conditioned to assume a role in which he himself feels trapped and stifled. The author offers the father's speculations in the third-person narrative voice: "Hadn't he read—it was in the Senate subcommittee report on juvenile delinquency—that delinquents are more frequently club members than nondelinquents . . . ? Yes, when you teach a child undue conformity to a group, when you take away his respect for the unique characteristics that make him different from all other human beings, then you create an automaton, ideal fodder for a juvenile gang—or a totalitarian mass movement."[27]

The author of the article perceives group conformity as a deterrent to innovation and creative thought, and also to the strength of his nation; curiously, the process of socialization said to produce mature Americans capable of resisting antidemocratic political systems threatens to turn on itself. But what would become of the adolescent who openly acknowledged his own uniqueness in the face of a society that was not prepared to accept it? Or of the father who decided to disrupt his daily routine and engage in social interactions according to his own volition? Although the article attacks conformity, it stops short of acknowledging alternatives. What it does intimate, however, is the possibility of a utopian state of social connectedness that tolerates difference, in which one would not have to forfeit one's individuality in order to be accepted.

Changes in the Hollywood Film Industry

"The difficulty in dealing with male rebelliousness," Barbara Ehrenreich suggests, "either on the scale of the individual, or as some psychiatrists feared, of the epidemic, was that it did have a certain seductive appeal."[28] In the medium of film, the representation of heroic, rebellious characters who harbored the potential to function as role models for adolescents was perceived as a threat to the prevailing social order, since such representations increased the possibility that young people would emulate antisocial behavior. Experts in the fields of psychology and sociology, as well as members of the clergy, repeatedly warned that attractive role models could not help but encourage audience identification. In its monitoring of the representation of role models in response to these concerns, the Hollywood film industry also participated in the regulation of reception strategies that might encourage such aberrant forms of identification. As a result of several developments in the Hollywood film industry after World War II, however, the representation of rebellious characters also harbored significant profit potential, and the designation of rebellion as a social problem on the national agenda made it ripe subject matter for exploitation on the screen. An examination of the film industry's strategies in the representation of two forms of rebellious behavior, juvenile delinquency and homosexuality, reveals both the success and failure of such attempts to regulate the ways in which viewers might construct role models of identification.

The separation of exhibition from the production and distribution sectors effected by the Paramount case (1948) facilitated the importation of foreign films with "realistic" treatments of adult subject matter. Additionally, with the film industry struggling to stabilize decreasing attendance and to differentiate its products from those of the television industry, Hollywood had more leverage to challenge the Production Code Administration's (PCA) policies regarding the representation of morally objectionable material and increasingly individual films were themselves rebellious.[29] In conjunction with its decision in the Paramount case, the Supreme Court agreed to support the protection of motion pictures under freedom of the press. Spurred in part by the controversy surrounding the closing of a New York theater that exhibited Rossellini's controversial film *The Miracle* in 1952, the Court overturned a 1915 ruling and granted First Amendment rights to the film industry.[30] During the remainder of the decade, the Supreme Court overturned additional censorship laws, and the film industry modified the Production Code to permit the introduction of much previously unrepresentable subject matter. Additionally, the major studios had some financial success with the exhibition of films that were not granted Code approval, beginning with United Artists' release of *The Outlaw* in 1946.[31]

Because of concerns over a burgeoning youth culture in the late 1940s, governmental committees expressed increasing concern over the negative effects of media institutions on youth behavior. These concerns were exacerbated by the publication of *Seduction of the Innocent* (1954), in which Fredric Wertham made causal connections between crime comics and criminal behavior among youth.[32] Between 1954 and 1956, the Senate Subcommittee to Investigate Juvenile Delinquency, chaired by Senator Estes Kefauver, solicited the testimony of experts and representatives from the comics, television, and film industries in an attempt to discern the responsibilities of media institutions regarding the delinquency problem.[33] Although the film industry investigations did result in recommendations for stricter enforcement of the Production Code, none of the above studies offered any conclusive proof that media incited delinquency.

As Barbara Klinger argues, Hollywood's exploitation of social problems and contemporary issues in the 1950s was a response to increasing demands for realism and verisimilitude partially stimulated by the popularity of foreign films.[34] The representation of the supposed delinquency problem of the mid 1950s was especially well-timed, since such films would appeal not only to concerned parents but also to a youth market which, as revealed by marketing analyses in the early 1950s, comprised the largest remaining portion of the diminishing film audience. In fact, the Senate subcommittee targeted both *The Wild One* (1954) and *The Blackboard Jungle* (1954) for their valorization of criminal and antisocial acts among adolescents, as the Senate subcommittee held special concern for any instances of imitative behavior that suggested that the audience was using film protagonists as role models. Observing the presence of young males wearing black leather jackets at screenings of *The Wild One*, a witness from the Catholic Tidings organization commented, "It was clear they identified themselves with the arrogant character [Brando] played in the film." The Chief of Staff of the Hacker Foundation for Psychiatric Research and Education testified that acts of gratuitous violence in these films were actually "hostile manifestations of a perverse sexuality."[35]

Both the Senate subcommittee and the Production Code Administration (PCA) expressed similar concerns over the representation of violence in *Rebel Without a Cause* (1955). Jack Warner's suggestion to the Senate subcommittee that the film highlighted "the juvenile delinquency of parents" was ill-received by both the Subcommittee and members of the Subcommittee's audience.[36] The PCA recommended extensive cuts to scenes portraying Plato's (Sal Mineo) brutal punishment by gang members.[37] The PCA's standardized "Analysis of Film Content" form included the question, "Does story tend to enlist the sympathy of the audience for the criminal?" Both the "Yes" and "No" boxes on the forms were marked with an "X."[38]

As it had done twenty-five years earlier with the gangster film, the Hollywood industry profited from the controversy surrounding the prevalence of juvenile delinquency in the 1950s, as well as from the accusations of its complicity in the severity of the problem. The industry "claimed to be helping in the national fight against delinquency, while it exploited public interest in, and fear of, juvenile culture."[39] As suggested above, the constraints of conformity imposed upon Americans in both the public and private sphere helped to make representations of rebellion especially attractive (fig. 1). Two additional aspects of this social problem made it not only ripe for exploitation, but also suitable for representation in the prevailing cultural climate. First, even before the film industry treated the theme, public discourse was already portraying delinquency as a problem whose solution could be imagined within the family and the domestic setting, and it had become urgent to rectify the problem in the interests of national security. Second, as Gilbert clarifies, the description of delinquency as a psychological problem was gradually yielding to its alternative description, through the introduction of sociological subculture theory, as a form of social integration (however thwarted) in a culture that overemphasized notions of success and ostracized those who failed to achieve it.[40]

As a problem prevalent in many forms of public discourse in the 1950s, homosexuality shared many of the attributes that made juvenile delinquency acceptable for representation in Hollywood cinema. It was deemed no less urgent to study and rectify. It certainly presented no less of a threat to national security, and through the discourse of "momism" its origins were often traced to family environ-

1　James Dean as the consummate rebel. Author's personal collection.

ments in which parents failed to provide proper role models. Despite such treatments of causality, and despite the findings of the Kinsey Report, however, dominant public discourse paradoxically continued to maintain homosexuality as a problem of identity—one that might be adopted, discarded, or resumed at any point in one's life, yet no less definitive a mark and distinction of one's individuality. It was, however, also considered to be a mark of what Richard Dyer describes as one of the most distinctive threats to the concept of individuality during the Cold War—namely, totalitarianism.[41] In the cultural context, homosexuality functioned as an indelible mark of identity and as a sign of the loss or surrender of individual identity to the demands of the group. As such, it certainly could not constitute an acceptable mode of resistance to a culture that overemphasized the necessity of social conformity. If juvenile delinquency could eventually be described as a subcultural form of social adaptation, the very existence of a gay subculture only strengthened the connection between homosexuality and Communist conspiracy: for example, Arthur Schlesinger described the way in which Communists could instinctively recognize one another as analogous to the practice of homosexual cruising.[42]

Certainly, the PCA's upholding of the prohibition against the representation of "sexual perversion" until 1961 provides the clearest explanation for its virtual absence in Hollywood cinema of the 1950s. Still, homosexuality was exploited thematically to a limited extent during the decade. When the topic did explicitly emerge, as in *Suddenly, Last Summer* (1958), however, it did so only in spite of the censors' deliberate efforts to disguise its ability to be identified incontestably as homosexuality, rendering itself visible primarily through descriptions in film reviews and critical responses that the PCA had no power to regulate.[43] If the sign of homosexuality was made visible, then, its visibility emerged only through unsuccessful attempts to render it absent.

This problem of the visibility of the sign of sexual difference in Hollywood cinema runs parallel to a crisis between identity and its absence that informs the contemporaneous discourse that male homosexuals were producing to describe themselves, and their place in society, at the beginning of the 1950s. Some gay men found that the most effective way to serve as productive members of society was to assimilate with the prevailing social order, thereby eliminating any recognizable signs of their sexual difference. Others, who rejected a social order that would not accommodate them, elected to foreground an identity-in-difference and find their own place by locating others who shared this difference. The latter group attempted to take control of the sign of homosexuality by adopting a discourse of rebellion most clearly linked to youth culture and the problem of juvenile delinquency. In doing so, they began to assume control over the construction of their own identities, and they articulated reception strategies for the construction and identification of visible homosexual role models in culture.

Gay Resistance and Assimilation in the 1950s

The Los Angeles-based Mattachine Society was founded in 1951 in an effort to assert the status of homosexuals as an oppressed minority. Beginning with the organization of small discussion groups, the Society attempted to provide a forum in which the dominant culture's pathological formulations of homosexual behavior could be challenged. As John d'Emilio explains, Mattachine's founders expressed that the normative roles of the "heterosexual nuclear family" had been unduly imposed upon a segment of the population that shared none of its concerns. A primary objective of the Society was to enlighten its members to the insidious ways in which mainstream society formulated normative gender roles as "natural," so that the logic of heterosexual oppressors could be overturned rather than appropriated. The Society inspired homosexuals to perceive themselves and their difference from the mainstream with pride—one that would be strengthened through community building.[44]

Mattachine's founders had been active members of the Communist party since the early 1930s, and, as its membership grew, the Society assumed a structure of "orders" designating a hierarchy of levels of responsibility.[45] Because the Society was growing at the same time that the persecution of Communists in the McCarthy era was at its most severe, Mattachine's Communist affiliations were kept secret from the outside world as well as most of its own members. These affiliations were inadvertently publicized in 1953, however, and the dismay of anti-Communist sectors of the Society eventually resulted in the resignation of the original founders and changes to both the organizational structure and philosophy. Instead of emphasizing acceptable difference, the "new" Mattachine stressed that the objective of its members was to gain "acceptance and full assimilation into the communities in which they live."[46]

The ideological differences of the two successive Societies become readily apparent in the first two major gay male periodicals in the 1950s. Edited by the Society's new regime since its initial publication in 1955, *Mattachine Review* promoted a positive image of homosexuality by foregrounding the potential for homosexuals to make significant contributions to mainstream culture. The opening volume set forth the aims and principles of the Society. The journal certainly acknowledged discriminatory practices, but it emphasized that these had been a result of the circulation of a set of inaccurate stereotypes. Public education was therefore a primary goal: the Society sponsored research on the causes of homosexuality, and many of the journal's articles include the testimony of experts (psychologists, sociologists, anthropologists) who challenge and dispel notions of homosexuality as aberrant behavior.[47] The journal also served to educate its members in matters of proper and acceptable public conduct and demeanor, and it discouraged any behavior that might reinforce common stereotypes. Although the "Aims and Principles" statement indicates that the Society promoted the revision of laws that permit undue discrimination, it also vowed to act in accordance with the law and democratic practices, and much of the document emphasizes the Society's anti-Communist stance.

Incontestably, the *Review* provided a sense of community and belonging to a sector of the population that had been rendered invisible and silent. The "Readers Write" column attests to this spirit of community: a letter in an early issue states that "Mattachine is, I sincerely believe, an answer to my problems of many years standing. I have long searched for a group to which I could belong and have the opportunity to establish a happier life, find peace of mind, and seek equality for persons like myself."[48] Reiterating dominant discourses of pathology, however, the Society and the *Mattachine Review* reflected the paradox of promoting homosexual identity and solidarity through the obliteration of any recognizable signs of homosexuality. The journal was not only reluctant, but openly opposed, to the formulation of any political or sexual identity-in-difference. One of its mission statements called for psychiatric rehabilitation and adjustment of the homosexual through group therapy, with "a view to reducing the high incidence of homosexuality in future generations. . . ."[49] Aligned with the discourse of anti-Communism, the Society opposed the formation of a homosexual subculture, encouraging gay men to "assume community responsibility" and "affiliate" rather than "withdraw into an invert society of their own."[50]

Homosexual identity was treated much differently in *One*, the journal initiated in 1953 by the original, Communist-affiliated founders of the Mattachine Society. *One* argued for a recognition and celebration of homosexual difference, and the journal aimed to dismantle rather than accept or tolerate the dominant, paradoxical formulations of homosexual identity with which the *Mattachine Review* more democratically contended. *One* refused either to deny or affirm the presumed connections between homosexuality and communism, electing instead to render them irrelevant. Instead of being relegated to silence and fear of exposure by the proponents of McCarthyism, the journal reversed the oppressor's logic. The strategy becomes apparent in "And a Red Too . . . .", a piece that responds to the question, "Are communists homosexual?" first by clarifying that Communist party doctrine not only denies membership to known homosexuals, but actively expels members who are revealed to be homosexual. Lest the parallels between these practices and the HUAC witch hunts be missed, the author refers to a "fashionable red hysteria" and adopts and refigures the very language of the investigative committee: "Is it reasonable, then, that any sizeable number of homosexuals are now or ever have been communists?"[51]

One did not resort to the testimony of psychological or social experts from the mainstream to validate or justify its existence to heterosexual society; indeed, the journal emphasized that homosexuals can develop self-respect and pride in their difference only by rejecting a dominant social structure that defined their behavior as reprehensible. In his pseudonymously published *The Homosexual in America: A Subjective Approach* (1951), Donald Webster Cory is especially attentive to the contradictions of social oppression: "The dominant group creates a system of social superstructures in which no place is left for the homosexual; then denies to the invert access to these institutions; and ends up by denouncing inversion because it does not fit into the very institutions from which it has been banned."[52] The only way to contend with such contradiction is not to attempt to integrate with the social system, but actively to rebel against it.

Rebellion figures prominently in both works as the logical path for attaining a necessary self-reliance. Rebellion begins with the epiphanic realization that, because the rules governing acceptable social behavior disavow the existence of the homosexual, they merit and demand violation. A 1954 *One* article entitled "The Importance of Being Different" asserts that "homosexuals are natural rebels." The author explains that "most homosexuals are inured to breaking the rules. They must somehow reject what they learned as children and still hear repeated about them. But when people break rules and know they have done so, and are not sorry, they usually are forced to decide that the rule is either irrelevant or wrong. Here, a new factor enters. They put their own judgement above the rules, which represent society's judgment, in short, they become rebels."[53] In somewhat similar terms, Cory explains that "as my being rebels against the hypocrisy that is forced upon me, I realize that its greatest repercussion has been the wave of self-doubt that I must harbor."[54] Here and elsewhere in the minority discourse of *One* and Cory's book, the concept of rebellion involves two interdependent yet necessarily sequential acts. The first is a separation from, or "casting off" of, a set of imposed social constraints deemed to be obtrusive. The result of this separation is the distinction of a "self" that has now to contend with a state of being unanchored, so that the subsequent act of rebellion involves a reclamation of the true and authentic identity, a return to an essential core of the self, which a deceitful and inauthentic mainstream culture has rendered unworthy of respect or even acknowledgment, has castigated and restrained from emergence.

In the logic of rebellion there is therefore an intimate, causal connection between a rejection of artifice and the location of an essence that functions as its opposite. The search for this essence is also a search for "identity," a word derived from the Latin *idem*, meaning "the same." The location of a core identity involves the search for a place where the self recognizes itself. Whereas the discourse in the *Mattachine Review* encourages the homosexual to find this place in the world by assimilation and integration with the society that harbors oppression, *One* and *The Homosexual America* suggest that the place of the self must be located from within.

Yet the attempt to locate such an identity, a place where the rebellious, unanchored self finds a sense of sameness and recognition, necessarily becomes a search for *connectedness* as well as authenticity and essence. This connectedness is figured as an introspective as well as an interpersonal problem: if rebellion were only to establish an authentic self through a recognition of difference, the individual would remain fragmented and isolated. To establish one's place in the world, it becomes necessary to recognize oneself in others as well, and the discourse of homosexual rebellion in the 1950s emphasizes the interdependence of personal connectedness and the emulation of role models. In a 1954 *One* article, Arthur Krell confirms that "every man's basic problem is to establish relatedness with others." [55] This search for connectedness becomes a therapeutic process, since "psychic health is impossible to the emotionally isolated." The process of identification with others is what ultimately permits the individual to constitute himself as a coherent being, and Krell makes frequent reference to the concept of an ideal "wholeness" of the individual that might be established through connections with others who have found themselves similarly cast off from mainstream society. Through such connections, one develops the resilience to live in a world whose ideology one has rejected.

What complicates the process, however, is that the social stigma of homosexuality prevents the rebel from locating others who share his plight. Public acknowledgment of sexual difference results in public persecution, thwarting the attempts of homosexuals to identify their place within a community. Although Krell acknowledges that the circulation of knowledge in the gay periodicals in which his own words appear helps to ameliorate this problem, he also perceives the need for a historical connectedness, for "patterns to copy" in the lives of public figures or the portrayal of fictional characters who share his sexual difference. The presence of "hero-ideals to emulate" is, however, severely lacking: Krell finds the models in contemporary gay fiction and theater to be inadequate since they either mimic the mainstream conception of homosexuality as pathological and tragic, or advocate the assimilation of the homosexual into the mainstream and thus deny his difference.[56] Cory reiterates this problem, one that he sees compounded by the fact that heterosexual culture has suppressed the circulation of public knowledge that might help homosexuals to identify their historical precedents in successful figures such as Marcel Proust or Walt Whitman.

This search for role models also constitutes an act of construction, a reconfiguration of cultural signs for the purpose of assembling a core identity. Lacking a set of identifiable figures in history or in contemporary culture, Krell clarifies that the homosexual seeks patterns in "Greek myth, SatEv-Post romance, newspaper sports page, or Bible, movie or comic strip," and by such means he learns "to develop piecemeal the patterns that may help him live in society as a whole man." [57] Krell's description here suggests that this act of textual poaching serves two interrelated purposes: the development of a coherent self through the development of a coherent role model who responds to the self.

Because the identity politics of the 1990s has posited the notion of a coherent or stable self as a fiction that disavows the necessarily fractured subjectivities that each individual harbors, it is important to stress that the search for "coherence" is posited here as a historically specific phenomenon — one that a subculture, and the individuals who comprise it, attempted to use in resistance to dominant ideological discourses that thwarted the attempts of homosexuals to construct their own identities (be they fractured or stable) and identifications in culture. The search also constitutes a response to a paradox imposed on homosexuals in the 1950s. The dominant ideology denied homosexuals the discursive power to appropriate role models, thereby forcing them into what Krell describes as "piecemeal" assembly; at the same time, however, this ideological discourse also insisted that homosexuality was a definitive sign of identity. Homosexuals were, simultaneously, "there" and "not there" in culture, and assimilation and rebellion constituted two responses to the identity discourse imposed on them — responses comprising different strategies by which one could find a place in the world. The assimilationist strategy required the elimination of the social stigma; rebels rejected the pathological identity imposed on them, but this rejection did not preclude the need for identification, for finding one's place by connecting with others who possessed a common difference. The search for coherence thus suggests parts that are held together as a recognizable whole, which 1950s homosexuals needed in order to affirm their own presence as well as the presence of a community to which they might belong.

Although the list of sources appropriated by the homosexual includes contemporary visual media texts, it is significant that both Cory's book and the *One* articles in the 1950s focus more intently on the identification and appropriation of literary figures. Krell suggests possible reasons for this preference. The first concerns the emerging homosexual subculture's awareness of differences in the enforcement of censorship practices among contemporary texts: "Our new freedom to discuss homosexuality (but not to advocate—a fine distinction) arises in an epoch when, for the first time since the Elizabethan age, the code permits speaking of practically anything on the stage, in a book or in a specialized magazine—but not in the movies, press, radio, T.V. or general magazines."[58] Regarding the film industry, at least, Krell's perceptions are accurate: at the time that his article appeared in 1954, even though the representation of homosexuality in film was protected by First Amendment rights, it was not yet permissible under the stipulations of the PCA. Literature is perceived as a less repressive public forum, and the strategy of emphasizing the importance of establishing literary precedents is consonant with the efforts of an emerging homosexual subculture not only to acknowledge its own accomplishments, but to have these accomplishments recognized by mainstream, heterosexual culture. As Krell explains, "When the homosexual appears widely in literature, not as a doomed weakling, but as a man whose supposed handicap becomes the very foundation of his achievement, the same literature that sets useful patterns for the homosexual will be read more widely, affecting society as well, creating human friendliness toward the whole man where none existed before."[59]

In the mid 1950s, then, it is clearly much more conceivable that openly homosexual characterizations might appear in literary discourse, whereas in film and television homosexuality would have to be surreptitiously inferred and constructed piecemeal.[60] Yet this piecemeal assembly of the "whole man" was constituted as an integral part of the process of rebellion, a theme that was granted extensive representation in both print and visual media in the mid 1950s because of its prominence as an issue of national concern in relation to the social problem of juvenile delinquency. Although homosexuality was still figured as a problem of identity and thus could not be overtly represented, it borrowed and adopted the discourse of social rebellion as a means of expression.

The rise of the "beat" culture attests to the ways in which discursive connections were formulated between rebellion and homosexuality in the mid 1950s. The beats challenged and rejected constricting codes of middle-class conformity as well as traditional literary respectability. As Richard Dyer explains, the beat writers "opposed a cult of authenticity, of being 'real' and one's 'self' over and against conforming to moral and social convention."[61] The inauthenticity of social conformity also became linked to artificially imposed restrictions of sexual desire, and several of the beat poets such as Allen Ginsburg openly acknowledged their homosexuality. Other associations of the beat movement with homosexuality were geographically rooted, since the two "cultures" converged in the North Beach section of San Francisco.

Mainstream culture certainly did not valorize beat social rebellion. As John d'Emilio explains, the popular press often used beat culture's sanctioning of homosexual practices as a justification for berating the beatnick as "hedonist," and "literary critics used homosexuality as a labeling device that allowed them to dismiss out of hand the work of San Francisco writers and others who were lumped into that category."[62] The attempts to dismiss beat culture also took the form of legal action when the San Francisco Police Department unsuccessfully attempted to outlaw the sale of a volume of Ginsburg's poetry on the basis of obscenity (178). Still, as d'Emilio suggests, the media attention devoted to the beats provided gays with evidence of a thriving subculture, as well as a means to "perceive themselves as nonconformists rather than deviates, as rebels against stultifying norms rather than immature, unstable personalities" (181). Despite their association with the social stigma of homosexuality, the beats struck a responsive chord in heterosexuals who perceived their individuality as being constrained by imposed demands of social conformity (181).

Rebellion and Identity in Melodramatic Fantasy

If, for both homosexuals and heterosexuals, the process of rebellion in the 1950s enacts the struggle to separate oneself from an established social order, to locate one's authentic self as a consequence of this separation, and to effect a state of connectedness with others so that one might live in the world, melodrama provides a most appropriate vehicle for the dramatization of this struggle. The texts of James Dean's star persona articulate the stages of rebellion through the melodramatic fantasy of origin in ways that were arguably particularly appealing to gay male spectators of the 1950s.

In the structure of the family melodrama, which comprises each of Dean's three Warner Bros. films, the various manifestations of the fantasy of origin are set into a system of conflict. David Rodowick argues that the family melodrama is typified by a displacement of problems of social and institutional authority onto the domestic setting. Here, the problems are often played out as a struggle between a symbol of patriarchal authority (usually, but not always, the father) and another male figure (the son) whose social and sexual identity is determined by the extent to which he accedes to the demands of patriarchy.[63] As Geoffrey Nowell-Smith suggests, "What is at stake [in this struggle] . . . is the survival of the family unit and the possibility for individuals of acquiring an identity which is also a place within the system, a place where they can be both 'themselves' and 'at home', in which they can simultaneously enter, without contradiction, the symbolic order and bourgeois society."[64] The conflict between father and son is thus organized as a crisis of identity in relation to the social and domestic order, a crisis that may be "resolved" by the male child's acceptance of his father's authority. According to Rodowick, in 1950s family melodrama this resolution is complicated by the paternal figure's ineffectuality, weakness, or absence, and he thus fails to provide a model of authority or moral integrity worthy of emulation. Also, since the family melodrama configures sexual identity in terms of social identity, this resolution via acceptance of authority is effected only in a channeling and containment of the son's desire through "a social economy defined by marriage."[65] "Excess" sexual desire that cannot be contained within this social economy manifests itself as violence — physical violence that the son directs against a patriarchal system that determines his place within it, as well as a "violence against the text in a manner which maximises the potential for disruption and incoherency."[66] Accordingly, if the domestic melodrama enacts a struggle between father and son whose successful resolution guarantees the perpetuation of the stable nuclear family (and, in broader terms, a stable social order), the struggle itself suggests that the patriarchal system is unstable, susceptible to challenge and disruption from within.

Yet the son's resolution through acceptance is complicated by an additional factor, one that follows logically from Rodowick and Nowell-Smith's assertion that the problem of identity is fundamental to the operations of family melodrama, and one that is pertinent to the appeal of Dean's onscreen persona in his three films. The complication concerns the place of the self and the determination of individuality in relation to a dominant social and sexual order. The assumption of "an identity which is also a place within the system," of negotiating personal identity through the established social order, constitutes an act of assimilation that might be attractive for individuals who perceive their difference from this social order as negotiable *in terms of it*—that is, if they desire to overcome or disavow their difference. In the context of the family melodrama, however, the plight of the son is also readable as the origin of a crisis of rebellion *against* the social order in its denial of the individual's right to determine his own place outside of it. The process of rebellion involves a separation from an imposing, dominant order, a consequent reclaiming of an authentic, essential self undetermined by this order, and a desire for connectedness with those who share a difference perceived as fundamental to individual identity. For the rebel, consequently, there is no place where one can be oneself and at home within the dominant order, and no place where one might recognize himself in others. The rebel negotiates the necessity of living within the dominant social order by perceiving its incongruities and desiring to change them, not by adapting himself to them (fig. 2). The melodramatic fantasy of origin accommodates the impulse to rebel, since it involves not only a desire for a return to a state of wholeness, essence, and connectedness symbolized by a return to the mother, but also a desire for the ability to determine one's origins and filiation so that one might reconceptualize a social order determined to be oppressive.[67]

Singly or collectively, Dean's roles in *East of Eden*, *Rebel Without a Cause*, and *Giant* certainly constitute no clearly articulated manifesto of rebellion, yet neither are they documents that demonstrate the protagonist's desire to assimilate into the dominant social order and find his place within it. The narratives retain an ambiguity that accommodates readings of the protagonist as either assimilationist or rebellious, and sometimes, paradoxically, as both. None of the three films either codes Dean's character as gay or articulates homosexual desire overtly, but the discourse of rebellion and resistance that is employed in each

2 Rejection of the dysfunctional family: Dean as Jim Stark with parents Jim Backus and Ann Doran in *Rebel Without a Cause* (1955). Courtesy Wisconsin Center for Film and Theater Research.

film addresses the concerns of those whom the dominant order has situated as outsiders, and each film responds to the ways in which these concerns were articulated in gay male discourses of assimilation and rebellion in the 1950s. Through the dramatization of the melodramatic fantasy of origin, each film enacts its protagonist's struggle to find a place where he can be both himself and at home. While it would be erroneous to suggest that homosexual men in the 1950s adopted the interpretive strategies utilized in the following textual analysis, the films' articulation of the process of rebellion within the structure of melodramatic fantasy aids in understanding one important way in which these films and this star enabled potential queer reading strategies in the historical context of the 1950s.

In all three films, external forces threaten the integrity and cohesion of the moral and social order. In *East of Eden*, Kate (Jo Van Fleet) describes her brothel in Monterey as successful because "half of city hall" can be found there on any given night. With the onset of World War I, the citizens of Salinas organize a posse to intimidate a German shopowner whom they considered to be their friend months earlier. In *Rebel Without a Cause*, the law enforcement institution impedes the applications of justice and order: when Jim Stark (James Dean) arrives at the police station late one night to confess his involvement in the death of Buzz (Corey Allen) in the "chickie-run" incident, the police officers on duty treat him as though he were only disrupting their more important bureaucratic responsibilities. At the end of the film, Jim stabilizes the "threat" that Plato (Sal Mineo) poses to the safety of others by removing the bullets from his gun; nonetheless, Jim's efforts to resolve the situation peacefully are undermined by the police officers stationed outside the planetarium who, by reflex reaction, shoot and kill Plato on the first glimpse of a gun in his hand. In *Giant*, the stability of the social order is linked to prejudice, intolerance, usury, and greed: Jett Rink (James Dean) explains to Leslie (Elizabeth Taylor) that her husband Bick Benedict's (Rock Hudson) claim to the 695,000-acre Reata ranch is a result of the Benedicts' exploitation and trickery of the Mexicans, the original owners of the land. The Mexicans currently employed by Bick are treated as subhuman creatures. Confined to a remote village, they have become victims of poverty and disease, and Bick deems them unworthy of medical treatment by the physician who treats the Benedict family.

In each film, the external subversion of moral order is mirrored by tensions within the nuclear family. Within the Trask family household in *East of Eden*, the father Adam's (Raymond Massey) attempt to represent moral decency through the Christian virtues of tolerance and respect is rendered hypocritical by the preferential treatment he gives to his elder son Aaron (Dick Davalos). Aaron is cast as the "good" son who has earned his father's pride through intelligence and attentiveness to his father's needs. Aaron is also preparing to preserve and perpetuate the integrity of the family name through his relationship with Abra (Julie Harris), who does volunteer work for the local hospital. Undermining his father's authority, and unattached to a respectable female figure, his other son Cal (James Dean) is treated with scorn and disrespect. The father also demonstrates his hypocrisy by maintaining to his sons that their mother died years ago, although she actually left Adam shortly after the birth of Aaron and Cal.

The configuration of the nuclear family in *Rebel Without a Cause* is revealed to be no less corrupt according to standards set in the 1950s. Judy's (Natalie Wood) father scorns her need to express affection toward him; both of Plato's parents are absent from the household, and he is reminded of his father's presence only by the child support checks that he receives in the mail each month. Although *Rebel* is the only film in which both of Dean's parents are present within the household, the narrative reverses their traditional gender roles, so that the father (Jim Backus) functions as domestic caretaker, while the mother (Ann Doran) assumes a position of dominance and control. This configuration certainly provides an explanation of Jim's juvenile delinquency by referencing the problem of momism and the absence of an authoritative father figure worthy of the son's emulation. What the gender role reversal highlights, however, is the more prominent problem that *any* stratification of authority and responsibility between parents complicates their ability to guide their son to make effective decisions. As Jim struggles to decide whether or not to inform the police that he knows the circumstances of Buzz's death, he seeks parental advice only to be told not to get involved with a matter that will mark him for the rest of his life: "You can't be idealistic all your life," his father advises, while his mother suggests that they evade the problem altogether by moving away.

Gender roles assume the more "correct" stratification within the domestic setting throughout the first third of *Giant*, echoing the dichotomy of inside/outside the home. When Leslie graciously thanks the Mexican servants for assisting with her luggage upon the newlyweds' arrival at Reata, Bick sternly reprimands her, reminding her that "you're a Texan now." He qualifies her assertion that "I'm still myself" by explaining that "you're my wife, honey. You're a Benedict." When Leslie attempts to sit in on a discussion of politics with her husband and male companions, she is ostracized and dismissed with the explanation that "this is men's stuff." Bick's intolerance of Leslie's challenge to his authority is later reproduced through his insistence that his firstborn son maintain his obligations to the family with respect to gender, tradition, and lineage. He forces the terrified, four-year-old Jordan Jr. to ride the pony that he has given him as a birthday present because Bick himself learned to ride before he could walk, and he is perplexed that the child seems more content to play with his doctor toys. It is not until the more compassionate Leslie gives Bick an ultimatum by departing with the children for Virginia that he is forced to temper his inflexibility.

The rights of inheritance within the patriarchal social order also become the basis for Jett Rink's (James Dean) sense of alienation and separation. Having worked on the Reata ranch as Bick's employee for most of his life, Jett is nonetheless an outsider since he lacks blood ties to the family. That he is disposable and replaceable becomes apparent on his initial entry into the narrative: as Leslie and Bick return from Virginia to Reata, we learn that Bick has fired him, and that he has been retained only because of the good graces of his sole friend on the ranch, Bick's sister Luz (Mercedes MacCambridge). After Luz dies in a riding accident, she wills him a small tract of land on the Reata estate, and Bick attempts to buy the land from him at a premium to keep the ranch solely within the family. Whereas Leslie and her children struggle to release themselves from the constraints of tradition and inheritance that Bick attempts to maintain, Jett's sole motive is to demonstrate that he is worthy of, and entitled to, the same privileges that Bick has enjoyed as a result of his lineage.

Each of the three films emphasizes the alienation of the Dean protagonist through devices of mise-en-scène and editing. Jett is usually placed at a great distance from the Reata household, permitted to enter only on the occasion of Luz's death. Later in the film, when he once again enters the home to negotiate a deal with Bick to install oil rigs on the Reata estate, Jett's presence is intrusive, tolerated only because of financial need. During the party to celebrate Leslie and Bick's marriage, the uninvited Jett reclines with his hat over his eyes in the Benedicts' convertible, his presence indicated only by crosscutting with shots of the party guests. His alienation is most prominent in his final scene in the film: in an extreme long shot, a drunk and virtually incoherent Jett delivers a speech to an empty auditorium in his new hotel, before he collapses onto the podium, knocking over a table that falls on top of him.

Although Aaron initially disavows the notion that Adam treats him preferentially, *East of Eden* signals Cal's alienation from the nuclear family through similar devices. He assumes the role of observer in several scenes toward the beginning of the film, watching and following Adam, Aaron, and Abra, as well as the woman he believes to be his mother, from a safe distance where he will not be perceived. His alienation is emphasized by his confinement to the edges of the CinemaScope frame, his placement in the extreme foreground of deep focus compositions that situate the objects of his vision in the distant background, and a volley of glance-object cuts. He almost never appears within the same visual plane with others, and when he does so, he casts his glance downward or offscreen. In one scene, Adam refers to Cal in the third person with a business associate, even though his son is standing next to him. Not only is Cal rendered apart from others, but also from himself, through the shadows that obscure his human frame in darkened settings, and the shadows that his figure casts in narrow, backlit hallways.

Rebel Without a Cause intensifies Jim's alienation through a number of stylistic devices. Within the CinemaScope composition, Jim arcs his body tightly into the upper left-hand corner of the frame in the first scenes at the police station, as his parents and grandmother look on in fear and disgust. Jim is separate from his peers as well as his family. In the first planetarium sequence, the camera crosscuts between medium shots of Judy, Buzz, and other members of the gang who sit together, and close ups of Jim sitting alone in a row behind them. When Jim befriends Plato, the other teenager ostracized because of his difference, the camera crosscuts between the two boys outside of the planetarium, looking down as the gang members hover around his car and puncture a tire with a knife on the street below. Jim is marked as different from others even in scenes where his presence is integrated with groups within the mise-en-scène. In the "chickie-run" sequence, his bright red jacket effects a sharp color contrast with his peers. His clothing also isolates him in the crowd as he ascends the steps of his new high school on the first day of class; unsure of himself, he inadvertently bumps into his classmates, and commits the drastic error of stepping on the school insignia that the other students carefully dodge.

Each of the three films marks the protagonist's alienation and disconnectedness in terms of ambiguities of location that play on the dichotomies of inside/outside and here/there. Speculating on the stars in the planetarium's sky theater, Jim tells Plato, "I was just thinking—once you've been up there, you know you've been someplace." Shortly afterwards, however, the lecturer predicts the earth's inevitable destruction in colliding with an asteroid; describing the silence of the aftermath, he ruminates that "man, existing alone, seems an episode of little consequence." The unnamed town where the Stark family currently resides is a temporary destination rather than somewhere to call home: the family itself has become nomadic, drifting from place to place whenever Jim gets into trouble. In *East of Eden*, Cal is a wanderer with nowhere to go, yet crouched atop a freight train car, he oscillates between two distinct points twenty miles apart: Salinas, where he was raised and where he currently lives, and Monterey, where he suspects that his mother still lives, even though his father has told him that she died many years ago. In *Giant*, Jett's placelessness is initially a function of his lack of historical connectedness in relation to the firmly rooted, multigenerational Benedict lineage. Jett's parents are never mentioned in the narrative. No past is ascribed to him, and he wanders in the unbounded space apart from the home on the vast expanse of the Reata estate.

In remarkably different ways, the Dean protagonist of each narrative attempts to reconcile locative ambiguities through a process of self-discovery that involves an attempted return to origin, and a reconfiguration of alliances of filiation. Early in *Rebel Without a Cause*, Jim tells the police officer who interviews him, "If I had one day when I didn't have to be all confused, and didn't have to feel that I was ashamed of everything, if I felt that I belonged someplace. . . ." Yet this sense of belonging comes about only when he and the other two ostracized teenagers vow never to return to the domestic spaces of the biological parents who have rejected them. Jim's self-exile is made the most emphatic, as he violently kicks and destroys a portrait of his mother on his way out the back door of his parents' home. Jim, Plato, and Judy find safety and comfort within the space of the deserted mansion where they hope that their presence will remain undetected. The relocation to the mansion functions as a return to origin in which the conventions of the traditional nuclear family and the society that demands their conformity are mocked and revealed to be superficial. Within this space, the threesome enacts a parody of their bourgeois roots and the breadwinner ethic: Plato takes the role of realtor, who tries to sell the mansion (at the most reasonable cost of $1 million per month) to newlyweds Jim and Judy, who deliberate whether they should "rent or buy." "We'll scrimp and save," Judy declares, and with affected distress the happy couple ruminates on the limitations of their budget, and the "crucial" matter of which rooms their children will occupy.

This tender mockery of heterosexual family conventions and dynamics serves as a prelude to the reconfiguration of the family that disrupts power relationships and resists the stratification of acceptable behavior according to gender roles and parental function. What is valued within this reconfigured family is not the demonstration and enforcement of parental authority, but a spirit of equivalence—a sameness to oneself and to others, and a spirit of mutual understanding that becomes possible whether one elects to enact the role of parent, child, or both. Earlier in the film, Plato has told Jim, "If only you could have been my dad." He later clarifies to Judy what is particularly appealing in this fantasy of choosing one's parents, and of selecting Jim as his father: "You have to get to know him. He doesn't say much, but when he does, you know he means it. He's sincere." The ideal parental figure thus becomes the ideal friend, one who listens and advises without judgment, and transcends the role of authority figure, which the dominant culture perceives as ideal. The dissolution of boundaries between father and peer is expressed through a correlative equivalence of word and deed (fig. 3). This equivalence corrects the verbal conflict that Jim finds so oppressive in the bickering between his mother and father early in the film, when Jim cries, "You're tearing me apart. You say one thing, he says another, and everybody changes back again" (fig. 4). Throughout the sequence in the deserted mansion, this fantasy of equivalence is enacted effortlessly, as the three outcasts find themselves in an environment where it is no longer unsafe to say what one means to say, and where words express what they mean.

Judy's formulation of the ideal companion demonstrates another, related aspect of this fantasy of origin, in which the distinctions between the roles of father and lover are rendered ambiguous:

JUDY: What kind of person do you think a girl wants?

JIM: A man.

JUDY: Yes, but a man who can be gentle and sweet. Like you are. And someone who doesn't run away when you want them. Like being Plato's friend when nobody else liked him. That's being strong.

JIM: I'm not going to be lonely anymore. Ever. Ever.

3   Jim Stark (Dean) at the police station, acting as the ideal father to Plato (Sal Mineo), as Judy (Natalie Wood) looks on. Courtesy Wisconsin Center for Film and Theater Research.

The qualities she finds in Jim are the same qualities that she has discovered her father lacks so severely—he does run away when she wants him, repulsed by her attempts to kiss him on the cheek because she is "too old" to do so. Within the fantasy, however, the boundaries imposed upon desire and filiation are revealed to be arbitrary.

Judy's description, however, also reconfigures the ideal man so that he embodies qualities that have been rendered contradictory and irreconcilable according to the cultural constraints that both of her own parents, as well as Jim's, have accepted. In Judy's utopic configuration, to be "gentle and sweet" is an indication of strength, and the ability to reveal one's vulnerabilities makes a man more of a man. At various points in the film, Jim demonstrates both of these seemingly contradictory attributes. In the opening sequence, he lies helpless in a fetal position on the pavement as he plays with a toy monkey; later, as Ray interviews him in the police station, high angle shots of Jim emphasize his helplessness as the man whom he has attempted to strike hovers over him. Jim's contact with his own pain remains intimate and un-

4   The isolated and misunderstood loner at the police station in *Rebel Without a Cause*. Courtesy Wisconsin Center for Film and Theater Research.

disguised after he pounds his fists violently against the wooden desk, Ray having incited him to release his anger toward his parents. Jim can also be resourceful and very strong, although he demonstrates these qualities only when he perceives his own safety to be threatened. He agrees to play the "chickie-run" game, but he is unwilling to get so close to the edge of the cliff to risk death in the process; in an earlier scene, he rests the tip of his switchblade against Buzz's throat to warn him definitively that he will not endure provocation. In the presence of his father, Jim struggles to articulate his reticence to resort to such demonstrations of invulnerable masculinity as a guiding principle in his life: "I think that you can't just go around proving things and pretending like you're tough. And you can't—even though you gotta—you look a certain way." Yet he receives no affirmation or guidance from a father who appears to have lost his ability to relate to the quandaries of adolescence, and whose weaknesses are not counteracted by demonstrations of strength and assertiveness.

Within the deserted mansion, the threesome establishes an empathy and mutual understanding in which it poses no threat for the individual to function alternately as the giver and recipient of care and compassion. Judy delivers her speech on ideal masculinity as the man who embodies this ideal rests his head comfortably upon her lap (fig. 5). Judy and Jim are similarly positioned in another scene, as Plato comes to join them by resting his own head against Jim's hip. It becomes impossible to deny the allusions to the Madonna image, and in comparison with the traditional configurations of the nuclear family, this variation would seem to be polymorphously perverse: Judy becomes both mother and lover to the man whom she perceives as both the ideal lover and father; Jim is portrayed both as Judy's son and as mother to Plato, and if the mysterious conflations of desire and filiation between Judy and Jim are extended to the two men, Plato also perceives Jim as both the ideal father and the perfect lover. Within the utopic space of the mansion, however, the binaries and polarizations of gender and sexuality, and the "proper" assignment of these variables between mother and father, become neutralized in relationships of equivalence and tolerance. The configuration of the triad thus transcends a description as simply homosexual, heterosexual, filial, or incestuous—it need not be any single one of the above, and yet it harbors the potential to function as all (fig. 6).

5 "What kind of person do you think a girl wants?" Judy and Jim in *Rebel Without a Cause*. Courtesy Wisconsin Center for Film and Theater Research.

6   The perfect family in the deserted mansion, before the ideal configuration is destroyed in *Rebel Without a Cause*. Courtesy Wisconsin Center for Film and Theater Research.

That this utopic state of equivalence and interchangeably can only be maintained temporarily is less a testament to the impossibility of its being imagined than a structural necessity if the melodrama is to yield to the demands of narrative closure. After all, Plato's perception of Jim as his father is sustained within the subjunctive mode of the "if only," and as the gang members intrude on the safe haven of the mansion, the illusion suddenly snaps. Plato once again perceives himself as alone and abandoned; realizing that Jim cannot be his father, he randomly fires his gun at both Jim and another boy. Although this intrusion permanently disbands the triad and forces them to leave their place of safety, in the process drawing Jim and Judy closer together as a heterosexual couple, Jim fails to confirm the police's characterization of Plato as the threatening, pathological menace who must be fired back at. "He needs us," Jim asserts, and when Judy attempts to qualify his statement with "he needed you maybe, but so do I, Jim," he returns, "He needs you, too. . . . He wanted to make us a family. I guess he just wanted us to be like his. . . ." Jim's affection for Plato remains nonexclusive even after the boy has been shot and killed, renewing the offer of a warm coat that Plato rejected in the opening scenes at the police station. "He was always cold," he explains, with an intimacy that suggests a lifelong affiliation with the boy whom he has known only briefly.

Certainly, the ending of the film does suggest that Jim and Judy are capable of sustaining their affection for each other in Plato's absence, and this is confirmed by the looks of mutual approval that Mr. and Mrs. Stark exchange after Jim introduces his new friend to them. In a script synopsis, story analyst Elma LeCron explains that at the ending "it is indicated that Jim and Judy will fall in love and find emotional security at long last," and the final script describes the ending as follows: "[Jim's] voice is warm and brimming with the new found pride in his parents as he introduces Judy to them. . . . there is a warmth emanating from the tight little group. Changes have happened to them. Old things have been shed and a new start has been made."[68] While the ending is intended to secure the journey of the two adolescents as a movement toward assimilation, the description of the ending as simply a "new beginning" oversimplifies and unduly limits the impact of the utopic configuration of human relationships that the narrative established minutes earlier in the mansion. In Jim's own words, Judy is described as a "friend," as someone with whom he has established a mutual trust, and both Jim and Judy feel the loss of the third figure who momentarily shared this trust with them.

The actions of Jim's father at the ending are no less significant to a qualification of the ending as purely assimilationist: his pride in his son stems less from the knowledge that Jim has ultimately learned to accept family life and parental authority on his father's own terms than from his understanding that as a father, he must learn from his own mistakes and from the example that his son has set *for him*. Mr. Stark's expressions of affection and concern for Jim directly echo Jim's treatment of Plato: vowing to stand up for himself and for his son, Mr. Stark offers his coat to keep Jim warm. Given that the discourse of the 1950s situates rebellion as an attractive prospect even while failing to fully articulate its consequences, I find it somewhat limiting to suggest, as Peter Biskind does, that "at the end [the film] delivers these children into their [parents'] hands, integrates them into the consensus."[69] Biskind's evaluation offers one possible reading strategy, yet an alternative reading is easy to make: the ending offers little to suggest that Jim and Judy have any interest in perpetuating the binaries of gender and parental authority that have victimized them throughout the film. The assimilationist reading denies the extent to which the narrative manages to articulate the original fantasy of individuality, connectedness, and mutual understanding—a fantasy that attempts to change the prevailing social order rather than blindly accede to it. In the logic of the family melodrama, this utopic state is rendered all the more powerful because it can be sustained only temporarily, in terms of the "if only." Whether or not the film ever definitively suggests a homosexual desire between Plato and Jim (as some have suggested) is less crucial than the fact that the film does present a character who is capable of not merely tolerating, but also accepting, difference, on the basis of a perception of his own difference from mainstream culture.

East of Eden enacts its protagonist's journey to reclaim a sense of origin as a more literal return to the mother. Arguing with his father, who refuses to discuss the reasons for the mother's departure after the birth of the sons, Cal insists: "I gotta know who I am. I gotta know who I'm like. I gotta know—where is she?" His journeys between the two cities promise to reveal the secret of his identity. Cal wants to find his mother because he instinctively perceives her as the source of his "bad" disposition. As he explains, "I guess there's just a certain amount of good and bad you get from your parents, and I just got the bad."

When Cal finally does induce Kate to verify that she is his mother, the resemblances between mother and son turn out to be more extensive than he had anticipated. She explains that she left Adam and the children because of her husband's hypocritical self-righteousness and his attempts to contain her activities within the home. In an ultimate act of rebellion, she shot and wounded him. Sensing that Cal empathizes with her perception of Adam as a tyrannical figure, and suspecting that he shares her own business savvy as the owner of a brothel, she agrees to lend him money to invest in bean crops so that he can replenish his father's finances. In one sense, this return to the mother satisfies Cal's curiosity by confirming his suspicion that she is alive; however, the disclosure of her motivations for leaving the family, as well as her trust in his ability to profit from her financial investment, thwarts his perception of her as a source of the "bad" in him. In fact, after his meeting with her, he begins to perceive himself dif-

7   The unaccepted gift:
Cal Trask (Dean) with
father (Raymond Massey)
in *East of Eden* (1954).
Courtesy Photofest.

ferently, as he realizes his potential to save the family from financial
disaster, and, hopefully, to gain his father's love and trust. Rather than
defeating his father, his journey is reconceptualized as a new gesture
of connectedness.

Yet both mother and father deny Cal any emotional bond. His
mother turns away from his stare, and she jerks her hand away in re-
pulsion as he moves his own hand over hers to stroke it, retorting bit-
terly, "I've got a business to run!" Adam's rejection is far more devas-
tating. His refusal to accept the money that Cal has earned from the
bean business reduces his son to despair: the devastated Cal cries and
winces, advancing with the money in his hand as his father steadily
backs away. The bills dropping from his hands, he grasps his father
tightly in a final attempt to be comforted, yet Adam shows only disgust
for his son's actions (fig. 7).

To a degree, Cal's individuality has been imposed on him — as others
persist in reminding him of his difference, he just as persistently lives
up to their expectations by performing seemingly unmotivated acts
of rebellion and defiance. Surreptitiously listening to Aaron and Abra
discuss their love for one another in a private corner of the ice house,

Cal disrupts their intimacy by hurling blocks of ice down the chute. Instructed to read aloud passages from the Bible at the dinner table as a penance for his antisocial behavior, Cal reads in a monotonous, disaffected tone; when his father tells him not to include the chapter and verse numbers, he proceeds to recite these *with emphasis*. Still, his individuality and difference from others just as often take the forms of exuberant and gleeful expression: he prances around merrily in his newly acquired beanfield, suddenly dropping to the ground to listen to the earth as though his excitement and anticipation might invigorate the roots of his crop. His impetuousness is also linked to demonstrations of resourcefulness and ingenuity. He installs a coal chute to streamline the loading of his father's lettuce crop into the freight cars, momentarily earning his father's praise before he learns that Cal has stolen the chute. He witnesses his brother's involvement in a conflict between the townspeople and the German shopkeeper from a car at the top of a stranded ferris wheel; without hesitation, Cal jumps from the car and climbs down the narrow spokes of the carnival ride to rescue Aaron.

These attributes of resourcefulness, ingenuity, and individuality are precisely what Abra grows to find attractive and endearing in Cal. At the beginning of the film she says that he frightens her, yet she soon begins to understand that he is the only person in whom she can confide. He understands her because they share common qualities: her mother died when she was thirteen, and she felt alienated when her father decided to remarry; she, too, perceives herself as different from others, "bad" in the same way that Cal sees himself, and therefore unworthy of the love that Aaron bestows on her. Abra shares with Cal a vulnerability that has rendered him suspicious of any good graces that others may offer him: convinced that something will inevitably happen to spoil his father's birthday party and the impact of his gift, he asks Abra to assist him with the preparations; unwilling to believe that she might want to do so, however, he pleads repeatedly, "Will you help me? Will you really help me?" More importantly, Abra sees in Cal not only a difference from others, but a tolerance for difference *in* others that progressively sets both of them apart from Aaron. Cal encourages her to speculate on this insight. When Abra tells him that "sometimes I think I'm really bad. Sometimes I don't know what to think," Cal responds scornfully, "Well, Aaron'll knock that out of you," thus marking the bond between his brother and Abra as a repetition and continuation of the bond between Adam and Kate when they were married: a union based on a conformity to the established designations of good and evil enforced through male dominance and the privileges of patriarchal authority. Aaron's subsequent actions confirm Cal's predictions in a way that Abra cannot fail to recognize. Aaron's birthday gift to his father is a proclamation of their engagement, unbeknownst to the fiancée herself. That the father receives this gift with much greater pleasure than Cal's monetary gift—one that resulted from hard labor and self-sacrifice—is hardly surprising given that it guarantees a transfer of authority to the male child whom the father feels he most resembles.

Yet this successful transfer of authority, and the upholding of clearly delineated distinctions between good and evil on which it relies, is based on Adam's perpetuation of a deception. As long as Aaron believes that his mother is dead, Adam may remain complacent in his disavowal of his complicity in driving her away. Cal is the only figure within the family who is capable of shattering this illusion, and when he does so, the integrity of the patriarchal order is irreversibly compromised: unable to bear the knowledge of his living mother's identity as the embodiment of "evil" according to his father's own laws, Aaron exiles himself by enlisting in the army, laughing at his father as he shatters a train car window with his own head, taken off to a war whose causes he believes to be unjust. Unable to reconcile himself to his own part in Aaron's undoing, Adam falls victim to a stroke that renders him paralyzed and virtually mute.

Certainly, the ending of *East of Eden* can be read as a taming of Cal's rebellious spirit, since he does agree to care for his now bedridden father, and he recognizes his own responsibility for Adam's condition. It can also be read as the reconfiguration of a moral order ultimately revealed to be corrupt. If Adam's ability to maintain patriarchal control has been sustained by withholding the truth from his sons, Abra makes it clear in the final scene of the film that such secrecy can no longer be tolerated. Uncertain that Adam can hear her words, she pleads: "It's awful not to be loved. . . . You never gave him your love. You never asked him for his. . . . You have to give him some sign that you love him. Else he'll never be a man. He'll just keep on feeling guilty and alone unless you release him." It is within the father's power to withhold such a "sign" from Cal (he can speak only in a whisper), and his silence might constitute the ultimate act of vengeance against the "bad" son who has driven the "good" son away. Yet he does provide this final sign, as Cal relates to Abra: "He said don't get anybody else. He said you stay with me and you take care of me."

That the father's final words in the film constitute an attempt to correct the wrongs he has committed in the interests of upholding patriarchal authority provides a validation of Cal's return to his origins. Attempting to identify his mother as the source of his own "badness," and assuming that he has been unworthy of his "good" father's love, the investigation of Cal's filiation ultimately reveals to him that neither parent emblematizes either of these opposites, and that consequently, he need not define himself in terms of the polarized categories of good and evil that his father has constructed. He begins to resemble himself (or, as Abra describes, "a man") more than he resembles either parent. The process that results in a recognition of this "self-resemblance" is facilitated by Abra's own recognition of her similarities with Cal. Although the ending of the film suggests that Cal has taken his brother's place in relation to both Adam and Abra, it is more accurate to say that Cal has found his own place, one which Aaron could never have assumed without renouncing the absolute distinctions between good and evil on which he relied in order to maintain a sense of entitlement to the privileges of the patriarchal order. Indeed, the ending of the film offers no indication that Abra and Cal will repeat the mistakes of their fathers, yet Abra and Aaron as a married couple inevitably would have done so.

If, in *Rebel Without a Cause*, the surfacing of homoeroticism between Jim and Plato is enabled by a briefly sustained utopia of equivalence in which gender and parental roles become flexible and interchangeable, this utopia requires that each of its participants assume identities as outsiders to the patriarchal order, and this difference permits them to discover similarities to one another. *East of Eden* affords Cal and Aaron no such mutual perception of difference, because Aaron sees himself in his father, at least as long as Adam continues to represent what is good in patriarchal authority and dominance. Still, the clash of perceptions that constitutes the brothers' sibling rivalry results in violence and homoerotic tensions that the studio itself did not fail to recognize.[70]

The issue of sibling rivalry is resuscitated and the homoerotic tensions renewed between the primary male protagonists in *Giant*, although here the character of Jett Rink harbors a curious combination of the attributes of both of the male brothers of *East of Eden*. Like Cal, Jett assumes the position of outsider, though here he is ostracized not because he is perceived as inherently bad, but because he lacks blood ties to the privileged lineage of the Benedicts. Like Aaron, Jett assumes that the only way to find his place in the world is by perpetuating the patriarchal order as it exists, and both characters value their similarities to figures that represent patriarchal privilege more than the "sameness to oneself" that ultimately constitutes the individuality of Cal Trask and Jim Stark. Jett believes that he must demonstrate his worthiness of the privileges through his ability to wrest them away from his male rival. Although the narrative provides Jett with no biological father to emulate or resist, Bick assumes the role, symbolically at least, through the fact that he is Jett's employer on the Reata estate. Because Leslie is Bick's wife, she is figured at various points in the film as a maternal figure and as an object of desire (fig. 8).

In the first half of the film, Jett threatens Bick less through domestic subversion than by the occupation of his rival's territory, the tract of land that Luz has left him, and that he dares to name "Little Reata," much to his rival's distress. While Jett is certainly proud of his acquisition, from the beginning it is clear that he considers Little Reata as a stopping-off point on his way to bigger and better things. When Leslie visits the home he has built on his estate, he is noticeably embarrassed to be serving her tea in such a dilapidated environment. A copy of a manual entitled "How to Speak and Write Masterly English" rests on his table, and he tells Leslie that "Someday, I'm gonna have a place I won't be ashamed of." Accordingly, Jett's dedication to the effort of self-improvement begins with the desire to be perceived as successful and sophisticated in the eyes of the world that has denied him a birthright. As the film progresses, he values his land less as a place to call "home" than as a piece of property that yields seemingly unlimited opportunities for exploitation. Once the land is revealed to be rich in oil, it is not long before he earns the right to drill outside of the domain of his small tract on the Reata estate, and he eventually fulfills his prophecy by acquiring ever larger and more expensive properties, culminating in the purchase of his own airport and the hotel where he will invite others to bear witness to his incontrovertible success.

8   Impossible mother/son relationships. Jett Rink (Dean) and Leslie Benedict (Elizabeth Taylor) in *Giant* (1956). Author's personal collection.

Jett's strategy in this territorial expansion is made clear when he rushes to the Benedict estate immediately after he first strikes oil. When Bick asks the purpose of this unexpected visit, Jett initially remains silent, letting his appearance speak for itself: his body is coated with a thick spray of black oil, in marked contrast to Bick and Leslie's clean, pressed, white clothing (fig. 9). "Me, I'm gonna have more money than you ever thought you could have, you and all the other stinking sons of Benedicts," he exclaims as he lumbers slowly toward the front porch, resting his soiled hand on the whitewashed railing. Bick responds with a strong blow to Jett's jaw once he begins to make sexual advances toward Leslie, and Jett returns three stronger punches, gleefully leaving the scene before the fight can progress. For Jett, financial success becomes sweet only if it can rouse the ire of his rival, and throughout most of the film it remains unclear whether his threat to add Leslie to his set of acquisitions is made out of a desire for her, or a stronger desire to spite her husband. What *is* clear, however, is that Leslie is wholly unimpressed by these arrogant demonstrations of masculine privilege, power, and authority; in fact, by the time of this first gush of oil on Jett's Little Reata, Leslie has already proven herself to be successful in curbing similar tendencies in her husband.

In its configuration of the melodramatic fantasy of the origin of the self, *Giant* is remarkably different from *Rebel Without a Cause* and *East of Eden*. Actively renouncing or ostracized from the patriarchal order, the rebellious outsider is also the subject of the fantasy in Dean's first two films; in *Giant*, it is the patriarchal figure himself who gradually learns to establish a sense of individual authenticity and perfect union through connectedness, while the rebellious figure remains ostracized from the fantasy network. Bick's heritage places him in a position of privilege that carries with it preconceived notions regarding various forms of stratification: an inherent racial supremacy, as well as a proper distribution of gender attributes between both husband and wife and his male and female children. Consonant with the obligations of heritage, the enforcement of his authority guarantees that the family order will be preserved and replicated from generation to generation. In her attempt to reverse and disrupt a perpetuation of patriarchal privilege that dictates her own place within it, Leslie becomes an ideal maternal figure, a role model whose goal is to reeducate her husband to overturn his assumptions. Step by step in the second half of the film, Bick

9 The despised black sheep. Dean and Taylor in *Giant*. Courtesy Photofest.

learns to assimilate the virtues of tolerance and compassion, becoming more and more like his wife. He relinquishes ultimate control over his children by accepting their right to determine their own careers, and by the end of the film he accepts (albeit reluctantly) the mixing of races within his family lineage, gazing with pride and bewilderment at the noticeably dark-skinned grandson who does bear his name, yet who will perpetuate something remarkably different from the privileges that Bick has inherited. As Leslie announces in the closing scene, Bick has become her "hero" by losing a fight with a restaurant owner who refused to serve a Mexican family. Having revealed his own vulnerability in the process of standing up for a set of moral values that are worthy of being upheld, Bick becomes the embodiment of an ideal masculinity.

In *Giant*, then, a utopia of connectedness is established by rectifying moral order within the family itself, and when Bick tells Leslie that he will understand if she feels the need to go "home" to Virginia after his "failure" with the restaurant owner, Leslie responds, "Home? Where do you think I've been this last breathless quarter of a century?" Bick and Leslie's shared place has never seemed more like "home" than in these closing moments of the film, when the couple finally shares in a relationship of understanding and compassion, seeing themselves in each other, yet simultaneously having returned to a state of authenticity that nurtures their own individuality.

The sense of loss that is retained within this melodrama is experienced through the figure who has failed to conceptualize his capacity for redemption in terms other than those established by the prevailing, corrupt moral order. Perceiving success in terms of recognition by others rather than by himself, Jett guarantees that he will never attain a sense of the place that Leslie and Bick can call home. Drunk, crying, mumbling, and virtually incoherent as he delivers his final speech in perhaps the only moment of introspection that the narrative affords him, Jett ultimately realizes the workings of his own failure: "Poor Jett. Fighting for what is good. Lucky. Lucky for Bick Benedict. Her husband. Poor Jett. Pretty Leslie . . . Rich Mrs. Benedict. The woman a man wants. . . ." In the context of Bick's moral redemption through Leslie, Jett's failure to attain the object of his desire simultaneously becomes a failure to return to the origin of the self, and to a place of comfort and compassion that the maternal figure emblematizes. The narrative construes his responsibility for his own isolation paradoxically: Bick's ability finally to return to the origin of the self through Leslie has come about only because the privileges of his lineage were initially instrumental in "winning" her; Jett, however, has had no control over his heritage and his lack of family roots. This very lack has guaranteed that a redemptive maternal figure, as represented by Leslie or any other woman, will remain inaccessible. Jett has thus been provided with no means with which to imagine a return to his own origin, and he is accordingly reduced to a position of self-pity, bemoaning possibilities that have never been available to him. Yet he wants to return, and he wants to be loved, and it is through this yearning for a state of connectedness rendered impossible that *Giant* formulates melodramatic pathos: if only Jett had had the family that Bick has; if only he had been able to imagine his redemption in other terms. Here, in Dean's final scene of his last film, it becomes clear that it may indeed be "too late" for the self that has ultimately begun to show signs of emergence ever to be fully revealed.

In each of his three film narratives, then, Dean's character explores the possibilities of attaining a state of connectedness and belonging through the emergence of an authentic self that is dramatized as a melodramatic fantasy of origin. Whether this state of authenticity is figured as absent or irretrievably lost, as it is in *Giant*, or attainable, as in *East of Eden* and *Rebel Without a Cause*, it retains the status of a possibility, a limit that the viewer is invited to perceive in a number of ways that seem inherently contradictory. Dean desires to assimilate with the world that ostracizes him, yet he also rebels against this world and can imagine integrating with it only on his own terms. The configuration of the authentic Dean persona depends entirely on the ability of the texts to maintain a construction of this persona as ambiguous—as emerging yet never fully revealed, as both integrating and alienated. Dean is consistently "neither here nor there," yet he is also portrayed as constantly emerging, and thus maintaining the promise that he might yet be revealed as a full presence that responds to the needs and desires of his audience.

The liminal state of presence-in-absence organized by this ambiguity is integral to Dean's appeal to audiences across the lines of sexual orientation. In conjunction with extratextual discourses of rebellion and sexuality that demonstrate the state of crisis in which 1950s American masculinity found itself, Dean's ambiguous, ever shifting, onscreen persona resonates and crosses over from the concerns of heterosexual audiences to gay audiences—both those who struggle to define themselves outside of the mainstream, and those who want desperately to do nothing more than fit in. On another, related level, the ambiguities of crossover operations within the film narratives begin to reveal how the star persona accommodates the roles of identificatory figure, with whom audiences may relate on the basis of perceived likeness, and object of desire, requiring a more dynamic interplay of self and other, without in the process alienating either self-defined gay or straight audiences.

Yet the narrative and extratextual discourses examined here only begin to touch on the implications of a crossover potential articulated more extensively and elaborately through the voices of studio press agents, journalistic commentators, biographers, and ultimately individual film viewers, before and after the star's premature death at age twenty-four. The interplay of these voices is the subject of the next chapter.

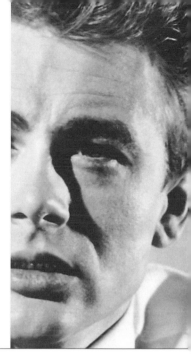

CHAPTER TWO

Stories without Endings:

The Emergence of the "Authentic"

James Dean

A s we have seen, the concept of melodramatic fantasy operates as a structure within individual cinematic narratives, as
an extension of the discourse of rebellion at a specific historical and cultural moment in the 1950s. The dynamics of melodramatic
fantasy are not, however, limited to such narrative and textual operations. The fantasy of star accessibility maintains a temporal dimension as well, through a progression of texts and discourses that evolves
over years, and even generations. In conjunction with Dean's three
primary film roles, publicity, promotional, and critical star texts in
popular cultural discourse extend and reinforce the fantasy of Dean's
authenticity and accessibility by structuring a more expansive melodramatic narrative in terms of the star's career progression. This narrative becomes susceptible to the changing reception practices and
strategies that were developing in American culture after the star's
death in 1955. In fact, the notion of premature death is integral to the
persistence of this melodramatic fantasy. Coterminous historical developments in gay subcultural empowerment from the 1950s to the
1970s would witness the emergence of Dean as a gay icon who no
longer required "piecemeal" assembly by a closeted and silenced sector of the American public. Through this empowerment, Dean would

continue to serve as a figure of identification, but the subculture would also find new ways to access and speak openly of the star as an object of desire.

The Authentic Self in Non-narrative Texts

It would be misleading to suggest that Warner Bros. publicity department was the sole agent in constructing Dean's authenticity and alienation; the development of these and other aspects of his persona resulted from several discursive forces which often acted in conjunction, but were just as often at odds with one another. By the time that Dean was contracted to Warner Bros. in 1954, his star persona had already been developing through a Broadway role in *The Immoralist* (fig. 10) and over two dozen appearances in television narratives, and a James Dean fan club had been formed shortly after the first of these appearances, as John the Baptist, in "Hill Number One" (*Family Theatre*, March 25, 1951).[1] Although the studio regulated star publicity by issuing official press releases and a number of biographical sketches, much of this material functioned as a form of damage control in response to factors that they could not monitor; these included unofficial reports of the star's offscreen behavior and activities, as well as articles on the star in popular magazines. Through efforts that were both deliberate and reactive, however, the studio attempted to regulate the circulation of the star's image as an alienated rebel. At the same time, in response to the consumption patterns of the teenage market, the popularity of the rebel figure that had already been secured by such actors as Marlon Brando, as well as the prominence of the social problem of juvenile delinquency on the national agenda, the studio came to recognize the advantages of exploiting the image of Dean as an alienated figure—even when the studio system itself was revealed to be one of the roots of this alienation. Here and throughout Dean's career, the inherent paradox of managing the persona of an actor whose rebellion reflected a disenchantment with the constraints of Hollywood studio image production, and whose image was developed in part outside of the studio system, was resolved by configuring this disenchantment as a sign of inherently marketable "character."

While it would be difficult to attempt to establish any sense of continuity in Dean's thirty-one television roles between 1951 and 1955, it is

10   James Dean with
Geraldine Page in the
Broadway production of
The Immoralist. Courtesy
Photofest.

interesting to note that several of the most popular of these play upon
the dynamic of alienation and assimilation. As a teenager who leaves
home to find fame and fortune, Dean's role in Sherwood Anderson's
"I'm A Fool" (CBS's *General Electric Theater*, 14 November 1954) prefigures the trajectory of his character in *Giant:* in both roles, Dean attempts and fails to find a sense of place by transforming an unworthy
heritage in a way that will make him appear acceptable in the eyes of a
desired love object. As the youngest of three sons in "Harvest" (NBC's
Robert Montgomery Presents the Johnson Wax Program, 23 November
1953), Dean portrays Paul Zalenka, an outcast on the basis of class, and
a confused adolescent who struggles with the conflict between personal identity and family heritage. In despair over how to tell his parents that he would rather enlist in the army than assume the responsibilities of his father's farm, Paul's alienation is accentuated by the
chorus of the nondiegetic ballad, "And it looks like I'm never gonna
cease my wanderin'."[2]

If several of these television roles establish Dean as an outsider,
Warner Bros. carefully monitored the information that would be
released to the public about the new star, and the early "persona-
in-process" accentuates the sense of Dean's eccentricity and individuality while simultaneously attempting to explain these attributes as indications of something other than antisocial behavior. Even though

Warner Bros. filmed *East of Eden* on a closed set, permitting no interviews with Dean, the press often reported on his bad manners and unconventional attire as indications of his disrespect for an institutional authority that extended to the Hollywood film industry. In a March 1955 assessment of the rising star, *Life* magazine states that Dean's "militantly independent offstage behavior and his scorn for movie convention have studio executives at Warner Bros. apprehensive."[3] This apprehension was confirmed early on, in a letter from Jack Warner to Elia Kazan at the time of casting in March of 1954: "About the boy, Dean. . . . You said he is an odd kid. I hope he isn't too odd as it is getting to the point that when we make pictures with odd people, the whole machine is thrown out of order. You know it only takes one odd spark plug to make the motor hiss."[4]

Dean developed a reputation for being "difficult" and uncooperative on the set of his first major film for the studio. According to Randall Riese, the time which the star needed to prepare himself for a scene frequently stalled production, to the frustration of cast and crew members; at other times, Dean would show up late on the set. He regularly refused to deliver his lines according to the director's specifications. On location in Mendocino, Dean frequently complained about distracting noises which kept him awake at night. Back in Los Angeles, "he began staying out at all hours of the night, hanging out at Googie's coffee shop, going on midnight motorcycle cruises down Sunset Boulevard."[5]

Yet with a single exception, in which the actor is described as "clowning around" on the studio set, the early biographies issued by Warner Bros. do not allude to Dean's status as a problem actor. Throughout Dean's brief career, in fact, the studio press releases frequently attempted to counteract his eccentricity when it could be construed as a sign of social deviance or irrational behavior that might compromise the star's favorable image. To explain obvious acts of eccentricity, the studio shifted the meaning of the act to one that could be interpreted as a sign of character. A press release for *Giant* reports that the conscientious star ordered 10,000 pictures for a fan mail answering service before leaving Hollywood for on-location shooting in Texas, and a *Rebel Without a Cause* release reports that "the usually brooding James Dean surprised everyone on the Warner Bros. lot the other day by greeting all his friends with a hearty handshake and a beaming smile."[6] Eccentricity could also become a sign of the performer's industriousness: the studio's first biography of its new star emphasizes Dean's well-roundedness and resourcefulness by itemizing his various interests and talents, which include athletics, music, theater, and academics.[7] Later in the star's career, press releases highlight not only his dedication to the craft of acting, but also his desire to purchase filmmaking equipment so that he can eventually direct his own films.

One of the most noteworthy strategies for coping with the star's eccentricity was to frame it as a natural extension of Dean's film roles, thus positing a continuum between the actor's history and the development of his onscreen characters. The star was thereby maintained as both eccentric and "in-character," and this combination served to heighten the star's authenticity instead of dispelling it. The popular press cooperated in this venture: the aforementioned *Life* magazine article states that "in Eden [Dean's] skillful portrayal of the elder son of a California rancher stems partly from his own complex personality and from elements of his own farm-bred life."[8] The first two Warner Bros. biographies of Dean, both issued before the release of *East of Eden*, accentuate the correlations between onscreen and offscreen life, and the portrayal of character becomes a natural extension of the actor's roots in America's heartland. In the second biography, Dean explains that "cows, pigs, chickens and horses may not appear to be adequate dramatic coaches, but believe it or not, I learned a lot about acting from them." After a detailed account of his childhood in Fairmount, Indiana, the biography states that "coincidentally, Dean portrays a farm boy, Cal Trask, in the CinemaScope-WarnerColor filming of John Steinbeck's 'East of Eden.'"[9]

By positing a continuum between the star's onscreen and offscreen personas, the star discourse generated by both the studio and the popular press did more than secure the star's authenticity and individuality; it also made nonconformity a symptom of his alienation and loneliness, and ultimately a sign of his vulnerability. As a result, his character portrayals gained more depth, since his biographical past began to function as intertextual "backstory" for his onscreen characterizations. At the beginning and throughout his film career, the star was frequently depicted as having to cope with a loss of origin—a maternal figure—that anticipated a desire to return to a state of connectedness.

If he behaved unconventionally, it was argued, he did so because he was misunderstood, alone; he was alone because he lost the only person capable of understanding him. The fact that Dean's mother died when he was nine years old is emphasized in the first two studio biographies, both of which correlate this loss with Cal Trask's search for his mother in *East of Eden*, and popular press accounts of the star persona frequently associate the loss of the mother with a vulnerability that invites the fan to comfort the star.[10] *Photoplay* columnist Sidney Skolsky suggests that "a woman wants to take care of Jimmy because he looks as if he needs help and kindness," and Dean's friend and biographer William Bast traces a series of "second mothers" that the actor sought in order to relieve his feelings of depression and isolation—the list includes Bast's own mother and Beulah Roth, the wife of Sanford Roth, the still photographer for *Giant*.[11]

The loss of the maternal figure is frequently correlated with a loss of place that accentuates the sense that Dean belongs nowhere and to no one. The roots of this locative ambiguity are also traceable to Dean's childhood: the boy originally lived with both biological parents in Indiana; the family then moved to the West Coast, where Dean resided for four years until the death of his mother; Dean's father then sent the boy back to Indiana to be raised by his aunt and uncle. The sense of placelessness continues even after Dean's acting career begins, as he shuffles back and forth between New York and California in search of work. Studio publicity materials consistently portray the star as homeless, transient, and unsettled: a press release for *East of Eden* states that Dean "has been sleeping in his air-conditioned studio dressing room during the day, while working at night."[12] On location in northern California, Dean takes residence in a Southern Pacific freight train car, after "complaining about passing automobiles keeping him awake in his motel at night."[13] While working on *Rebel Without a Cause*, a press release indicates that Dean "is giving up his Sunset Plaza apartment and is looking for a new abode."[14] The actor's homeless status continues until the end of his career. While he is on location for *Giant* in Texas, the studio suggests that he "has given up, for the present, searching for a house to rent. . . . Dean said he'll keep his one-room apartment until he returns to Hollywood,"[15] yet the actor's final place is only a temporary residence, a rented home in Sherman Oaks.

If Dean's nomadism becomes an indication of loss, it is simultaneously associated with a struggle to locate a state of authenticity, the search for a place where the star can be at home with himself. This search is figured as a return, a recuperation of an authentic self that becomes threatened by the notion of celebrity. The first studio biography draws a clear distinction between the natural, down-to-earth qualities of the farm-bred actor and the superficial and alienating spaces he is compelled to inhabit in his search for public recognition: "[Dean] was overwhelmed by the big city and during the first few weeks [in New York] didn't stray far from the hotel just off Times Square. He would see three movies a day to escape the loneliness and depression he felt." [16] The intentional separation from all one's roots and ties— including those of the more "natural" country space of Dean's childhood—is often figured as a prerequisite to self-discovery. The caption of a famous Times Square photograph of Dean in *Life* magazine reads, "WALKING IN RAIN, Dean wanders anonymously down the middle of New York's Times Square. His top floor garret on Manhattan's West Side is no more home to him, he says, than the farm in Indiana. But he feels that his continuing attempt to find out just where he belongs is the source of his strength as an actor" (fig. 11).[17] Here, the actor's dislocation from both country and city spaces becomes instrumental to the search for an authentic identity from within—the return to origin is predicated on the successful rebellion against origins that have been imposed on the self.

In many of the Dean articles, a tension develops between the identities attributed to the star on the basis of his original country roots, his current star status, and the unanchored, rebellious self that struggles to emerge in defiance of all social and cultural ties. In these cases, the rebel is authenticated specifically by means of his rejection of an artifice most often associated with the Hollywood film industry. Dean's refusal to behave as a star renders him more sincere than if he were to take his celebrity status too seriously, and his sincerity can only be enhanced by the fact that his behavior is often interpreted as antisocial. The rejection of social convention becomes a sign of complexity, and the star's depth of character is accented by the fact that he is willing to endure the risk of being misunderstood and misinterpreted. A writer for *Modern Screen* comments, "He acts awkward and this awkwardness is interpreted as rudeness. Actually, it seems that Jimmy retreats into his shell when he can't handle a new social situation, such as a studio

11 *Life* magazine's representation of the alienated rebel. Author's personal collection.

shindig or a top-level interview or a swank Hollywood get-together. He appears sullen and non-cooperative, but largely because he feels out of place and doesn't know what to do. Also, he is by nature fiercely independent and resents doing anything that rubs against his grain." [18] Dean's appeal, then, is paradoxically rooted in an insecurity, or a sense of placelessness, that can be explained and justified by his sudden and abrupt rise to a celebrity status that offers him no place where he can be himself. His behavior can be described as resilient in that it demonstrates a rebellion against the superficial trappings of success, or it can be deemed compensatory and unpremeditated, "a youthful cover-up for not knowing quite how to handle his sudden stardom." [19] In either case, the star offers the promise of an emerging individuality in relation to which even his own alienation becomes liberating: "At this point, James Byron Dean is living strictly for himself. He has no one to support, no one to please, no one in the world to cater to except James Byron Dean." [20]

Authenticity and Individuality in Film Reviews

Despite these attempts to construct the star as an emblem of authenticity and individuality, the critical responses to Dean's three films demonstrate the extent to which reviewers rigorously scrutinized his persona in relation to contemporaneously held standards of authenticity in film narrative, representation, and acting style. All three of Dean's films were melodramas, and he adopted the Method acting style in each of his roles. Both of these factors connoted a superficiality and excess that 1950s reviewers frequently associated with the products of the Hollywood film industry. These associations initially appeared to compromise Dean's critical reception as an authentic figure. At the same time, however, the critics used Dean's alienated rebel image as ammunition against the studio system that employed him, thereby revealing the roots of inauthenticity to lie in the system rather than the individual whom it exploited. Accordingly, through his critical reception in the 1950s, Dean emerged as an authenticated figure.

In her discussion of the reception of Douglas Sirk's films, Barbara Klinger argues that film reviewers in the 1950s valorized a realist aesthetic traceable to the influences of "war documentaries, Italian neorealism, and developments in the theater," and that the Hollywood film industry was increasing compelled "to meet the criteria of [a] postwar verisimilitude" that demanded the direct and often sensational confrontation of social themes and problems.[21] The realist canon required a subordination of style to content and theme. Stylistic elements that were found to be extraneous to content became signs of a superficiality and artifice increasingly associated with "Hollywood glitz," and "critics insisted that the worthy drama demonstrate signs of alienation from the industry" (74).

Klinger's suggestion that melodrama was most heavily criticized when its narratives were deemed either implausible, morally suspect, or stylistically excessive is supported by the critical responses to each of the three melodramas in which Dean appeared. The same stylistic devices that Hollywood was using to differentiate its product from television in the 1950s are consistently scrutinized for their appropriateness to film content. Both the CinemaScope process and canted camera angles of *East of Eden* and *Rebel Without a Cause* are justifiable only when they support the narrative plot and character, and they are always evaluated in terms of their potential to figure as distractions. John McCarten suggests that "under the direction of Elia Kazan, 'East of Eden' offers a new wrinkle in CinemaScope. Not only is the screen as wide as California, but the camera angles are frequently distorted."[22] The *Newsweek* review of the film takes the criticism a step further, arguing that Kazan's style overemphasizes mood at the expense of acting and characterization.[23] Bosley Crowther finds that the widescreen device and the WarnerColor process constitute a "slickness" that is at odds with the film's intended "realism," and a reviewer from *The Hartford Times* complains that both devices create an "artificiality" that interferes with the "mood" of the narrative.[24] Critical evaluations of stylistic excess in *Giant* are confined to the unnatural and unrealistic effects of the WarnerColor process: John McCarten comments that "as people age in the film, their hair turns electric blue."[25]

Melodrama itself signals accusations of stylistic excess in the film reviews. Andrew Sarris praises *East of Eden* because it successfully aligns its form with its content, and also because "there is none of the superimposed melodrama in *Eden* that we find in [*On the*] *Waterfront* [directed by Kazan and released in 1954] just as there are no easy melodramatic solutions."[26] *Variety* diplomatically argues that the pleasures of this "heavy melodrama" will be determined by individual taste, yet the reviewer proceeds to criticize a film in which "Kazan often allows style to get in the way," formulating a curious distinction between degrees of verisimilitude: "Here, it's the staging of a realism of mood, rather than the realism of life, that predominates."[27] Whereas the realism of *East of Eden* is often redeemed by critics because it is based on a "respectable" novel of the literary canon, the critical responses to *Giant* often cite its more popular literary source as the root of the film's failure.[28] Sarris suggests that "what was false and pointless in the book—the melodramatic treatment . . . is equally false and pointless in the film."[29]

Especially in the case of *Rebel Without a Cause*, the studio publicity unit at Warner Bros. seemed acutely aware of the advantages of appealing to the realist aesthetic in the presentation of social melodrama. Nicholas Ray hired a criminology professor from Berkeley as a consultant during project development, and the production notes for the film include an extensive description of the research that "contributed to the earthy realism of the drama," which included interviews with police officers, juvenile court officials, welfare agency representatives, and psychiatrists. While the research was conducted in an attempt to justify the controversial representation of violence and juvenile delinquency in the film through recourse to "authenticity," it also served to redeem the film as an example of realism; indeed, the fact that Dean incurred minor injuries in the knife-fight scene outside the Griffith Park Observatory guaranteed the film's notoriety months before its release.[30] The studio's promotional strategies were largely successful, and with few exceptions, reviewers either ignored the melodramatic aspects altogether, or argued that they did not distract from the film's realistic presentation of a contemporary social problem.[31]

The discourse of realist aesthetics, and the dichotomy that it organizes between the authentic and the artificial, is extended to the subject of acting style in the film reviews. If, according to the standards of the realist canon, stylistic innovation and melodramatic form threaten the integrity of narrative content, the innovations of the heavily publicized Method acting figure more paradoxically as both an indication of, and threat to, authenticity of character in performance. Integral to this paradox is a fundamental premise of Method acting—the notion that an authentic self, derived from the actor's unconscious depths, can

emerge through performance in a way that obscures any differentia-
tion between the actor and the character he portrays. As Gledhill suggests, "The Method is the contemporary performance mode most able
to deliver 'presence,' the goal of both melodrama and stardom," yet she
also clarifies that in his struggle to attain an authenticity or "presence,"
the Method actor relies heavily on nonverbal systems of expression in
a process that reiterates one of the premises of melodrama itself—that
words have been deemed inadequate to bear the burden of meaning.[32]
In both melodrama and star discourses, the original self becomes a goal
that the actor strives to attain but can never ultimately reach, so that
the act of striving becomes the sign of the subject's authenticity.

As Steven Cohan elucidates, the symbiotic relationship between an
actor's performance and his authenticity plays itself out in the fan discourse of many young male actors of the 1950s. Cohan's study of Montgomery Clift's persona reveals that "the qualities of integrity and intensity make 'acting' and 'being himself' equivalent terms. . . . One
accounts for the other as its origin, and their equivalence turns him
into a cipher, which then causes the fan magazines to reinscribe his in-
decipherability as his most authenticating feature."[33] The notion that
the Method both produces and reflects an authentic self appears to be
at the core of what might be initially perceived as the "crisis of authenticity" that circumscribes Dean's star persona at the start of his career
for Warner Bros. The gradual emergence of Cal Trask's individuality
through a return to (and reconfiguration of) the origin of the self parallels the emergence of an authentic, clearly recognizable star persona
through the studio biographies and popular press articles; however,
the circumstances under which Dean "arrives" in Hollywood to become recognized as a talented actor undercut and disrupt this process
of emergence by the time that his first film is released. From the outset,
Dean is known not only as a rising star, but also as a Method actor. His
actual affiliation with the Actor's Studio in New York was very brief,
yet the fact that he secured his first starring role in a film directed by
Elia Kazan, who "discovered" the star and whose own affiliation with
the Actor's Studio was already known to the public, makes Method acting an integral component of Dean's public identity. A related and no
less integral component of this identity derives from Marlon Brando,
another actor with close ties to the Actor's Studio, whom Kazan had
also directed the previous year in *On the Waterfront*, and whose "re-

semblance" to Dean is frequently articulated by the popular press on the basis of mannerism and style of dress.

The reviews of *East of Eden* begin to reveal a star whose identity is consistently compromised by these affiliations with Kazan and Brando: Dean is defined less as distinctly "like himself" than as the construction of his mentors and historical antecedents, and his identity is linked to an acting style that the reviewers acknowledge as innovative, but which they also describe as no less stylistically excessive than melodramatic form, the aspect ratio of CinemaScope, or the Warner-Color process. The dichotomy between the authentic and derivative makes for some rather curious critical evaluations of Dean's performance. Having clarified that the film avoids the "superimposed melodrama" of *On the Waterfront*, Andrew Sarris goes on to berate *East of Eden* for espousing crucial elements of melodramatic form—namely its overreliance on the actors' "stylized mannerisms and movements" that take the place of much needed "meaningful dialogue." Arguing that the film avoids "easy melodramatic solutions," he yet renounces Kazan's "elliptical style that never fully explains or resolves any situation with language."[34] While Sarris perceives no inherent connection between melodrama and Method acting as forms of expression, he groups them together in a category of stylistic devices that compromise the realist aesthetic.

Almost invariably, when the contemporary critics describe Dean's work in *East of Eden* as a failed performance, it is because the actor has been victimized by an acting style that has been imposed on him in much the same way that style is unduly imposed on narrative content. The star around whom so much publicity has been generated has turned out to be derivative, an imitation of something or someone else. Some, like the reviewer for *Time* magazine, are generous enough to grant that Dean does what he can within the given limitations of this acting style: "Like many Studio students, who have been brought up on 'the Stanislavsky Method,' Dean tries so hard to find the part in himself that he often forgets to put himself into the part."[35] The most consistent criterion for criticizing Dean's performance, however, is that the actor is imitating Marlon Brando onscreen in the same way that he has adopted his style of dress offscreen. Some critics describe the imitation as entirely intentional on Dean's part: Louella Parsons complains, "Aren't Jimmy Dean's imitations of Elia

Kazan directing Marlon Brando a little too biting for appreciation in certain quarters?"[36]

In most cases, however, the critic's observation that Dean's performance is derived from Brando results in the *authentication* of both Dean's onscreen and offscreen personae. This is accomplished through one of two strategies, used singly and often in conjunction. First, the responsibility for the imitation is displaced from Dean onto Kazan, who is accused of attempting to re-create his creation of Brando in Dean through the Method, thus imposing on the newcomer a style that denies the actor's ability to emerge as an individual on his own terms. A writer for *Saturday Review* explains that "Kazan has apparently attempted to graft a Brando-type personality upon Dean." If "the result is less than successful," it is not because Dean lacks talent: indeed, the critics proceed to describe the considerable merits of Dean's Broadway performance in *The Immoralist*. The failure occurs because the director has become guilty of an "artful construction," an imposition of style that denies the natural development of a promising actor.[37] Even when critics do not cite the talents of Dean's past acting work, Kazan's imposition of the Brando mimicry begins to generate curiosity about the actor's capabilities in the hands of a less controlling director. *Variety* describes the process of Dean's individuation as a struggle for emergence against insurmountable odds: "Just how flexible his talent is will have to be judged on future screen roles, although he has a basic appeal that manages to get through to the viewer despite the heavy burden of carboning another's acting style in voice and mannerisms. It should be interesting to see what he can do as Dean."[38]

Even the most scathing assessments of Dean's performance participate in the process of authentication. Describing Cal Trask as "a mass of histrionic gingerbread," Bosley Crowther continues: "Never have we seen a performer so clearly follow another's style. Mr. Kazan should be spanked for permitting him to do such a sophomoric thing. Whatever there might be of reasonable torment in this youngster is buried beneath the clumsy display."[39] Kazan's imposition of style also yields to the critic's assessment that the derivative is more talented than the original: a reviewer for *Catholic World* suggests that "at times [Dean] is forced too consciously into the Marlon Brando-Montgomery Clift mold but I suspect that he has more individuality and scope than either of them."[40]

The second strategy of authenticating the star involves a direct disruption of the authentic/derivative dichotomy, with the intention of displacing Brando as Dean's mentor, so that the new star's behavior is seen as indicating the natural expression of the individual. In an attempt to redeem the star on his own terms, this strategy is adopted primarily by those who react favorably to Dean's performance as Cal, and it often involves the participation of the Warner Bros. publicity department. In an interview shortly after the release of *East of Eden*, Nicholas Ray, the director of Dean's forthcoming Warner Bros. film, offers a point-by-point analysis of the Brando attributes that Dean has been accused of imitating. He clarifies that Dean's interests in car races and motorcycles predate Brando's, and that "the only similarity between the two is that James also is a serious and sensitive young actor." Ray also uses the studio's strategy of defending Dean as a well-rounded individual with a variety of interests: "I've seen him come to my apartment, take off a heavy leather coat, pick up a piece of sheet music and play Mozart very delicately."[41] *Newsweek*'s assessment of *East of Eden* is hardly favorable: the reviewer decries Kazan's emphasis on mood over narrative and characterization. Ironically, the dismissal of the film as failed narrative is followed by a four-paragraph biographical sketch of the praised actor, primarily comprising a number of studio press releases. The section includes the standard studio material on Dean as well-rounded individual, but it also offers the actor's own assessment of the accusations of "Brandoism": "People were telling me I behaved like Brando before I knew who Brando was. I am not disturbed by the comparison, nor am I flattered. I have my own personal rebellion and don't have to rely on Brando's."[42]

Filtered as it is through the voices of the Warner Bros. publicists, this strategy of authenticating and individualizing the star by permitting him to defend himself in his own voice prevails in several of the reviews of Dean's first film. While in the reviews of *Rebel Without a Cause* several critics continue to be annoyed by the similarity of Dean's acting style to Brando's, now that they are presented with a second Dean performance, the locus of the authentic/derivative dichotomy shifts from an evaluation of past mentors and influences to past roles and characterizations. The *Rebel* reviews often foreground the links, relationships, and continuity between the Cal Trask and Jim Stark roles and the ways in which the actor portrays his characters. This continuity is occasionally marked as further evidence of Dean's derivation: a review in *The Morning Telegraph* points out that "Mr. Dean's performance is, of course, a copy of that sliding, slithering, upside-down kind of thing he did in 'East of Eden,'" yet the reviewer immediately qualifies the attributes of this self-imitation as "hallmarks of the distinctive James Dean style."[43] Even as Eugene Archer associates character continuity with imitation by identifying Jim Stark as "a simplified variation of the part he created in *East of Eden*," he notes a coherence and individuality in this role repetition, in which Dean becomes "a confused adolescent in revolt against his surrounding environment, motivated by an unhappy relationship with his father."[44] Whereas many of the unfavorable assessments of Dean in *East of Eden* link inauthenticity to Method acting, Archer's review of *Rebel* associates the style with a *natural* quality that he finds in Italian Neorealist performers such as Anna Magnani: "The mannerisms employed are natural ones, frequently encountered in American life, and consequently approximating reality much more closely than the graceful movements and evenly-modulated delivery of previous styles."

With the accumulation of just two major film roles, Dean begins to emerge as an individualized persona who is no longer deemed derivative so much as he redeems and vindicates whatever is artificial, imposed, or unnatural in his films. No longer associated with a Kazan project, the actor is said to have "overcome" his Brando-like tendencies, and "he reveals completely the talent latent in his 'East of Eden' performance."[45] This sense of redemption is even more apparent in the reviews of *Giant:* the *New Yorker* review describes Dean's mannered performance as the only sign of authenticity in a film with an overinflated narrative scope and an inappropriate use of WarnerColor: "He proves that Stanislavsky is just as much at home among the cattle as he ever was off Broadway."[46] The *Film Culture* review entirely reverses the authentic/derivative dichotomy by defending Dean's style as "straight 'method' acting," arguing that the "actor's studio interpretations" of Texans adopted by Dean and Carroll Baker constitute more "authentic regional characterizations" than those supplied by the "native" Texan actors in the film, Chill Wills and Jane Withers.[47] The *Giant* reviews either praise Dean's Method acting style or refrain altogether from referencing it as a salient point of critical assessment.

Evidence does not support the conjecture that, between the time of release of *East of Eden* (March 1955) and Dean's two latter films (October 1955 and October 1956), the canonical standards of the realist aesthetic were drastically modified to accommodate as natural and authentic an acting style that had previously been perceived as an affected, self-conscious construction—in many ways the ultimate sign of artifice. Nor is it reasonable to assert that the status of melodramatic form and narrative was in the process of being vindicated during this time. What *had* changed, however, was the status of the actor himself: Dean died approximately one month before the release of his second film, and thirteen months before the release of *Giant*. While the accumulation of character portrayals certainly contributed to critics' redemption of Dean as an actor, death figures as a more prominent factor that informs and continues the shift in critical reception of the star from the derivative to an authentic and individuated persona.

Death and (Dis)closure

In his illuminating assessment of the popularity of the postmortem star, Edgar Morin postulates that "the supreme escape is death, just as the absolute is death, just as the supreme individuality is death."[48] If Dean's death prevents the possibility of any future film narratives that might further individuate the star persona, it also invites film reviewers to attribute distinction and individuality to a figure whose popularity was at its apex at the time that his career was abruptly curtailed. The reviewers also attempt to make the star's life story "coherent," such that the arrangement of parts in this story would begin to make logical sense as a recognizable whole. Many of the *Giant* reviewers formulate this coherence by attempting to secure a sense of closure to the Dean "story" on the basis of the star's death. For Bosley Crowther, *Giant* becomes "a haunting capstone to the brief career of Mr. Dean,"[49] while the reviewer for *Time* magazine discovers in this final performance a sense of the full presence of the star: "James Dean . . . in this film clearly shows for the first (and fatefully the last) time what his admirers always said he had: a streak of genius."[50] Hollis Alpert attributes full and ultimate emergence of the star persona to the consistency of his three film roles, less on the basis of acting style than in terms of character and identity: "In each [film] he played a young, tortured rebel, a renegade who was basically good, who got into trouble with his environment because he was incapable of conforming." [51]

If death helps to resolve and authenticate the star persona, in Dean's case the sense of closure that might be provided by death comes too early. Premature death leaves unresolved the issues of how the star's life and career might have progressed "if only" there had been no car crash: "[Dean] played one part, emotionally, in all his pictures— a lonely, rejected, rebellious, confused and dangerously idealistic adolescent—and he played it with a passionate demand to be understood that came off the screen like a blow. What he did was utterly convincing and indescribably touching, but whether he could have done anything else we won't know." [52] What reviewer Robert Hatch makes clear here is that the use of death as an endpoint to secure the star's individuality and the coherence of his life story is wholly inadequate in Dean's case: if his roles demonstrate a consistency of character, they also provide the viewer with access to only a very limited portion of a larger emotional spectrum that necessarily remains indeterminate and therefore becomes boundless. The range of the spectrum that has been made accessible to view reveals a figure whose location remains unfixed ("lonely," "rejected," "confused") yet who is moving toward or away from some fixed point ("rebellious"). The star's three character roles expose a persona suspended in a state of urgency, remaining fundamentally opaque at the moment of his death because there can no longer be any definitive response to his "passionate demand to be understood."

If death fails to ensure coherence because it leaves aspects of the star persona unresolved, then the "solution" to this problem may be approached in many ways. Details from the star's offscreen life can be used to reconfigure his onscreen persona in a way that makes the fact of death appear to be inevitable; alternatively, the star's life itself (both onscreen and offscreen) can be situated as a logical prelude to other resolutions capable of being imagined *in spite of* the fact of death. Both strategies are used in the postmortem star discourses surrounding James Dean, and in both cases, death becomes less a definitive mark of closure than a signal to start over again from the beginning, to write the history of the star subject so that the story's ending makes sense. Because of the incontestable fact that there can be no more screen narratives to supply depth of character, however, this writing also becomes a rewriting, one that necessarily depends on the imaginative faculties of the individual whose affective investment in the star requires a formulation of the star persona's history as coherent and intelligible.

This process of rewriting inevitably involves the melodramatic fantasy, figured once again as a reconfiguration of the origin of the self. It both interprets and attempts to complete the process of rebellion, a movement from an unstable, unanchored, and unfixed location to a stable place of connectedness and self-recognition. Although the star persona functions as the catalyst that initiates the fantasy, the pleasure here is that of the participant, guided not exclusively by the series of primary narrative texts (there are, after all, only three and no more) but also by extracinematic discourses that extrapolate from the onscreen persona. Following the logic and structure of fantasy, the pleasures to be derived lie less in the possibility of ever attaining a definitive solution to the problem of origin, than in the elaboration of settings of desire in which this problem can be staged. Since the premature death of the star as the emblem of truth and meaning guarantees that his identity ultimately remains ambiguous, it becomes impossible, and indeed irrelevant, to confirm the accuracy of the fantasy scenarios, and the specific pleasures of fantasy necessarily depend on the desires of the individual participants.

In the fantasy network, the fact that the star can no longer verify the "truth" of his identity facilitates the generation of a number of possible truths, each of which serves to authenticate Dean's persona. As Morin suggests, in the postmortem discourses "the 'heroic' life and character of James Dean are not prefabricated by the star system, but are real, revealed. There is still more."[53] In the years immediately following Dean's death, the public demand for additional details about the star's life was so strong that any new (or recycled) information was deemed preferable to silence. After publishing William Bast's three-part Dean biography and several other articles on the star in 1956, *Photoplay* published a letter from a fan who thought that by continuing to perpetuate Dean's name in the press, the star's image was being dishonored. In an editorial appearing beneath the letter, *Photoplay* concurred with the fan's perspective and announced that there would be no more Dean stories.[54] Not more than three months later, however, the journal's "Readers Inc." column published a letter from another fan who be-

12   Dean in his Porsche Spyder, en route to a road race he would never reach. Author's personal collection.

lieved that *Photoplay*'s silence was itself disrespectful to the memory of Dean: "I keep thinking about the thousands of Dean fans who *want* to hear more. . . . Jimmy's fans have not forgotten him." In a diplomatic editorial comment, the journal announced that its sole interest was to accommodate reader demand, and since so many readers had responded angrily to their previous decision, *Photoplay* agreed to recommence the publication of Dean materials immediately.[55]

The attempt to rewrite the history of the star as an individual whose life story is made coherent through death is a feature of several articles in *Photoplay* and various scandal magazines in the late 1950s; in the years immediately following Dean's death, these efforts coincided with the interests of Warner Bros., who also participated in this effort to "make sense" of the star's life by issuing two final biographical sketches in 1956 and 1957. Indeed, the studio had considerable stakes in this venture, and each of these biographies strategically anticipates the release of a new film that promises to "complete" the star's life story for his audience. Teleologically, in both biographies, death is figured as an incident that makes sense because of the star's interest in racing, yet both pieces also accentuate an irretrievable loss that is about to be abated by new narratives featuring the star (fig. 12). Issued two months before the release of *Giant* in November of 1956, the first of these biographies includes a comprehensive retracing of the star's life. Outlining the significant stages of Dean's development from birth to death, the sketch has the feel of a rags-to-riches story tragically interrupted by a car accident occurring at a moment when the star appears at last to have attained depth of character and a sense of purpose as a public performer.[56] Released as publicity for Robert Altman's forthcoming biopic *The James Dean Story* in 1957, the final studio biography is the only one to stress Dean's individuality and rebellion, and it describes his death as "a tragic close [to] a brilliant career that had only begun to bloom"(fig. 13).[57]

Neither of the biographies needs to introduce "new" information about the star in order to configure death as both a logical outcome and a tragic, unforeseen interruption of his life: the fact that Dean

13   The funeral service, from Robert Altman's *The James Dean Story* (1957). Courtesy Photofest.

for solitude is sometimes taken for separateness or a distaste for companionship." [65]

A mythological figure brought down to earth and revealed to harbor the same problems and concerns as other unextraordinary men and women, Dean becomes accessible to a public who comes to understand his personal rebellion as an extension of its own. In the postmortem texts, the fact of death provides a critical distance from which to assess fans' affective investment in the star as the recognition and confirmation of a likeness that is overtly described, in an increasingly popular psychological discourse, as an identificatory phenomenon. Both the popular press and fans themselves participate in this process of recognition. With remarkable psychological clarity, *Saturday Review* proposes that "Dean provided a symbolic channel for [the public's] own rebellions against the pressures of conformity, lacks of love and feeling." [66] *Look* magazine explains that Dean's success as a star resolves the primary conflict among adolescents between "the pressure to conform and the drive to develop individuality." [67] There is often a considerable urgency for fans' perceived likenesses to the star to be confirmed by those who have attained an "authority" status through their interactions with Dean—especially George Stevens, who directed his last film, and Hedda Hopper, who presented him favorably in her interview.

If there is additional information about Dean to be revealed in these testaments to identification and likeness, it is an affective sensibility that the fans suspect has been overlooked or misrepresented in the sensational, profit-oriented Hollywood film industry, as well as by the popular press. The identification reveals a private, intimate, and sometimes almost inexpressible connection between star and fan, both of whom have been misunderstood. In the process of revealing the star as sincere and authentic, the correction of misunderstanding also validates fans' identities, since they are now provided with a vehicle for self-recognition. The connection is often established through a common quest for a truth that can be indicated but never defined. In a celebrated, ethereal poem published in *Photoplay*, Dean fan Evelyn Hunt expresses an inability to reconcile herself to the actor's death; several months later in Hunt's letter to the editors, she explains that "from one of Jim's close friends I have learned that the qualities of character I ascribed to Jim by a kind of instinct for the truth were the qualities he actually possessed." In the follow-up poem appearing in the same column, she confirms the mutual likeness of star and fan by proposing that Dean possesses the qualities of the same "searcher for the truth" that she has revealed herself instinctively to possess.[68] Here and elsewhere, the more opaquely this truth is circumscribed, the deeper the potential connection between star and fan.

The most complex configuration of star and fan in the identificatory process arises through the effect of Dean's ambiguous constructions on his relationships with women. If the star is consistently portrayed as unanchored in terms of location, and either moving toward or away from a fixed point, he is also a victim of arrested development, occupying a nebulously defined position between childhood and adulthood. The ambiguity was constructed long before Dean's death: his physical features, mannerisms, and shyness define him as "boyish" in many of the *East of Eden* reviews. At the same time, the reviewers' observation that the childlike features are offset by attributes of strength and resolve serve to make his persona deeper and yet more indeterminate. The *Detroit Free Press* describes his portrayal of Cal Trask as "suitably boyish and uncertain, yet equally strong in determination"; from the perspective of a critic from the *Los Angeles Times*, Trask is a "kind of stumbling, tormented, but ultimately valid manboy."[69] With the release of *Rebel Without a Cause*, Dean's indeterminacy becomes associated with confused adolescence, and the same critic notes that he is "too old for kid stuff but not yet grown to responsible adulthood." The in-between status of the star is reflected by his embodiment of a wide variety of seemingly polarized attributes that mark the dichotomy between innocence and experience: his childhood vulnerability is tempered by adult strength, "sensitivity" is coupled with "force," and "pensive" and "moody" yield to "dominant" and "actionful."[70]

The ambiguity of these man-boy descriptions does not render him inaccessible as an object of sexual desire; instead, it becomes integral to what one columnist describes as "a new style of male sexual appeal": "He is not a muscle-flexing hunk of beefcake. It is not his chest expansion, but his brain power, his personality, his lost-soul mannerisms and his deeply philosophical approach to life that have made him so attractive to a tantalizing assortment of lovely young women. His shy, uneasy ways—a welcome contrast to the strutting

peacocks they are so accustomed to—stirs up the sentimental feelings in them."[71] The nature of these "sentimental feelings" is difficult to pinpoint: The same writer proceeds to explain that "Jimmy's
gals . . . have pretty much made a fad of mothering and understanding him." His female admirers are thus purported to respond to the
star as both mother and lover, in a sexualization of maternal instinct
that recalls the configuration of filiation, gender, and sexuality in each
of Dean's three films: within and outside of the narrative, his capacity
and need for "understanding" make the star an object of both identification *and* desire, while it also blurs the boundary between these
two forms of affective cathexis.[72] The conflation of parental and sexual
roles resists being defined as incestuous because it transpires in a utopic
realm in which the interchangeableness of roles indicates equivalence
and mutual understanding. Here, strength is no longer incompatible
with vulnerability; indeed, the need to be cared for becomes a sign of
strength. Resembling especially the dynamics between the members
of the ideal nuclear family in *Rebel Without a Cause*, the star/fan relationship plays itself out as a desire for connectedness in a fantasy of the
origin of the self—a fantasy that demands a reconfiguration of socially
assigned roles.

In the star texts published after Dean's death, the construction of
this fantasy of origin becomes more elaborate. The female fan continues to respond to the star as both mother and lover; perpetuating
the contemporary psychological discourse, however, the loss of Dean's
biological mother is configured as an *explanation* of his suspension in a
state of unconnectedness at the time of his death. Accordingly, the star
texts effect a historical reconfiguration that attempts to make sense of
Dean's life through his death; the story of James Dean is dramatized
as a return to the beginning, to the origin of the self where connectedness, understanding, and meaning are guaranteed and self-evident.
Yet the biographical facts of the star's childhood ensure that this ideal
reconfiguration of the star persona can only function as a limit that is
perceptible rather than attainable.

If the loss of Dean's mother already figures prominently in the promotional studio biographies and publicity texts during the star's life,
after his death the loss of his mother becomes integral to the construction of coherent narratives that extend the fantasy of origin beyond the three films in which the star appeared. For example, "The

Triumph and Tragedy of Jimmy Dean," a 1956 cartoon biography by Lou Cameron, structures the story of Dean's life as a literal return to the mother. While Bast's biography identifies three "second mother" figures, Cameron extends the list to include Dean's New York agent Jane Deacy, Natalie Wood, Elizabeth Taylor, Pier Angeli, and Ursula Andress. With Dean's mother identified as the only person capable of understanding him, his moodiness and antisocial behavior are consistently attributed to her loss. He attempts to regain this sense of understanding in all of his relationships with women during his acting career. In campfire conversations with Elizabeth Taylor on location in Texas, Dean begins to open up "just enough to hint at the presence inside him of that mystic vein left by his mother's death." He comes closest to finding a "sense of self-recognition" with his kindred spirit Pier Angeli, with whom "he felt confident and sure, almost for the first time since his mother had died." Dean is devastated when she subsequently marries Vic Damone, blaming himself for the fact that she has rejected him. Only by dying can the star effect the desired return to the mother: speeding down the highway in his sports car, with the fender of the vehicle he is about to hit figured prominently in the foreground, one caption reads, "I feel as if I'm close to my mother again, as if she's very near to me" (fig. 14). The subsequent image displays the looming headlights of the oncoming vehicle, refracted to resemble two large female breasts.[73]

Here and in several other scenarios that reenact the melodramatic fantasy of origin, the loss of the mother guarantees that it is always too late for the star to reclaim a desired sense of wholeness and connectedness, and Pier Angeli's rejection functions as a microcosm of the star's original, maternal loss. Paradoxically, while they conflate maternal care with sexual desire, the narratives also explain the failure of each of the star's heterosexual relationships as the result of Dean's realization that friendship is distinct from love, and that the maternal figure cannot simultaneously serve as an object of desire. This realization only exacerbates his sense of loss: Cameron stresses that "never did anyone yearn more desperately than Jimmy yearned to fall in love," but his maternalization of any potential object of desire guarantees a failure that becomes historically grounded as "fate."[74]

This explanation of Dean's single status lends coherence to a series of publicity and promotional texts that describe the star's relation-

14   "I feel as if I'm close to my mother again." The penultimate frame of Lou Cameron's "The Triumph and Tragedy of Jimmy Dean" (1956). Author's personal collection.

ships with women; at the same time, it offers a form of damage control to deter any suspicions that the star was anything but heterosexually inclined. Studio press releases frequently insinuated that there was romantic potential between Dean and Angeli, Wood, and several other women.[75] Not long before the actor's death, a press release groups Dean together with two other actors, Rock Hudson and Tab Hunter, identifying each of the men as an "eligible bachelor" who has not yet found the time to commit to a single woman: "They say their film rehearsals are in conflict with their marriage rehearsals."[76] After his death, his commitment to his career continues to serve as the perfect explanation of his unattached state; one source suggests that he shied away from committed relationships "not to hurt [the] girl but rather to prevent their being hurt in any way."[77] Another source explains that only through Pier Angeli did Dean begin to understand that he could have both a career and a relationship, but "by the time he *did* know — it was too late," both because Pier had already moved on, and also because the actor would soon run out of time (fig. 15).[78] The actor's conflict between maternal friendship and sexual desire was often reported to have had disastrous consequences: one writer suggests that Vampira may have been instrumental in Dean's death, because of a retaliatory rage at "being demoted to platonic palship."[79]

While many of the postmortem texts use the concept of personal or maternal loss as a mark of closure to the Dean story, another prominent strategy is to speculate on alternative scenarios that configure this loss as either avoidable or already avoided. Responding to the question of what might have happened "if only" the actor had found the ideal companion before it was too late, one writer argues that Dean had already done so: her name is Betty Lou, and she lives on a farm outside of Baton Rouge, where Dean met her one day as he was driving in his sportscar. Positing that Dean's plans to return to Louisiana to marry her earlier were disrupted by his car accident, the author attempts to gain credibility by situating the marriage proposal as a resilient demonstration of Dean's defiance of Hollywood producers who tried to force him to date more publicly recognizable women; his act

15   Dean with Pier Angeli, on the set of *East of Eden*. Courtesy Wisconsin Center for Film and Theater Research.

is therefore perceived as consonant with a private persona whose own farm roots resemble Betty Lou's. This secret proposal brings a sense of closure to the actor's long series of unfulfilling relationships, enhancing the resonance of his ultimate discovery of true love because it has never been publicly acknowledged. At the same time, the piece anticipates Betty Lou's own disclosure of her private relationship with the star.[80] A piece entitled "Did Jimmy Dean Leave a Son?" makes it much less likely that disclosure would confirm the truth of a rumor that "Mary B.", a carhop at a Sunset Blvd. drive-in restaurant, was carrying Dean's child at the time of his death. Confirmed by unnamed, close acquaintances, the circulation of the rumor is enough to preserve the possibility that "James Dean would live on—in the material form of another person—his own son."[81]

The Emergence of the Homosexual Dean

If a common feature of these texts is a tendency to authenticate and anchor the alienated star persona through a historical reconfiguration of his origin that explains why Dean never committed to a sexual relationship, they also function collectively as an attempt to negotiate the star's sexuality so that he may remain accessible to a desire configured as exclusively heterosexual. According to the hypothetical logic of the "if only" construct, even the fact that Dean was twenty-four years old when he died supports this assertion: he was, after all, young enough for public discourses to reconcile his single status to an extended (if interminable) period of youthful experimentation that would culminate in his discovery of the woman who could satisfy his desires and bring to an end his search for connectedness. At the same time, however, these numerous attempts to settle the star in either a hypothetical or actual heterosexual relationship only serve to draw attention to the fact that his identity, as well as his sexuality, remains unanchored and ambiguous at the time of his death. In the process, Dean's image becomes more open to appropriation in queer readings of the star.

During the star's brief film career, the film industry participated in this negotiation of Dean's sexuality not only by issuing press releases that emphasized the star's accessibility as an eligible bachelor, but also by attempting to regulate the reception of his image. Scenes from *East of Eden* that were deemed to be too overt in their suggestion of

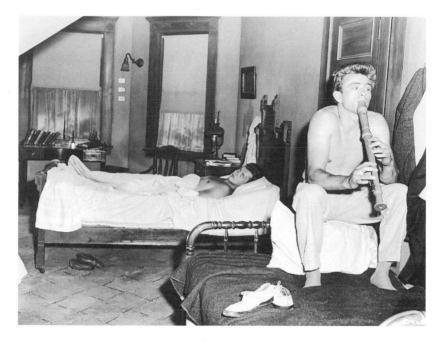

16   Cal Trask (Dean) with brother Aaron (Richard Davalos) in a scene deleted from *East of Eden*. Courtesy Photofest.

homosexual tension in the sibling rivalry between Cal and Aaron were deleted from the film (fig. 16).[82] Additionally, in a letter from Geoffrey Shurlock to Jack Warner several months before the release of *Rebel Without a Cause*, the head of the PCA advised the studio that "it is of course vital that there be no inference of a questionable or homosexual relationship between Jim and Plato."[83] Yet even though the PCA regulated both the inference and representation of homosexuality in the 1950s, magazine and film journal reviews brought homosexuality into discourse since they remained outside of the PCA's domain.[84] Chon Noriega argues that while such references to homosexuality in 1950s film commentary were primarily negative, they still served to acknowledge the existence of viewers who might read mainstream cinematic representations against the grain. In the case of *Rebel Without a Cause*, these inferences were occasionally reattributed to the film through the same popular psychological discourse that the film itself used to suggest the instability of the nuclear family. After identifying the characters portrayed by James Dean and Natalie Wood as "victims" of an

Oedipus and Electra complex (respectively), a reviewer for *Presbyterian Life* explains that "there is also the suggestion of a latent homosexuality among teen-age boys." [85]

After Dean's death, when the studio relinquished any control over the circulation of his image, criticism and commentary extend this acknowledgment of alternative readings to the star outside of his film roles. Using the star's own voice in his 1957 biography, William Bast narrates Dean's attempts to secure stardom on his arrival in Hollywood by ingratiating himself with (unnamed) influential figures in the studio system: "I did a little dancing myself, and it was dumb. I thought it might pay off. But it doesn't take long to find out it won't. I'm not performing for any of them. Not anymore. And if I can't make it on my talent, I don't want to make it at all. I know, maybe I'll never work in this crummy town, but at least I'll preserve some dignity." [86]

While euphemism and indeterminate pronoun references confine homosexuality to the realm of inference and subtext in the biography, the issue of sexual orientation surfaces in the more open discussion and negotiation of the star's sexuality in scandal magazines. By protesting that Dean was incontrovertibly heterosexual and attempting to dispel any rumors that suggested otherwise, the scandal pieces open up a space for alternative and contestatory readings of the star's sexuality. The nature of Dean's "dancing" is anything but opaque in an article by Lynne Carter, who reportedly "learned about love from Jimmy Dean" when Dean was in Philadelphia for previews of *The Immoralist*. Dean confided in Carter that "a noted producer . . . made a play for him," and although she certainly emphasizes that the star declined the offer, her description of Dean's reaction to homosexuality is ambivalent: "As for the slimy insinuations that Jimmy himself was a sex pervert because he frequented certain Greenwich Village hangouts, I find them ridiculous and unfounded. He never felt it was right to openly judge any one person or thing. He accepted people on the basis of their character and not their color or class." [87] Carter's attempt to dispel rumors that threaten the star's accessibility as a heterosexual results in the introduction of additional rumors that can be neither confirmed nor denied by her own interpretation.[88] While this commentary invariably continues to configure homosexuality as pathological, it also stresses the star's capacity to accept difference in others unjudgmentally, thereby establishing itself as consonant with Dean's film roles (in the first two films at least) and his offscreen image as an alienated rebel who is perpetually misunderstood and misinterpreted, but who also has a great capacity for compassion. At least as much as they express disdain for the homosexual act or person, Bast and Carter vilify a corrupt film industry that requires that actors do "a little dancing" in order to succeed.

Yet Carter's interpretation of Dean's reaction to homosexuality is significant for another reason: although it certainly does anything but attempt to establish the star as gay, it bears a curious resemblance to the descriptions of heroic behavior set forth by Donald Webster Cory six years earlier: "For an individual who is himself not homosexually inclined to find himself out of sympathy with society's treatment of the invert requires a combination of faculties that is indeed rare—a critical and imaginative mind, a spirit skeptical of socially accepted folkways, a deep insight into an alien group." [89] These are qualities that the star is revealed to have demonstrated not only in film roles such as Jim Stark through his concern for the outcast Plato, but also in his interactions in the reputedly homosexual milieu of Greenwich Village in New York City. If such behavior is rare especially because a "sympathetic viewpoint" might generate the suspicions of others, Dean continues to qualify as an advocate for homosexual behavior because he never cared what others thought, and because any future suspicions cannot affect the now deceased star.

While these confluences between rebellious and homosexual behavior are occasionally brought to the forefront in the popular public discourses of the late 1950s, it is not until the early 1970s that they begin to constitute deliberate attempts to identify the star himself as homosexual.[90] Throughout the 1960s, public interest in the star appears to wane. There is little consistency to contemporary explanations for this shift in the star's relevance. In a 1964 piece for *Film Culture*, Taylor Mead postulates that the public continues to crave stars who can serve as figureheads for revolutionary ideas, but a stale and sterilized contemporary Hollywood film industry has failed to provide them.[91] In 1965, *Films and Filming* speculates that in the current world in which "the real social problems . . . are either impersonal or out of control of the individual," audiences can no longer be encouraged or inspired by the efforts of heroic figures who emblematize individuality.[92] In another retrospective twelve years later, however, the same journal attributes the waning of the cult to the "cynical or apathetic

attitudes" of the 1960s and 1970s, in which Dean's "brand of uninhib-
ited emotion" seems out of place.[93] A 1976 piece in *New York* magazine
suggests that Dean's undirected and unfocussed rebellion became an
"anachronism" during the 1960s, by which time "rebels had causes and
some were prepared to die for them."[94]

Anachronistic or not, it is pertinent that most evaluations of Dean's
popularity in the 1960s and 1970s continue to indicate rebellion as
the most salient feature against which to assess the star's place in the
contemporary cultural climate. If the rebel hero is identified as unanchored or out of sync with the times in relation to teenage rebellion, he becomes yet more pertinent to homosexual rebellion in the
process. Some critics trace this claiming of the star as a "gay icon" to
Kenneth Anger's appropriation of the Dean image in *Scorpio Rising*
(1964), which, according to Juan A. Suarez, "made visible the gay community's reception of Dean, whose screen persona as a sensitive, tortured outsider embodied some aspects of the subculture's self image."
Suarez speculates on the likelihood that Dean had an established gay
following by the mid 1960s, on the basis of the gay undertones of the
Jim/Plato relationship in *Rebel Without a Cause*, as well as "rumors
about Dean's homosexuality" that may have circulated by the time of
the release of Anger's film.[95]

Certainly, Anger's film facilitated the circulation of rumors that
scandal discourses of the late 1950s had inadvertently introduced
through their foregrounding of the issue of the star's sexuality. Still,
the differences between the negotiations of Dean's sexuality in the
early 1960s and the 1970s point to a set of changes in the discursive
construction of homosexuality in mainstream society, as well as in
the emerging gay subculture—medical, juridical, political, and representational changes that affected not only the ways that homosexuals
were perceived by society, but also the ways that they were invited to
perceive themselves. In the early 1960s, Dean's status as homosexual
icon is confined to the realms of "underground" and subtext; by the
1970s, however, gay cultural critics openly debate the matter of the
star's sexuality among themselves as well as with mainstream writers,
in a contestation whose stakes involve the open acknowledgment, recognition, and legitimization of homosexual identification and desire.

Changes in the representational practices of the Hollywood film industry indicate some of the ways in which homosexuals were becoming

more visible to the mainstream throughout the 1960s. In 1961, the Production Code was revised to permit the representation of homosexual characters, at least within the boundaries of "good taste." While this regulatory modification certainly resulted in more representations of characters who acknowledged their homosexuality, Vito Russo argues that the public's perception of this "other" sexual orientation experienced no correlative change: "An important by-product of the Code revision was the allowance of the American dream of staunchly heterosexual heroes to coexist with visible homosexuality so long as the two fought the classic battle and homosexuality and heroism did not occur in the same person."[96]

Yet even if the film industry's sanctioning of homosexual representation provided more opportunities to vilify and pathologize homosexuality in the media, it also provided homosexuals with onscreen verifications of their presence in culture, and it may even have contributed to the acknowledgment of an emerging homosexual community. In a 1982 *American Film* debate on the value of these early cinematic representations of homosexuality—a debate conducted among a group of self-acknowledged gay film critics and historians—Stephen Harvey argues that films such as *Advise and Consent* and *The Children's Hour* (both released in 1962) signalled a shift in mainstream cultural perceptions of homosexuals: "They were dealing candidly with the fact that there were gay people out there who were sensitive and intelligent and often hounded through blackmail to suicide. Depression and loneliness were the best that could be hoped for. But this is a relatively liberal attitude. These people were regarded as victims, not menaces. The movies represented tentative steps towards dealing sympathetically, if not positively, with the image of gay people in America."[97] In the same article, Stuart Byron explains that the increase in cultural representations of homosexuality made it easier for him to "come out" at this time, because "it was in the cultural air that homosexuals existed." He adds that "I also think that media visibility of gays certainly had its effect on gay consciousness. If they're going to be onstage for all the world to see, then maybe it's less threatening to go out on the streets when a bar is raided" (62).

Homosexuality's increased cultural visibility was certainly not confined to onscreen representation. Throughout the 1960s, an abundance of articles in popular magazines devoted themselves to the topic of homosexual life, signalling an "implicit recognition that gay men and women existed in groups with a network of institutions and resources to sustain their social identity."[98] A *Time* magazine article appearing just three months after the 1969 Stonewall incident provides a particularly cogent example of the proliferation of homosexual discourse and its potential effect on the lives of gay men and women who had remained culturally isolated and silenced for decades. Featuring a photo spread above the caption, "Homosexuals Watching Old Movies in San Francisco Gay Bar," the article traces the history of the gay movement since the early 1950s. Its historical trace is also extended through the listing of gay and gay-identified authors such as W. H. Auden and Oscar Wilde, as well as an acknowledgment that Geoffrey Chaucer represented homosexuals (albeit negatively) in *The Canterbury Tales*. The article includes anonymous interviews with four men and women currently involved in homosexual relationships, and it concludes with a symposium ("Are Homosexuals Sick?") among authorities in the fields of sociology, psychology, and religion. Significantly, however, the panel also includes noted gay activist and Mattachine Society ex-president Franklin Kameny.[99]

The importance of the presence of avowed homosexuals in open forums conducted in mainstream publications cannot be overestimated, and it evidences a gradual yet clearly noticeable shift in medical constructions of homosexuality in the 1950s and 1960s. As discussed earlier, sociological theories of subculture were instrumental in identifying juvenile delinquency as a form of social adaptation in response to increasing pressures to conform in the 1950s, and John d'Emilio reveals a parallel, yet much slower, shift in the discursive construction of homosexuality. Signals of this shift from psychological pathologization to sociological adaptation occur as early as 1954, with Lionel Ovesey's "The Homosexual Conflict: An Adaptational Analysis." Ovesey posits homosexuality as an effect of "the disorders of the mid-twentieth century" that manifest themselves in "the generalized anxiety of the nuclear age, intense competitive demands on males, pressure to conform, the rapid pace of technological change, [and] shifting roles and increased expectations of American women."[100] Nine years later, Howard Becker's *Outsiders* (1963) suggests that sexual deviance is an effect of a dominant culture that arbitrarily defines boundaries between normality and abnormality (142).

Stressing that such revisionist perspectives of homosexuality were out-weighed by the prevailing pathological definitions, d'Emilio yet insists that the introduction of these revisions "weakened the consensus sur-rounding homosexuality that had so hampered the efforts of homo-phile activists in the 1950s and that had helped to keep gay women and men away from the movement" (144). By 1974, partially resulting from the efforts of the gay liberation movement, the American Psychi-atric Association finally removed homosexuality from the list of social disorders.

Changes in the juridical construction of homosexuality coincided with these shifts away from the medical model. Increasingly through-out the 1950s, the American Civil Liberties Union successfully repre-sented homosexuals in discrimination cases. Longstanding sodomy statutes began to be challenged as early as 1957, and both Illinois and Connecticut overturned such statutes in the 1960s. Just as importantly, challenges to obscenity laws escalated in the late 1950s and into the 1960s, and the adoption of the "redeeming social value" clause resulted in the dissolution of barriers to the sale and distribution of gay fiction and pornography.[101]

During the 1960s, changes in the self-perception of homosexuals within the emerging subculture run parallel to these changes in main-stream cultural perceptions. As noted earlier, the Mattachine Society had taken an assimilationist stance since the mid-1950s, soliciting the testimony of noted social and psychological experts in order to legit-imize homosexuality in the public eye. In the 1960s, however, radi-cal and militant activists openly decried this assimilationist stance, in the process making gay politics more confrontational, encouraging the homosexual community to take pride in their difference, and ulti-mately rejecting the pathological model. In the early 1960s, activist Randy Wicker openly acknowledged his homosexuality to the press; in a letter to his mother shortly before an appearance on national television, he explained that "I will be reaching dozens, perhaps hun-dreds, even thousands of young men and women who are lost and confused, who are thinking of suicide, who are laden with guilt, who cannot face the world, who think they are the only ones in the world who feel as they do. I will be a 'symbol' of hope to these people."[102] Franklin Kameny's academic career at the University of Arizona had been ruined when his homosexual involvements were publicly disclosed, and his efforts helped to secure homosexuals with access to legal representation. Kameny also became a key figure in the Washington Mattachine Society, and in 1965, he was instrumental in developing and promoting an "antisickness" platform that caused internal rifts in the more influential New York Society's leadership. In the 1965 New York elections, militants successfully ousted the assimilationist faction, thereby overturning Mattachine's official, longstanding position on the pathology issue.[103]

It is in the early 1970s, with the onset of a more publicly visible gay liberation movement, when homosexuals begin to *participate* publicly and confrontationally in their own discursive construction—a construction which brings to the forefront issues of "identity" and "place"—that Dean appears in the press as not only an ally to gay rebellion, but also a potential homosexual himself. In 1951, Donald Webster Cory suggested that "by identifying men and women of indisputable merit with homosexuality, the cultured inverts hope to detect a clue as to the specific contribution that being sexually in a rejected minority might have made to the creative geniuses of these people."[104] In the star texts of the 1970s, Dean begins to qualify as a *historical* figure for the gay liberation movement, one who might attain "heroic" status on the basis of, rather than in spite of, his homosexual identity. Just as importantly, if the hero has remained spatially unanchored as a result of his rejection of mainstream culture, he finds a sense of place in a movement that espouses the virtues of self-recognition over self-denial. Focusing on matters of self-recognition and identity, the 1970s negotiation of Dean's sexuality is conducted both within and outside of a gay community that struggles to make its voice heard, and to have the accomplishments of its heroic figures recognized. Concerned with the location and production of coherence and meaning at the locus of the star persona, the debates continue to operate according to a melodramatic structure articulated in several different ways, depending on whether the author's intention is to confirm, deny, or render ambiguous the truth of the star's sexuality.

Although the matter of the truth of Dean's sexuality certainly informs most of the accounts of Dean's life published in the mid-1970s, not all of the biographers are interested in confirming that the star was gay; many confirm that what has been and will continue to be revealed about the star's life only serves to highlight a fundamental indeterminacy of character that leaves his persona accessible to audiences of all sexual orientations. This debate concerning truth thus constitutes a struggle over the meaning of the sign of homosexuality. In a piece published in *The Advocate*, William Bast explains that he decided to write the screenplay for a 1975 made-for-television biopic in order to protect the star's image from recent rumors and allegations, arguing that his close friendship with Dean makes him eminently qualified to present an objective assessment of the star's life. Bast had used these same justifications eighteen years earlier when, at the height of the postmortem Dean cult, he wrote the first book-length biography of the star. Extending the studio's construction of the star persona as a well-rounded individual to the matter of his sexuality, Bast argues that "he dabbled in everything. He wanted to experiment with life"; his interviewer explains that while "Bast won't say that [Dean] is gay . . . he will say that Dean is definitely bisexual. He will go even further and say that he believes that Dean was basically heterosexually inclined." [105]

John Howlett's *James Dean: A Biography* (1975) echoes Bast's earlier study of Dean, conceding that the star engaged in homosexual acts only out of a sense of desperation in his first years in Hollywood. While he does not attempt to construct the star persona as exclusively heterosexual, he identifies Dean's sexual encounters with men as only another sexually unspecific manifestation of the star's need for acceptance.[106] Venable Herndon's *James Dean: A Short Life* (1974) discloses recent accounts of rumors of the star's homosexuality more explicitly and sensationally, yet he ultimately concurs with Bast and Howlett's perspectives by configuring the star's homosexual tendencies less as a sign of gay identity than as an obligatory response to a corrupt Hollywood. For example, Herndon explains Dean's decision to move in with gay television producer Rogers Brackett as a convenient way of "dumping" Beverly Wills, a woman whom he was being pressured to marry but did not love.[107] David Dalton's *The Mutant King* (1974) constructs the star as an opaque, mythological figure whom he compares to the god Osiris, arguing that his malleability and quintessential androgyny made him "a universal . . . symbol for just about anything imaginable." [108]

Within the gay community itself, however, the debate unfolds as a radical reaction to an extended period of silence and historical obscurity that appears to be coming to an end. In 1951, Cory had already announced that if the homosexual had been accused of resorting to the strategies of "rationalization, illogical deduction, planned confusion, exaggeration and suppression" in his attempt to identify and construct common features with the public figures he appropriates as gay, the claim that these figures were by default definitively heterosexual had been deduced by similar means: "If the homosexuals are guilty of building their studies on a feeble foundation . . . the heterosexuals are no less guilty in arriving at the opposite conclusions. In fact the biographers who have been so anxious to leave their heroes 'untainted' have lied, suppressed, and distorted in a manner that must be much more shameful than anything in the lives of their subjects."[109] While homosexuals in the 1950s were relegated to a position of silence, the more vocal gays of the 1970s reactivate Cory's strategy by constituting the production of the truth of Dean's star persona as an act of defiance and rebellion. In the late 1950s, writers had attempted to rewrite the star's life in order to make sense of his death; the revisionist biographies of the 1970s are more purposefully political regarding the matter of a historical correction based on textual interpretation, rumor, newly revealed details of the star's life, interviews with those who can provide the most informed assessment of the star's identity, and citations of the star's own authentic voice.

The historical reconfiguration of the star persona in 1970s criticism by gay men situates Dean in a debate over identity politics, an issue that had polarized the gay community into assimilationist and minority factions since the 1950s. Attempting to organize a fragmented and silenced gay community into action against social oppression, the political platform of increasingly influential gay activists and militants of the 1960s stressed the importance of pride in difference and the rejection of pathological models that mainstream society had used to disable such pride. In these efforts, they were inspired by the rebellions of other 1960s social movements that aimed to empower disenfranchised minorities. John d'Emilio emphasizes that gay activists such as Franklin Kameny took the "direct action" strategy of the Civil Rights Movement as their model for effecting social change. A primary component of this strategy was to foreground difference instead of attempting to mask it; Kameny observed that "I do not see the NAACP and CORE worrying about which chromosome and gene produced the black skin, or about the possibility of bleaching the Negro."[110]

Adopting the Marxist politics of the Mattachine Society's founders in the early 1950s in conjunction with the "direct action" strategy of effecting social change, the revolutionary Gay Liberation Front (GLF) of the early 1970s was also inspired by the radical feminist movement in calling for a radical overturning of a heterosexist ideology that oppressed homosexuals by enforcing "the primacy of the nuclear family and the dichotomous sex roles within it." [111] D'Emilio and Estelle Friedman argue that the act of "coming out" constituted the most empowering demonstration of pride in difference: "Coming out of the closet was incorporated into the basic assumptions of what it meant to be gay. As such, it came to represent not simply a single act, but the adoption of an identity in which the erotic played a central role. Sexuality became emblematic of the person, not as an imposed medical label connoting deviance, but as a form of self affirmation" (323).

That this constitution of a core identity based on sexuality ultimately served to repolarize sex roles rather than render them fluid is a paradox that is foregrounded in identity politics of the 1980s and 1990s, yet the paradox inherent in the act of "coming out" also informs the contestations over the truth of Dean's sexuality in the biographies of the mid-1970s. In the first book-length study of gay representation in cinema (1972), Parker Tyler reveals Dean's homosexuality as self-evident, in a contestatory textual reading that could never have been tolerated in Cory's time: "We all know that the late James Dean's rather hard, but very pretty, physical shell was a homosexual parody of Marlon Brando, in that it . . . became a fetish of boy-man homosexualism." Describing the Jim/Plato relationship in terms of a master/slave dynamic, Tyler shamelessly discloses that the "*secret* cause" of Dean's rebellion is the redemption of homosexual desire.[112] Using a somewhat more methodical approach, Jack Babuscio combines textual interpretation with an enumeration of recently revealed biographical evidence to conclude that Dean's alienation and "rejection of social convention" is the root of a "gay sensibility" that can be discerned only by other homosexuals who find themselves on the fringes of mainstream society. Accordingly, Babuscio finds Venable Herndon's method of disclosing gay rumors that serve only to enhance the star's sexual ambiguity as evidence of a "heterosexual bias." He also renounces the early Dean biography *Rebel* (1962), in which Royston Ellis first pathologizes the star's homosexuality, and then excuses it only because the star managed to remain "discreet" about his illness. Babuscio's historical corrective demands that Dean's homosexuality be displayed and acknowledged in defiance of the stigma that mainstream culture will attach to it in an effort to protect the star's image: "A reminder, then, to future biographers: James Dean was a homosexual. This fact was crucial to the development of his personality and his art. Furthermore, as a member of an oppressed sexual minority, his orientation adds further psychological significance to his life experience and creative output. If this is not understood, then no sense can ever be made of the life of James Dean." [113]

As was the case in many of the star texts published in the late 1950s, historical correction in the 1970s texts does not always require an author to substantiate his claims with documentable evidence, yet the 1970s texts are far more gleeful, as well as deliberate, in their rebellion against conventional methods of discerning truth. While Tyler focuses specifically on matters of textual interpretation and appropriation, in his treatment of Dean in *Hollywood Babylon II* (1984), Kenneth Anger relays several intimate details of the star's life as though they were already common knowledge within the gay community. Anger reveals that Dean suffered from crab lice on the set of *Rebel Without a Cause*, and that the star was nicknamed the "Human Ashtray" because of his predilection for the pleasure of cigarette burns at S&M bars.[114] Even as he sardonically identifies rumor as "the vodka in America's screwdriver," *Advocate* writer Donald Von Wiedenman stirs the drink a few times by publishing a still from a porno film in which Dean was purported to appear. He comments, "It is difficult to say who is attached to that mammoth, erect cock, but to millions of men and women, it sure looks like Dean, a giant in more ways than one." [115]

In the process of historical reconfiguration, the rewriting of the star's life sometimes involves a return to origin that is quite overt. In a book-length biography, *The Real James Dean* (1975), the star's close friend John Gilmore extends the psychological discourse of the 1950s star texts in a lengthy discussion of Dean's childhood, arguing that the loss of the mother exposes the truth of the star's identity. His intent, however, is somewhat different from the 1950s accounts of this loss. Gilmore explains that "Winton [Dean's father] is on record as having complained to Mildred [Dean's mother] that his son was girlish at times and that no red-blooded boy should be satisfied to spend more time with his mother than with playmates of his own age." [116] Instead of attempting to reclaim the lost mother, however, this version of the Freudian scenario reveals a boy in search of a *father* substitute: "His own father never recognized him, and Jimmy was to spend the remainder of his short life seeking an alternative" (122). While the 1950s texts limited the "mothering" instinct to female fans, Gilmore extends it to "the girls and boys and the faggots" (63).

Yet Gilmore's reconfiguration of Dean's origin becomes as much an investigation of the author's own identity as a search for "the real James Dean," and it is here that the melodramatic fantasy most clearly intertwines identification with desire. Gilmore's biography is a curious combination of advance and retreat, confirming that Dean certainly experienced homosexual desire during his life, but simultaneously disavowing that he was exclusively gay. The intimate bond between author and biographical subject is much stronger here than in any of the other book-length biographies of the 1970s, and toward the end of the book Gilmore's relationship with Dean assumes a utopian construction that, however momentarily, stabilizes the scene of desire by suggesting that the two men recaptured a sense of origin through their mutual connectedness: "When he learned that I'd published some poetry and was doing quite a lot of writing, we got closer, and he began to enter more directly into my life. Eventually I was to feel as though I were mother, brother, lover to him, and that there were only Dean and myself and no others in the whole world, and he gave me the feeling that we were riding *against* the world, that we thereby shared a kind of common anguish between us" (115). In this almost metaphysical utopia, the blurring of boundaries between self and other is augmented by the multiplicity and interchangeableness of roles that the men enact, dissolving distinctions of gender and filiation in a way that echoes the radical reconfiguration of the nuclear family in the deserted mansion of *Rebel Without a Cause*. It is perhaps for this reason that Gilmore refrains from marking the star as gay—less from an intent to protect the star from public censure than from a suspicion that the label is inadequate to contain these polymorphous manifestations of identification and desire.

Gilmore's description does not, however, tell all there is to tell about either the "real" James Dean or John Gilmore, as is revealed by the title of his article-length, revisionist biography published in 1980: "I

Had Sex With James Dean!" Here, the author contends that the earlier book "tells the truth as I laid it out to the publisher," and his subsequent contention that the "whole truth" is a subjective matter that can never ultimately be known is demonstrated in rather graphic descriptions of his numerous sexual encounters with the star.[117] The piece provides a different slant to Bast, Herndon, and Howlett's suggestion that Dean's homosexual encounters were motivated only by his desire to become famous; in his account, Gilmore confirms that both he and Dean did have sex with noted Hollywood figures for this reason, that the encounters were humiliating, but that these shared experiences have only served to enhance the bond between them as self-designated outcasts. After one of the many sexual scenarios that the article describes between the two young actors, Dean explains that with Gilmore "it's different, isn't it? I mean, it's different than being with people that you don't like and that you think you have to be with, right?" (17) In Gilmore's account, their mutual respect, identification, and desire arose from a shared scorn for a film industry that requires them to be something other than themselves.

"Jimmy liked to cuddle in bed," the author explains. "He liked to be held and he liked to be kissed" (18). The sex scenes are played out with such softness and gentleness that what the two men actually do in bed is sometimes difficult to discern: an extended deliberation on who will assume the top and bottom positions is never clearly decided, yet when they awake the next morning, Dean asks, "You want to do it again?" (17) Although the climaxes are described vividly enough, the pleasures that Gilmore derives from these experiences clearly lie more in the suspension and delay of ultimate gratification, and even moreso from the ability to recall, narrate, and repeat these scenes of desire that have been etched in memory: "I have a great warmth inside of myself and a kind of place I can go to, that has to do with Jimmy. My feelings for him were a sort of pivotal point, you might say in a spirit sense, at that time of my life."

Both here and in Gilmore's account in the earlier book of Sal Mineo's experiences with Dean, biography becomes a therapeutic, confessional narrative whose goal is to locate this "place" where the author or subject can feel at home with himself.[118] Mixing identification with desire, the fantasy of connectedness serves to anchor and stabilize the identity of both biographer and biographical subject. In the fantasy scenario, repetition is central to this stabilization: discussing his own death scene at the end of *Rebel Without a Cause*, Mineo explains how much he relished the chance to experience "what it would be like for someone close, someone that I idolized, to be grieving for me." Mineo explains that "I wanted to do that scene over and over again, and each time we did it, he'd position me in the kind of repose that would work best for him to get the emotion going. It was very moving for me, because *he* was very moved." [119] That the fantasy facilitates the subject's own self-recognition becomes even clearer in an interview with Mineo two years before his own death, in which he explains that he never identified his attachment to the star as a manifestation of desire until years after Dean's death, when "I realized . . . that I was homosexually attracted to him" (figs. 17 and 18). Clarifying that the two men never had a sexual encounter, Mineo yet suggests that "we could have—like *that*." [120] These curious regulations of proximity to and distance from the desired object are rendered more haunting in a 1978 piece written after Mineo's death—reputed to be a "homosexual slaying"—that suggests that after Dean's death Mineo was perpetually haunted by a psychic connection with the star.[121]

In many ways, then, the debate over Dean's sexuality in the 1970s perpetuates several of the strategies used in the texts that have constructed his star persona since the early 1950s. Throughout his career and continuing into the star's "afterlife," a fundamental truth must be disclosed in order to render Dean's identity meaningful. During Dean's brief career, this truth is assessed in terms of a conflict between the authentic and the derivative; after his death, truth becomes a matter of a redemption of the star's life, an attempt to make sense of a tragic incident that would forever prevent the alienated figure from attaining the understanding that he was purported to crave. In the 1970s, truth becomes, more emphatically than ever before, a matter of sexual identity. In each case, the discernment of truth requires a return to the origin of the self, a repetition that must start from the beginning of the star's life to effect a coherent historical reconfiguration. Consistently, ultimate truth is perceived more as a limit than a goal of the investigations conducted by studio publicists, film critics, writers of the popular press, and gay men in search of role models to emulate. A primary difference between these two historical periods, however, involves a reconfiguration of power structures and the agents who participate in

17/18   Sal Mineo's looks of desire, reciprocated in the police station (Figure 17) and surreptitious outside the Griffith Park Observatory (Figure 18). Courtesy Wisconsin Center for Film and Television Research.

deciding how this truth may be configured, and for what purposes. These differences result from fundamental changes in the discursive construction of homosexuality in a span of over twenty years.

Even if those who knew the star most intimately appear to have privileged insights into the mystery of James Dean, Gilmore's suggestion that the truth is always susceptible to the interpretations of the perceiver leaves open the potential for the generation of a seemingly limitless number of possible versions of this truth. If there will always be additional details to be kept secret, and subsequently to disclose, about this ambiguously configured star persona, Gilmore and Mineo's fantasy scenarios—whether or not they can ever be historically verified—reveal that this may be because there always remains some distance to be covered in the search for a "place" of the self.

Clearly, in the early 1970s, the crossover phenomenon manifested itself in the coexistent expression and publication of straight readings of the star, as well as gay readings that would never have been tolerated twenty years earlier during the actor's career. It would not be long, however, before a much different form of crossover would make such a categorization of reception strategies by sexual orientation a much less discrete operation—one whose very ambiguity would begin to entice the same film industry that had earlier expended such great efforts in maintaining star images as exclusively heterosexual. These developments lead us to Hollywood in the late 1970s, and to Mel Gibson.

CHAPTER THREE

Identity Transformations:

Mel Gibson's Sexuality

*I*n January of 1997, Mel Gibson invited a select group of lesbian and gay filmmakers to the set of his latest film project,
Conspiracy Theory, in an attempt to make amends with an increasingly vocal sector of the American viewing public. Heavily publicized in both the gay and mainstream press, this "day-long seminar"
was organized through the efforts of the Gay and Lesbian Alliance
Against Defamation (GLAAD), a watchdog organization formed in 1985
to monitor and challenge stereotypical representations of homosexuality in the media. At a meeting between Gibson, his press agent Alan
Nierob, and GLAAD representatives in May of 1996, Nierob stated that
"the gay community should know [Gibson] is not homophobic, nor
has he ever spoken out against [gays]."[1]

Yet by the mid-1990s GLAAD had accumulated a substantial listing of grievances that challenged the accuracy of Nierob's statement.
The first of these concerned *Bird on a Wire*, a 1990 summer release
in which homosexuals are represented as flamboyant and stereotypically affected hairdressers who serve as objects of ridicule for the characters portrayed by Gibson and co-star Goldie Hawn. Three years
later, the script for Gibson's first directorial effort *The Man With-*

out a Face (1993) attempted to elide any implications of a homosexual relationship between teacher Justin McLeod (Gibson) and the student he agrees to tutor, even though Isabelle Holland's 1972 source novel had foregrounded McLeod's homosexuality. The most vituperative of GLAAD's accusations concerned *Braveheart* (1995). According to GLAAD representative Al Kielwasser, "The ostensibly 'fact-based' epic portrays Edward II (believed by historians to be gay) as an excessively foolish and vain homosexual, deserving the audience's ridicule. In screenings thus far, audiences have consistently laughed (on cue) every time the character appears on the screen, and have even cheered as Edward's lover is tossed out a window to his death."[2]

In addition to such character portrayals, Gibson's vocalization of his political position regarding the issue of homosexuality roused the ire of GLAAD. The actor's politics were rarely foregrounded in publicity discourses at the start of his career, but by the late 1980s his conservatism became too difficult to ignore: in interviews he began to speak out against abortion and birth control, and he expressed opposition to the Catholic church after the liberal reforms of Vatican II. In an interview with the Spanish newspaper *El Pais* in December of 1991, he lashed out against all forms of homosexual conduct, and actively distanced himself from the gay community with which he had been "mistakenly" aligned on the basis of his profession. Adding insult to injury, in a *Good Morning, America* interview he outwardly refused to apologize for his statements, arguing that "I have a right to an opinion."[3]

The gay community's response to Gibson's opinions included protests and boycotts. In 1992, National Gay and Lesbian Task Force (NGLTF) spokesperson Robert Bray urged for political countermeasures: "Gay fans of Mel Gibson need to throw away their Mad Max tapes and stop going to his movies until he stops defaming gay people."[4] Gibson was urged to decline an offer to appear at a January 1992 fundraiser for San Francisco's Bayview Opera House because his "recent anti-gay and anti-choice remarks make him too big a target for protesters."[5] At the summer 1993 premiere of *The Man Without a Face* at the Chinese Theatre in Hollywood, Gibson was greeted by "a half-dozen homosexual activists carrying placards reading 'Anti-woman, anti-gay, anti-choice,' condemning alleged past homophobic remarks by the actor."[6] In the summer of 1995, GLAAD urged gays to document

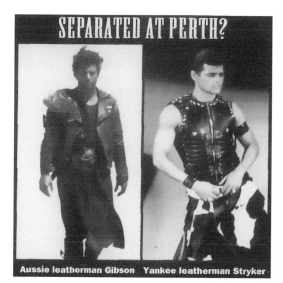

SEPARATED AT PERTH?

Aussie leatherman Gibson   Yankee leatherman Stryker

19 "Sissy of the Year" Mel Gibson, with gay porno star Jeff Stryker. From *The Advocate* (June 30, 1992). Author's personal collection.

their concerns over the homophobic elements of *Braveheart* by sending letters to the head of Paramount Pictures, and to entertainment magazines that either ignored or downplayed Gibson's homophobia in recent interviews and cover stories.[7]

Gibson's remarks in the *El Pais* interview also earned him the dubious honor of "Sissy of the Year" in *The Advocate*'s third annual Sissy Awards competition in June of 1992. Both the lead story and the cover recontextualize and legitimize Gibson's self-acknowledged fears of being perceived as homosexual by foregrounding gay readings of his persona. The cover story features a series of questions that Gibson posed in the *El Pais* interview: "Do I sound like a homosexual? Do I talk like them? Do I move like them?" And *The Advocate*'s response is that "Frankly, Mel, honey, you do!" To support this point, the story strategically juxtaposes two photos (fig. 19). On the left, "Aussie leatherman Gibson" is shown in torn leather regalia in a scene from *The Road Warrior* (1982); on the right, "Yankee leatherman [Jeff] Stryker," the celebrated star of gay porno films, poses decked out in a somewhat tighter-fitting, studded leather outfit. Under the caption "Separated at Perth?", the resemblance between the two figures is (pardon the pun) rather striking. On the magazine cover, a shirtless Gibson gazes intently at the camera in a waist-up shot as he presses his fingertips to his nipples, thereby suggesting a variety of potential responses to another of Gibson's questions to *El Pais*, placed immediately adjacent to the photograph of the star: "With this look, who's going to think I'm gay?"[8]

Gibson's question assumes, of course, that there is an identifiable "gay look"—one that is inconsonant with his own image—and this assumption points to one of the central concerns of the present chapter. Beginning in the mid-1970s and continuing through the early 1980s, at which time Gibson emerged as a rising star of the Australian New Wave cinema, gay style was sufficiently pervasive and influential in mainstream American society that it was often rather difficult to make clear distinctions between heterosexual and homosexual artifacts in culture. While this phenomenon of crossover between dominant and alternative sexualities was at its height, significant transformations in the cultural construction of masculinity were taking place—both within and outside of the gay community—and these transformations made the boundary between straight and gay identities yet more ambiguous. Many gay men began to actively and noticeably challenge a stereotype of effeminacy that had been imposed on them historically for decades, and this challenge resulted less in a disruption than in a reinforcement of boundaries between male and female. Coterminous with these newly masculinized gay self-representations, however, American consumer culture was also discovering new methods of scrutinizing and packaging the male body, which became vulnerable and accessible as an object of desire in ways that also suggested its feminization.

If industrial, political, cultural, and social changes from the 1950s to the 1970s were instrumental in the gradual transformation of James Dean's persona into a figure that many gay men were able to appropriate as a sexual ally, historical changes from the 1970s to the 1990s reveal a reverse trajectory, in which Gibson's initial crossover appeal is gradually narrowed. Unlike Dean, whose premature death rendered him susceptible to various appropriations that he could neither authorize or refute, Gibson actively participates in his own transformation. So how is it that Gibson's star persona is rendered accessible to both gay and straight readings from the outset of his career, despite the fact that he has never appeared as a self-acknowledged gay character in any of his films? And what later happened to change this so dramatically?

Identity Transformations: Sexuality from
Revolution to Commercialization

A useful starting point for understanding the crossover appeal that Mel Gibson enjoyed at the start of his career is the complex set of convergences and divergences of homosexual and mainstream culture in the 1970s—developments that had a profound effect on the representations of male sexuality and its reception by straight and gay audiences. The first of these developments involves the discourses and political strategies that an emerging and visible gay community used to define itself after the "official" birth of the gay liberation movement in the late 1960s. Two qualifications need to be specified at the outset, both relating to the inherent and inescapable problems of defining categories of group and individual identity. First, the use of terms such as "gay community" and any group subdivisions thereof in this discussion does not presume any uniformity or homogeneity among self-identified gay men. Such terms are used as a convenient means of denoting group alliances that were forming and that have been historically documented. Second, the use of the terms "gay" and "straight" (and also "dominant" and "subcultural") when describing cultural trends, artifacts, reading strategies, and identities threatens to maintain polarities between sexual orientations by positing origins. In the 1970s and afterwards, the assignment of sexual origins to cultural productions was often an integral component of strategies to identify, market, and promote culture products and phenomena. I have attempted to be as careful as possible to designate the existence and deployment of such practices in history while simultaneously stressing that the categories "gay" and "straight" are themselves social constructions rather than essences.

After the Stonewall riots, the Gay Liberation Front emerged with a revolutionary platform that targeted the dominant heterosexual ideology as the root of social and sexual oppression. It insisted that the sexual liberation of all Americans might be achieved only through a radical restructuring of accepted "family values" as well as the eradication of boundaries between sexual orientations previously assumed to be fixed rather than fluid. As such, it constituted a revolutionary attempt to liberate those who identified themselves as "straight" and "gay" from the psychological and social constraints of imposed categorical definitions; however, the social effects of this incitement to revolutionary action were short-lived. The gay liberation movement gradually began "pulling back from its radical critique of the effects of sexual repression and instead recasting itself as a movement in the long tradition of American reform," focusing its efforts on the elimination of discriminatory practices in society, media, and culture, thereby establishing the homosexual community as a distinct minority entitled to the same rights as all other Americans.[9]

Historians attribute the dissipation of the revolutionary platform to diverse factors. D'Emilio and Freedman correlate it with the advent of a more widespread conservative political climate by the mid-1970s, and David F. Greenberg suggests that since the radical interventionist factions "did not call upon anyone to do anything in particular, they inevitably fell to the wayside in favor of more modest requests of the sort that groups fighting discrimination typically make: the elimination of pejorative newspaper reporting and stereotyping on television, a stop to police harassment, an end to discrimination on the part of government agencies and private businesses, funding for research and social welfare."[10]

While gay American political history of the 1950s and 1960s had traced a struggle between discrete integrationists and separatists, the developments of the post-Stonewall era suggest less a reconciliation or compromise between these factions than a hybridization that demonstrates the paradoxical nature of 1970s identity politics. The emerging gay culture asserted that gays were people "just like everyone else" who yet followed a distinct and identifiable "lifestyle" separating them from the mainstream.[11] Unlike the anti-integrationists of the 1950s, the 1970s breed did not perceive itself as castigated; unlike the earlier integrationists, gays of the 1970s were less inclined either to make excuses for, or to disavow the importance of, sexual difference to the constitution of personal and social identity. Although homosexuality maintained an association with rebellion, the new emphasis on "coming out" signaled not only an embracing of self-ostracization, but also the promise of emerging into a welcoming and supportive community of other gay men and women who were gradually gaining wider acceptance within heterosexual mainstream culture.

Dennis Altman sees in this continuum between minority and community the beginnings of the social tolerance of homosexuality as an "alternative lifestyle." Certainly, straights did not accept this lifestyle universally, yet many did recognize its attractiveness in the context of changing social attitudes resulting from the sexual revolution of the 1960s, which brought with them higher divorce rates and a greater tolerance of nonmonogamous relationships.[12] A 1980 *Maclean's* article argued that "the truth is that society itself was changing long before the emergence of the homosexual culture. The contraceptive pill, the increased role of the state in taking care of the infirm or the elderly and the technological advances that made it possible for women to leave the family and go to work, all started heterosexual culture moving in the direction of gay values."[13]

Here and elsewhere, the mainstream press openly acknowledged what Altman describes as the "homosexualization" of American culture. If popular press articles of the 1960s had already begun to serve as road maps to the emerging homosexual community for both straights and gays, 1970s articles in *Time* magazine take these devices of orientation a step further. A 1979 cover story entitled "How Gay is Gay?" supportively documents the cooperative efforts of gays and straights to crack down on hate crimes in Chicago's largely gay New Town community, and reports on the organization of gay community support groups in cities such as Makato, Minnesota and Macon, Georgia.[14] The 1975 cover story "Gays on the March" includes a convenient guide that explains the connotations of such subcultural artifacts as color-coded handkerchiefs and the distinction between wearing key chains over the left and right hip, as well as the meanings of such vernacular expressions as "nellies," "butch," "aunties" and "abigails."[15] These and other media developments certainly fall short of suggesting any unqualified acceptance of homosexuality by mainstream society: continuing discriminatory practices provide the impetus for many of the popular press articles that document the largely indeterminate, yet admittedly influential, new "gay lifestyle." Still, these pieces range from the nonjudgmental to the openly supportive, with virtually no association of homosexuality with pathological activity.

While these developments signal a gradual shift in the social tolerance of homosexuals, they also attest to the extent to which the transformation of gay culture and identity in the 1970s remains a function of how homosexuality is perceived by mainstream society. The acknowledgment of the sexual identity of what many have called a new

"gay sensibility" in the 1970s has as much to do with the gradual commercialization of gay culture as it does with any broadening acceptance
of homosexual practices. As an alternative subcultural identity solidi-
fied into something openly recognizable by the mainstream, homosexuality was also transformed into an entity that could be readily targeted, packaged, and marketed. Critics have noted that for a number
of reasons, this factor of targetability is especially relevant to the developments of gay culture, which by the 1970s was acknowledged to be
a highly influential, trendsetting culture because of its longstanding
"outsider" status and its historical association with aesthetic production. According to Daniel Harris, many homosexuals had associated
themselves with an "aestheticism of maladjustment" long before the
1970s: their imposed roles as social outcasts encouraged them to formulate resistant aesthetic responses to their oppression in tolerant culture industries such as dance and theater.[16] At the same time, Harris suggests, this aestheticism was a form of elitism, inaccessible to
those who could not afford to participate in it or who were not sufficiently aesthetically refined to appreciate it. Reacting to this elitism, Harris argues, the more visible and widely recognized gay culture
of the post-Stonewall era gradually transformed aesthetic resistance
into conspicuous consumption, developing an "ersatz aestheticism" of
consumerism that yet demonstrated its own sense of distinction and
refinement, and that manifested itself in an obsession with designer
products. "The unfortunate consequence" of this move from aesthetics to consumerism, Harris argues, is that homosexuals' "need to produce art will begin to wane, and we will feel less inclined to assert ourselves as the proverbial tastemakers of our society" (7).

Harris's assessment of this transformation from aestheticism to
consumerism is perhaps overextended, and he reproduces the "snob-
bish sensibility" of the undifferentiated mass of homosexuals he sees
reaching desperately for their "Gucci bags and . . . designer fragrances"
when he bemoans homosexuals' abandonment of high culture for low
cultural artifacts. Still, links between the concept of a coherently defined gay community and its increasing consumer clout in the mid-to-
late 1970s are also noted by other self-acknowledged gay critics. Dennis
Altman asserts that purchasing power and rampant, refined consumerism functioned as signs of comeuppance, social respectability, and
acceptance by the mainstream for many gay men: "Indeed, talk of a

'gay community' often seems more a product of commercialism and conspicuous consumption than the sort of political identity associated with the early seventies." [17] Still, the concept of homosexual community that the mainstream popular press most often recognized and valorized was the trendsetting community that was as instrumental in the process of urban gentrification as it was influential in the culture industries. In 1979, *Time* magazine identifies gay trendsetting as a logical consequence of subcultural alienation: "Some open gays, feeling themselves to be rebels against conventional society, search restlessly for new fashions that run counter to the straight taste at the moment." [18] *Maclean's* magazine attributes the influence of gay style to the mainstream popularization of such phenomena as "Sunday brunch, wicker, Perrier, sandblasted townhouses and reconverted warehouses, moustaches [and] earrings." [19] The marketing departments of clothing industries such as Levi Strauss kept close tabs on the gay community for upcoming trends, citing the original button-fly jeans, painter's pants, and running shoes as examples of successful gay-to-straight crossover products in the fashion industry.[20] In a 1975 *Village Voice* piece, "Selling Gay to the Masses," John Lombardi notes the popularity of trendy "mass gay" products in Bloomingdale's successful campaign to market a line of bath towels and t-shirts from New York's Continental Baths.[21]

The concept of a gay community made increasingly visible by the presence of self-acknowledged homosexuals in urban centers, and helped along by devoted media coverage of the new "gay style," paradoxically obscures the very signs of alternative sexual identity that it simultaneously signals. This process of erasure in the crossover between gay and straight culture demonstrates the workings of consumerism on the mainstream's perception of homosexuals, as well as homosexuals' own self-perception. First, through a rather conspicuous process of mimicry and cultural "blending," popularizing products and cultural artifacts for mainstream consumption, the subculture loses its distinction from the mainstream. By 1975, gay culture was compromising its status as a rebel or outlaw culture: "The mythology of gay doesn't work anymore, precisely because in the traditional gay centers . . . gayness has lost its exclusivity and is busy becoming the dominant sensibility." [22] On the other hand, by embracing and consuming cultural products to which gay "origins" are ascribed, the mainstream merges with the subculture. Despite widespread media coverage and the open acknowledgment of gay influence, however, the "success" of this second vector of crossover works best when it remains undetectable: gay style sells to the general public as long as its promoters refrain from blatantly identifying it as gay style.

A brief examination of the disco/dance club phenomenon demonstrates how gay style was perceived as both "there" and "not there" in mainstream culture. Disco originated in black gay clubs, but by the mid-1970s it had become a staple of the white gay community.[23] Mainstream publications of the 1970s and early 1980s openly acknowledge the racial and sexual origins of this dance phenomenon. Arguing that disco combines "the new sensibilities regarding sex and race" that resulted from social movements of the 1960s, a 1977 piece in *Horizon* perceives the discotheque as a stage for the expression of contemporary social and sexual attitudes—a "place where new attitudes about sex roles can be freely played out," by both the self-acknowledged gay men who congregated there, and the straights who turned to dance clubs to find release from social conventions in the liberating combinatorial politics of the dance floor: "People get up and dance alone or in groups, and members of the same sex also dance together."[24]

The growing popularity of the discotheque and dance music in the mid-1970s made disco "an entertainment formula too hot—and too profitable—to remain the sole property of an urban subculture."[25] Despite the press's acknowledgment of the historical roots of disco dance culture, however, the marketing strategies used to effect the mainstream's appropriation of "disco fever" required that these roots be disavowed: "The mission [of the promoters] . . . was to make disco attractive to the family man, the working woman, and the student looking for an inexpensive date. If disco's homosexual origins had to be diluted in order to do that, so much the better—a fad which could be made safe as milk might hang on long enough to become a fixture in the shopping mall" (21).

The strategy used to secure disco's successful mainstream crossover was not so different from other mass-marketing strategies in 1970s entertainment industries: hybridize and amalgamate. The success of this crossover attests partially to the fact that while disco was popularized in gay clubs, it was not a specifically or inherently "gay" phenomenon, but one that rather recalled past musical forms and integrated contemporary cultural developments that could readily be dissociated from any homosexual origin. As a dance craze and a musical form, disco was from its beginnings an inherently hybrid form ripe for such amalgamation. The promoters' task was to assemble and synthesize "the disparate elements of 1970's society—progressive sexuality, computer technology, mind-stopping drugs, the fitness craze, and a nostalgia for Jazz age decadence." (21). Many of these elements had become associated with the gay lifestyle, but they were hardly indigenous to it.

Even moreso than with many other popular musical forms, disco quite often foregrounded its own sense of derivation. The beats and steady rhythms were easy to imitate and reproduce, and it relied heavily on the elaborate, technologically processed sound effects of that most hybridizing of musical instruments—the synthesizer. If Jamake Highwater is correct in noting that "there is something in disco—its combination of musical styles from several eras . . . that appeals to many people of different kinds and different ages," evidence of disco's cross-marketing potential and its inherent hybridization can also be found in its reliance on the "cover."[26] A musical genre less than half a decade old was already racking up many of its greatest commercial successes in remakes of established classics from a number of other disparate genres, from "If You Could Read My Mind" (Viola Wills, 1980) to "If My Friends Could See Me Now" (Linda Clifford, 1978), to the Moussorgsky-based "A Night on Disco Mountain" (1977).

In the case of disco, the marketing of gay style to the straight world was effected through a strategic masking of the gay sensibility with which the musical phenomenon had previously been linked. At the same time, this process of amalgamation also represented the only way in which any of the cultural form's associations with an indeterminate, yet highly marketable, homosexual lifestyle could be preserved: "Every time a minority culture starts to affect the mass sensibility, the mass has to water things down a little. . . . At first, when it was new and nobody thought it had a chance, gayness could afford to be more strident. Now, it's really affecting everyone's lives . . .so gayness has to be . . . quieter. What's really happening is the spread of a gay attitude, if not overt gayness, among the masses. . . . How many people want to be reminded of that?"[27]

Consumer Clout, Target Marketing, and "Window" Advertising

With the widespread recognition of gay men's influence as trendset-
ters, the 1970s advertising industry soon came to realize the profit
potential of targeting the very community that they were simultaneously reluctant to identify as the source of cultural trends and innovations. Still, such target marketing might never have taken place if an
awareness of the dangers of alienating the gay community had not been
forced on advertising agencies. Even as gay style was being surreptitiously marketed to the mainstream public, more visible and vocal gays
continued to exert political pressure to combat conservative and reactionary forces that would keep them socially invisible and silent. The
inception of nationally distributed gay publications such as *Christopher
Street* and *The Advocate* provided a forum that highlighted the inde-
cencies of the Moral Majority and Anita Bryant's 1977 "Save the Children" campaign, and these publications asserted that political clout
went hand in hand with consumer clout. For example, the threat of a
gay boycott of the Coors Brewery, which had been cited for sexually
discriminatory hiring practices, prompted Joseph Coors to place an
advertisement in a 1979 issue of *The Advocate* asserting that the brewery neither practiced such discrimination nor supported the efforts of
Anita Bryant.[28]

In a 1982 *New York Times* article, Karen Stabiner suggests that the
Anita Bryant campaign was itself responsible for provoking many irate
gays to assert their presence and to force themselves "into the business community's line of sight."[29] Gay culture also established its own
historical link between socio-political visibility and market potential,
through two readership surveys that *The Advocate* commissioned in
1977 and 1980, both conducted by the marketing firm Walter & Stru-
man Research Inc. As Stabiner indicates, these two surveys, which
provided virtually the sole basis of advertisers' assessment of the gay
community's marketability, revealed that gay men have (among other
things) much higher annual salaries than straight men, "a devotion
to particular brand names and styles," more discretionary income for
vacations, more concern with "physical well being," and (according
to a 1982 follow-up survey) a greater propensity to purchase personal
computers.[30]

The survey itself comprised no more than 1,100 respondents,

most of them well-educated, upper-income, white urban professionals. Nonetheless, the group constituted what *Advocate* editor Peter Frisch described as "a recession-proof market" that drew the focused attention of advertising agencies during the economic slump of the late 1970s and early 1980s—enough attention, it would seem, for many banks, car rental companies, record labels, and film studios to devote significant resources to advertising in *The Advocate* and other high-circulation gay weekly and monthly magazines. As Stabiner clarifies, the greatest risk in such direct appeal to the homosexual market was the possibility of either alienating straight men or rousing the ire of the increasingly vocal Moral Majority—in either case, the reputation of an advertising agency could be irrevocably "tainted." Accordingly, much of the attempt to appeal to the subculture was accomplished through strategies of covert infiltration: Seagram's representatives brought their gay-oriented advertisements for Boodles gin directly to gay bar owners to encourage product orders; in marketing the 1982 film *Making Love*, 20th Century Fox "distributed posters and match books in bars popular among homosexuals," while downplaying homosexuality and universalizing other themes of the film for the mainstream ad campaign.[31]

One strategy much more difficult to recognize (and consequently, less risky) involved the concept of "window advertising," which Stabiner describes as addressing "the homosexual consumer in a way that the straight consumer will not notice." In its images and scenarios, the window advertisement must remain sufficiently ambiguous to entice gay men into believing that they are being addressed without forfeiting the same sense of enticement for straight consumers. For the advertising industry, the concept is equipped with its own safety valve, by which an ad can appeal to the attractive gay market (or, at least, refrain from alienating gays) without any outright admission from advertisers that they are engaging in such targeting: "The only evidence of 'gay window' advertising is in the eye of the beholder: The whole beauty of the concept, for advertisers, is in being able to do something without confessing it" (82). Describing advertisements for Paco Rabanne cologne and Calvin Klein jeans as oft-cited instances of the "window," Stabiner explains that the marketing director with the agency for the Calvin Klein account initially admitted that the billboard of a half-clothed model was chosen to lure product-loyal gay men away from Levi's jeans; when later pressed on this issue, however, the director equivocated by saying that "I don't think it's politically smart to be talking about this. I don't think that a spokesperson from Calvin Klein, other than Calvin Klein, should be taking a position on this" (82).

The Man in the Window: Masculinity as Cultural Synthesis

If the crossover from the gay to the straight market was often successfully accomplished through a strategic synthesis of disparate cultural elements—a synthesis that thereby disavowed any evidence of the gay roots of the cultural product marketed—the window advertisement enabled another form of such disavowal by relying on images and scenarios whose appeal was sufficiently synthesized to accommodate both gay and straight readings. In both cases, the "sign" of homosexuality was used at the same time that it masked itself as something else. The window became a most accessible option for advertisers in the 1970s and early 1980s because of the already demonstrated ambiguity between straight and gay—even more directly enhanced by the solidification of the concept of a masculinity that could be thought to appeal to straight men's identification and gay men's (and straight women's) desire. As such, window advertising was a strategy often planned or calculated but just as often rather inadvertent, since it had become so difficult to distinguish between gay appeal and straight appeal due to solidifying concepts, shared by so many gay and straight males, of what it meant to be a man.

In 1982, as Altman notes, "The expectation that the growth of gay self-assertion would lead to a much greater degree of androgyny and blurring of sex roles seems, at least for the moment, to have been an illusion."[32] As the categories of homosexuality and heterosexuality were frequently intersecting in the 1970s, and as the notion of a gay community was becoming more visible to mainstream culture, many gay males were distancing themselves from a stereotypical association with femininity—an association that for decades had made gays visible and recognizable in the eyes of mainstream culture. A reciprocal exchange thus occurred between the culture industries that were discovering new ways of promoting alternative sexuality and the bodies of straight and gay men who became the target of these marketing strategies.

It would be misleading to suggest that, after Stonewall, the fact that gay men became more visible to the mainstream meant that they suddenly found it necessary to retreat from their past historical associations with effeminacy by assuming the convenient pose of "macho men." With the gradual transformation from revolutionary to reformist gay politics in the early 1970s, the radical notion of liberating society from the constraints of gender polarity yielded to an embracing of new sexual freedoms, making a political statement to mainstream society that it was acceptable to be gay. In the gay ghettos of major metropolitan centers, where the notion of gay community developed as a domain where such sexual freedoms could be explored and indulged without the past threats of legal censure, incarceration, or public humiliation, gay culture was commercialized primarily as a sexual culture. It was within such openly gay communities that "hypermasculinity" was first marketed as ideal masculinity—one that evidences a quite strategic interplay between identification and desire: "'The macho man' was the sole gender type openly marketed to the emerging gay male community as the appropriate sexual object choice. . . . On everything from advertisements for poppers to bathhouses, the hypermasculine male ideal appeared, beckoning gay men to *have* him and to *be* him. Indeed, he was the man gay men were to desire. But the only way to have him, gay men were being told, was to look just like him."[33] The version of masculinity that was most heavily and successfully commercialized, then, was a rugged masculinity that the working-class, heterosexual male emblematized, and into which many gay men attempted to transform themselves in a variety of "clone" types, including the beefy lumberjack and the well-muscled construction worker. Resulting in what Michelangelo Signorile describes as a "cult of masculinity," the commodification occurred not only in the marketing of clothing and products associated with the desired clone type, but also in the transformation of the male body into ideal sexual object through rigorous discipline and regimentation.

But why was this version of masculinity idealized instead of other forms? Daniel Harris traces its roots to the narrow spectrum of masculine ideals made accessible to gay males in the pre-Stonewall era.

For example, physique magazines recognized and appealed directly to gay male audiences in their objectification of the male body; forced to denounce their gay appeal to preclude censorship, however, they regularly printed testimonials to secure the notion that their male models were macho, threatening, and incontrovertibly heterosexual. Consequently, Harris suggests, gay men who purchased the magazines were conditioned to worship working-class, heterosexual emblems of an "unadulterated" masculinity; in the process, the "un-masculinized" homosexual body was left undesirable and unrepresentable.[34] Under the guise of unqualified self-acceptance, individuality, and newfound sexual freedom, then, the post-Stonewall gay clone only conceded his male inadequacy and insecurity by continuing to succumb to the limiting notion that the blue-collar male heterosexual was the ideal of masculinity.

Daniel Harris finds that the macho man image was at odds with another version of the homosexual body that also attained prominence in the 1970s: a bourgeois and feminized male homosexuality that was no less openly and rigorously marketed in conjunction with the product lines that it required: "The license afforded by the growing climate of tolerance and permissiveness [after Stonewall] ushered many gay men into a whole new era of pampering" (94). Because the macho man perceived the pampered type as artificial, inauthentic, and unmasculine, Harris argues that the conflict between the two types was internalized as a conflict within the body of the gay male macho man himself, who continued to perceive the heterosexual working-class body as an emblem of natural and authentic masculinity, despite the labor of construction required to (re)produce this authenticity.

Several critics have recently questioned the integrity of positing the 1970s gay macho man as either a recourse to acceptable heterosexual masculinity or a sudden reaction to an association of homosexuality with femininity. In his most recent study of masculinity, Robert Corber convincingly challenges the notion that, until the 1970s, "gay men [had] adopted a self-consciously effeminate mode of behavior to mark their identities."[35] On the contrary, Corber asserts that 1950s culture harbors substantial evidence of the construction of gay male subject-positions whose pronounced masculinity could be considered a direct reaction to the versions of acceptable male behavior emblematized by the roles of organization man and breadwinner: "The gay macho style represents the use of an oppositional form of masculinity that first emerged in the fifties as a means of staging a desire that does not conform to the domesticated values of the white suburban middle class" (146).

Thomas Waugh offers an extensive analysis of the production, circulation, and reception of the images of nude or semi-nude male bodies in physique magazines.[36] He traces the origins of physique culture to the late 1800s, explaining that in the World War I era the culture expanded because of national concerns with the physical fitness of American soldiers (206). By World War II, physique culture was disseminated through dozens of magazines, constituting one of the most prominent forums of access to images of the displayed male body. Throughout the 1950s, Waugh explains, censorship laws that attempted to regulate the images' homoerotic reception required producers and distributors to develop legal "alibis," protective devices designed to vindicate the culture as either a legitimate sport, an aesthetic celebration of the male form, or an expression of the male body's harmony with nature (217–223). He emphasizes that while some physique magazines were produced by self-identified straight men (who were often overtly homophobic) specifically for heterosexual consumption, many of the images and magazines were authored by gay producers, photographers, and models, and their consumption by gay men was widely recognized. By specifying the historical conditions of production and consumption, Waugh's study offers a significant qualification to Harris's argument that the image of the hard body of this culture was invariably the hard "heterosexual" body: Waugh argues that the loosening (and eventual abolishment) of censorship restrictions by the 1960s brought about a softening of the contours of the male form in many of the magazines — the male body became less imposingly rugged and more receptive to accommodation as sexual object.

These developments only serve to highlight the paradoxes inherent in any attempt to differentiate between straight and gay versions of representable masculinity in the 1970s, when rugged, macho hypermasculinity was once again rigorously promoted as an ideal. If the re-emergence of the macho type signaled changes within the gay male community as well as within the physical bodies that comprised it in the post-Stonewall era, gay macho had a no less demonstrable influence in mainstream culture in the 1970s. In a 1975 *Village Voice* piece, a representative from the McCann Erickson advertising agency notes a shift in advertisers' strategies in marketing gay style. John Lombardi explains that while gay culture had helped to promote the androgynous "glitter rock" image of artists such as David Bowie to mainstream audiences earlier in the decade, androgyny was soon replaced by a less flamboyant and decidedly more "straight-masculine" image. The change was attributed to the transient and impermanent nature of all cultural trends, but the representative emphasizes that "gays were always into straights. They really like them better, and things have just shifted back a little. At McCann Erickson we used to call it The Pendulum Factor."[37]

One indication of the influence of the macho look upon mainstream culture was the tremendous popularity of the Village People, a group that incorporated several exaggerated versions of rugged, elemental masculinity (including the construction worker, the leatherman rebel, and the cowboy), and that worked exclusively in that musical genre that, by 1978, had already made a successful gay-to-straight crossover: disco. Gay producer Jacques Morali had discovered two of the group's performers dancing in costume at leather bars in New York City. Morali admits that "I never thought that straight audiences were going to catch on to it. . . . I wanted to do something for the gay market. But the album was very big in discos."[38] Although the group received considerable record play in gay discotheques, its appeal was at least equally strong among straights, and "construction worker" group-member David Hodo explains that the group gave most of its live performances in straight discos. Certainly, there was little attempt at concealing the group's associations with the homosexual community (a fact to which the appearance of an article in *Rolling Stone* attests); still, Morali argues that "I don't think . . . that straight audiences know they are a gay group. . . . Anyway, the Village People don't look like queens, they look like boys. And the straight guys in America want to get the macho look" (30).

Indeed, the group members also appeared to understand the appeal to straight female audiences who, according to "leatherman" Glenn Hughes, perceived the Village People not as homosexuals, but as "six humpy guys," claiming that women "get off on the sex we're selling." Whether or not gay men were responding to similar aspects of the sexual commodity, the group's promoters had successfully tapped into a concept that appeared, by 1978, to transcend the boundaries of sexual orientation: a narcissism that had come to be associated with psychological and physical health and that conveyed self-acceptance. Hodo explains, "We went for a totally male, masculine celebration—that men can get up there and feel their tits and do bumps-and-grinds and still remain men. Narcissism is a good thing. Everyone does it, I don't care what they say." In relation to another group member's observation that "we make ourselves available to as many interpretations as possible," the marketing tactics of the Village People represent a most curious form of window advertising: a self-conscious representation of gay male sexuality that now defines itself as universal in its various manifestations of identification and desire. Its macho man, hard male bodies become what straight men want to be, what straight women want to have, and what gay men want to be *and* to have.

Even the lyrics of the group's songs are aligned with window advertising strategies: the emphases upon the release of inhibitions ("you know you don't need them"), liberated self-expression ("say what's on your mind"), and pride and faithfulness to the individual and authentic self ("I am what I am," "I did not choose the way I am"), carry distinct yet curiously overlapping inflections to a gay community in the process of "coming out," and a mainstream culture whose obsessions with finding healthy ways to feel good were emblematized by the popular product slogan of the early 1980s: "I believe in Crystal Light, 'cause I believe in me." Lest some might infer any ironic social commentary in this self-absorption, Morali confesses in earnest: "Listen. Seriously you know, I want to tell you something. I am gay, you know, myself, so I am not the kind of person to joke about the statement. Because it's my statement, you know? Knowing that the group is gay and that I'm really believing and trusting what I'm doing, it's not a parody at all" (30).

Surface and Depth in the Window of Fantasy

The fantasy of an idealized masculine body accessible "to as many interpretations as possible" finds its most convenient marketable outlets in those media based on still images—images that clearly connote sexuality but that also refrain from specifying the sexual orientation of the fantasy participant or her/his object. With the minimizing of narrative content and context came the broadest ranges of potential narrative inference. The image of the Marlboro man, who (according to *Advocate* editor Peter Frisch) "emphasizes masculinity and talks about Marlboro Country as being 'open and free,'" was ideal in its crossover appeal because he provided an expansive space for such inference: his identity was confined to the frozen image, and it was never necessary to reveal what he did before or after he posed in front of the camera, riding the wild country.[39] A print advertisement for Paco Rabanne cologne attained a similar effect by depicting "a man lying in a rumpled bed talking on the phone to someone the dialogue vividly portrays as a just departed—and deliberately ambiguous—lover" (82). Even the construction of the Village People's sexuality, however animated in elaborate dance routines, basically involved the marketing of a set of related masculine types drawn together to celebrate the male body, but required to do little else.

The Hollywood film industry of the late 1970s and early 1980s certainly discovered effective means of capitalizing on this new freedom to represent the male body as an object of both identification and desire, but the medium's reliance on narrative required that the marketing of the male sexual object also function as a marketing of *character* in a series of causally linked scenarios, and all of this without making any definitive pronouncements about the sexuality of the character or the actor who portrayed him. The construction of Mel Gibson's accessibility to gay and straight audiences at the start of his career responds to the necessary modifications to the male body in its transformation to sexualized and "cinematized" object at a historical moment when gay culture influenced definitions of acceptable masculinity. In the early version of Gibson's star persona, the transformation from "image" to "character" correlates with a transformation from "surface" to "depth." Gibson becomes an amalgam or synthesis of physical and character traits that might be read as contradictory under other historical circumstances, but that star discourse and film roles in the early 1980s configure as ambiguities connoting depth. The narratives that effect this transformation comprise individual films as well as progressions of extracinematic star texts. Through constructions as both hard and soft, strong and vulnerable, and Australian and American, Gibson's deep yet ambiguous persona also becomes readable as both straight and gay, and accessible to audiences across the lines of sexual orientation.

Popular press articles from as early as the middle of the decade proclaim the advent of a new era of tolerance and acceptance of homosexuality in the Hollywood film industry. In a 1975 *Village Voice* article, Cliff Jahr suggests that this new attitude in Hollywood liberates actors to play a wider range of roles without concern for being labeled "gay," and even that electing such roles demonstrates an "audacity [that] reaffirms their masculinity."[40] Such a notion suggests a transformation in prevailing definitions of straight masculinity traceable to changes in the discursive construction of male homosexuality. The culture industries found new ways to sell a masculine sexuality, regarding which the concept of a "new macho," inspired by the visibility of gay culture, was instrumental in defining. It may have been audacious and masculine to risk "playing gay," but it was much safer to employ strategies of addressing gay viewers without the risk of directly acknowledging such address—to appeal to a spirit of rebellion that might continue to appear to target homosexuals even as it appealed to a related, yet more universalized, concern with personal well-being, individuality, and authenticity. In a revealing 1983 cover story in *Newsweek*, David Ansen traces the popularity of new "incredible hunks" such as Tom Selleck and Mel Gibson to the recent gay-to-straight crossover phenomenon that has popularized male underwear ads, beefcake calendars, and fitness planners. "Homosexuality always celebrated male beauty," Ansen argues, "and there's little doubt that the general acceptance of a gay subculture has encouraged an outspoken appreciation of masculine sexuality in the mainstream culture."[41] Ansen explains that this trend suggests a redemption of handsome actors who had, until very recently, been stigmatized as shallow and one-dimensional. Michael Medavoy, an executive at Orion Pictures, concurs that "we're looking for a new generation of Paul Newmans" (49). "A few years ago, there was a stigma against good-looking actors," Selleck observes, but "now the pendulum has moved back to the middle" (49).

The attempt to market masculine icons of desire thus necessitated a construction of the male body as a sexual object that was also more than *just* a sexual object. Instead of shallowness, this new model of masculinity required a sense of depth. Ansen describes the fantasies that Selleck and Gibson offer as purely escapist, and that fantasy subjects indulge in them with "no mess, no fears of intimacy." Clearly, however, the fantasy of Mel Gibson constructed in both popular press articles and early film narratives is a fantasy *of* accessibility—one that requires temperings and modifications of the macho image to produce a more universally accessible star body. In order to suggest the persona's depth, the objectified body becomes a curious conflation of strength and vulnerability, remaining sufficiently hard and impermeable to perpetuate an image of ideal masculinity, but also portraying this masculinity as natural, authentic, human, and within reach as an object of identification and desire. As Ansen argues, these "incredible hunks" promote fantasies that cross the lines of gender and sexual orientation: "Men and women [are] blissfully free to project whatever sexual scenario they choose onto whichever objectified gender they prefer."

The early star discourse of Mel Gibson in the mainstream press offers less an attempt to reproduce the stereotypical hard-male beefcake macho of the Village People than to adapt it to human and accessible terms. Instead of being rendered impermeable, the body is transformed into a site of receptivity and invitation: it is firm, agile, and muscular, but not in a way that calls attention to itself. Facial features resonate with an emotional depth: in 1982, Richard Corliss remarks that "since *Gallipoli* . . . [Gibson] is more mature and authoritative; his moon face is cratered with character."[42] If narcissism and excessive muscularity had come to represent an unashamed celebration of masculinity, in Gibson these attributes are considerably tempered so that they do not register too overtly as signs of obsessive self-interest. The star is very comfortable with his own body, but not overly obsessed with its magnificence. Gibson's sexuality keeps its macho roots in ruggedness and even in working-class male heterosexuality that had come to connote a natural rather than constructed masculinity. The source of the early Gibson's appeal is his very lack of self-consciousness. The star never takes his constructed screen image too seriously. According to *Newsweek* in 1982, Gibson's *Road Warrior* persona emanates "a quiet, unnarcissistic intensity" and "easy, unswaggering masculinity."[43] *People* magazine's 1983 story of this male "heartthrob" notes "the astonishing dichotomy between the image and the man" who never actively seeks the desire that his fans invest in him.[44] Gibson's modesty in describing his own appeal reinforces the notion that his sexuality is unforced and natural, drawing attention to the work that he performs for his audience while simultaneously discounting the image as construction: "I don't think physical good looks and some kind of empty shell is appealing to anybody. . . . Every now and then you get onto something that . . . strikes a chord with most people. You have to provide a mirror for them."[45]

Gibson's "naturally" rugged body conforms to the stereotypical image of the working-class male heterosexual that was promoted to pre-Stonewall gays as an ideal, and this image was integral in establishing the actor's authenticity as well as his dissociation from the superstar image that was being imposed on him. Pointing out what would be repeatedly emphasized in the star discourse throughout his career, *Newsweek* explains that Gibson's father was a railroad worker and that his roots are unmistakably working class. These roots are reiterated in Gibson's role in his first two box-office successes in the early 1980s: in *Gallipoli*, Frank is identified as a poor railroad worker from Perth, and *The Road Warrior*'s Mad Max is an ex-police officer.

Gibson is strong but not maniacally aggressive, hard but not impermeable, masculine but not stereotypically masculine, a sexual object who never solicits his own objectification. That Gibson's universal appeal is the result of an ambiguous identity that attempts to reach several audience sectors without definitively aligning itself with any of them can be demonstrated by the locative ambiguities that construct the star persona as well. Gibson's popularity in America is at least partially the result of a hybridization of nationalities that refers back to the inception of the Australian New Wave cinema as a successful concept transcending any specific national allegiance. Prior to the release of *Mad Max* in 1979, Bob Villard explains, Australian cinema had historically proven to be too insular for the international market, "especially the highly lucrative American market," and producer Byron Kennedy and director George Miller "conspired to overcome the 'ethnicity' of their homeland" with a film that attempted to "obliterate the fact that the story's action was filmed in Australia."[46] The construction of a "*cross-cultural*, mythical hero, one who could triumph over evil in all markets" was prosperous in countries as culturally diverse as Japan, Germany, and England, yet the film's relative lack of success in the United States has been attributed to the distributor Filmways' deci-

20   Gibson as *Mad Max* (1979). Filmways dubbed the American release of the film.
Courtesy Photofest.

sion to dub the voices of the Australian actors; Miller explains that
Filmways "adamantly maintained that our actors' accents were unin-
telligible" (fig. 20).

The substantial American successes of Gibson's two subsequent
and undubbed American releases, *Gallipoli* (Paramount, 1981) and *The
Road Warrior* (Warner Bros., 1982) proved that the accent was not
nearly as much of a problem as anticipated. Curiously, the star texts
that help to construct Gibson's image for these films both foreground
and obliterate national identity. Certainly the biographical facts of
Gibson's upbringing dovetail nicely with a construction of the star as
ambiguously rooted to geographical location: while Gibson's grandmother was Australian, the star was born in Peekskill, New York, and
spent his childhood there until his father moved the family back to
Australia when Gibson was twelve years old. Gibson's emergence onto
the American celebrity scene in the early 1980s is therefore also a return to his own homeland.[47]

The star is sometimes Australian, sometimes American, and just as
often neither Australian nor American—he remains capable of assum-

ing both national identities while he carefully skirts any definitive association with either. From a promotional standpoint, Gibson's heritage
readily transcends national boundaries: both Paramount's production
notes for *Gallipoli* and Warner Bros.' production notes for *The Road
Warrior* list his numerous screen and stage acting awards as evidence
of "an ever-growing international following."[48] The star texts of the
mainstream press preserve the notion of Gibson's cross-cultural marketing potential, but also occasionally describe his national outsider
status as instrumental to his popularity with American audiences.
Newsweek remarks upon his "hint of Down Under humor [that] may
be quintessentially Australian but is also the stuff of an international
male star."[49] Yet throughout his career, his "quintessence" is just as
often described as a set of neutral attributes that counterbalance ethnic
difference with features that make Gibson accessibly and specifically
American. *People* magazine would comment that "Andy Warhol thinks
Mel Gibson's short-cropped hair, smoky blue eyes and strong chin give
him a 'pure, clean-cut American look.' 'His mystery,' concurs Gloria
Steinem, 'comes from his ordinariness.'"[50]

Beginning with the star texts of the early 1980s, the construction
of locative ambiguities enforces a tension between city and country, and between derivation and authenticity, suggesting that the road
to stardom has made Gibson an outsider who belongs in neither of
the two places he has chosen to call home. In the city/country dichotomy, these locative ambiguities echo similar tensions surrounding the star person of James Dean, whose origins in the homeland of
Indiana always threatened to be compromised by the artificiality of
Hollywood glamor. With Gibson, however, the ambiguities are much
more elaborate: while the actor's origins remain in the rural setting
of upstate New York, it is his inherited home of Australia that serves
as the heartland whose roots he risks losing, even though the home
where Gibson resided at the time that he made both *Gallipoli* and
The Road Warrior was not located in a rustic, rural community, but
in metropolitan Sydney. In one of the few biographical pieces circulated in the mainstream press before he acquired a new residence in the
United States, Gibson is found to be "in no hurry to get to Hollywood.
'It's not a question of Australian loyalty. I just want to do interesting
work. I'm not going to go to Hollywood just because it's Hollywood.'"
Yet this same article later suggests that although Gibson "remains an

American citizen . . . his outlook is totally Australian. 'I'm in tune with this place [Australia]. . . . But I can speak with an American accent—with a bit of effort.'"[51]

Although in such statements Gibson is careful never to rebuke the American film industry, the price of international acclaim here becomes a loss of identity and a compromise of authenticity. Early star texts also identify Gibson's authentic Australianness as an almost fetishized exoticism. Discerning the core of Gibson's appeal to American audiences, David Ansen hypothesizes that "perhaps it's the Australian accent, a new sound to American ears, the slightly brutish vowels a sharp rebuke to the cadences of upper-class British speech. Mix that suggestion of crudity with huge baby blues and a classic profile that evokes Redford, and the elements of a new screen Apollo are in place."[52] In such descriptions, Gibson's national heritage is linked to the "secret" of his sexual appeal. Through whatever is quintessentially Australian about the star, he embodies a rugged and unrefined masculinity whose naturalness stems from its "crudity," its distinction from a Britishness that suggests a derived affectation. It is, however, this same Australian quintessence that enables him to transcend definitive connections with any national heritage, giving him a more universal, classic look that makes his appeal still more elemental and natural as it is tempered and made vulnerable by his "huge baby blues." For American audiences, his Australian "otherness" enforces his sexual objectification, even while the transformation of this otherness into "quintessence" makes him accessible as an identificatory figure.

If Gibson harbors any quintessence, then, it is certainly a very malleable quintessence, capable of transforming itself in a variety of ways without ever compromising the star's originality or an authenticity that enmeshes nationality with sexual appeal. His quintessence remains elusive and ambiguous primarily because, in the construction of his star persona, he retains the capacity to emblematize a wide range of features that constitute the self without ever settling on or being limited to any one of them. His versatility and "pan-accessible" appeal is as much a result of the universality of the fantasies he promotes as the variety of spectatorial positions of access that his image enables, according to the variables of a human "subjecthood" that Teresa deLauretis describes as "not only [the subject's] psychic or fantasmatic configuration, the places or positions that she or he may be able to assume in the structure of desire, but also the ways in which she or he is located in social relations of sexuality, race, class, gender, etc., the places she or he may be able to assume as subject in the social."[53] Gibson's identity consistently eludes definition even as it retains specific character attributes in the categories that deLauretis itemizes, and the star texts construct a persona who acknowledges and accommodates the specificity of the spectator-subject's own constitution of identity. Within such categories as class and ethnicity, the persona offers a range of available options that may be diversely assembled, but that never fail to accumulate into the composite of the "natural man."

He can appeal to his audiences as a working-class, heterosexual, male Australian who denies his status as a sexual object. Given the historically specific circumstances of the early 1980s, however, these attributes of identity can also be drastically reconfigured: his working-class roots also make him accessible as an embodiment of a masculinity that addresses the desires of many gay men as well—indeed, a version of elemental masculinity that gay American culture was instrumental in promoting as an ideal to be emulated and desired. The star texts even manage to transform a male sexual objectification—also promoted by gay culture—as an aspect of feminine vulnerability that curiously reinforces his status as a strong, deep, elemental, and entirely masculine man. His biographers would later elaborate on the star's skillful execution of this gender sleight-of-hand: "Close-ups of his unusual green [?] eyes show up over and over, and in *Mad Max* the camera repeatedly focuses on his black leather boots and then pans slowly, tantalizingly upward.... If that sounds like a treatment usually given only to female stars, it is. But the only thing remotely feminine about Gibson is the vulnerability he projects.... Audiences sense that there's a peculiar mix of elements in this particular psyche, and they're right."[54] Referring again to the early Gibson of *Mad Max*, Neil Sinyard reiterates this peculiar synthesis of gender attributes, noting that the star possessed "a certain attractive 'feminine' vulnerability," and that "already a kind of duality was becoming apparent in his screen persona, as he seemed able to switch between a virile and vulnerable masculinity.... At this stage of his career [he was] able to communicate vulnerability...without any sacrifice of masculinity."[55]

Speaking specifically of his national heritage, Gibson would verify in 1985 that "I think it's good to be a hybrid."[56] What the star does not acknowledge in such statements is that the consequences of this admixture of nationalities that his image promotes, and that secures his appeal to a wide range of audiences, are inseparable from a sexual hybridization. Indeed, the promotional strategies used to construct Gibson's pan-accessible appeal overlap significantly with the window advertising strategies used to construct multiple consumer access to print advertisements for products such as Calvin Klein jeans and Marlboro cigarettes. As with window advertising, the promotion of Gibson's image in star texts relies on a minimizing of narrative content that affords a maximum number of subject positions of access, relying on the consumer's ability and desire to "fill in the gaps" in the construction of the fantasy scenario. Like the print ad strategies, Gibson's crossover appeal remains mostly unacknowledged by its promoters. This lack of acknowledgment is, however, insufficient to refute the fact that Gibson's construction accommodated gay-accessible readings of his persona. Placing this window in historical context, two responses arise to Gibson's question, "With this look, who is going to think I'm gay?": Gibson embodied an objectified masculinity that was idealized by specific sectors of gay culture; he also accommodated a subject position from which many gay spectators could readily access both the star's image and his narratives.

Gallipoli *and* The Road Warrior: *Melodramas of Loss and Emergence*

"To those who complain that the movie lacks a love affair, Gibson responds, 'But there was a love story—in a male sense. It was a very strong mateship. At that time, those fellows really depended on one another'"(fig. 21).[57] What Gibson may have intended as a statement of mere camaraderie between the two male leads of the 1981 film *Gallipoli* is complicated by its appearance in the journal *After Dark* that, since its inception in the mid-1970s, had a large gay following. Daniel Harris describes the journal as "an audacious mass-marketing experiment in gay eroticism [that] arose like a phoenix in all of its subversive splendor."[58] Masquerading in its early years as a high culture journal devoted to "impartial coverage of homoerotic dance and theater," it "never officially declared its [gay] allegiances but played an endless game of hide-and-seek" (65). Between 1980 and 1982, however, the journal featured articles on Christopher Reeve's daring de-

21 "But there was a love story—in a male sense." Archie Hamilton (Mark Lee) and Frank Dunne (Gibson) in *Gallipoli* (1981). Courtesy Photofest.

cision to "play gay" in *Fifth of July*, condemnation of the Moral Majority's censure of straight and gay sexual content in television and Hollywood film, editorials upholding homosexuals' right to promiscuous sex, Vito Russo's synopsis of his forthcoming *The Celluloid Closet*, a rash of media celebrity beefcake photos, as well as full-page advertisements for *Making Love*.[59] *Gallipoli* was also produced by mogul Robert Stigwood, who had become known for his successful experiments in crossover and hybridization by popularizing the rock opera (*Hair, Jesus Christ Superstar, Evita*) as well as the 1970s "rock music film," from *Grease* and *Sgt. Pepper's Lonely Hearts Club Band* to the movie that became instrumental in disco's gay-to-straight crossover, *Saturday Night Fever*.[60] Although popular press reports never acknowledge Stigwood's own homosexuality, *Newsweek* emphasizes that the producer "has never been married and centers his social life around a surrogate family made up of those he works with."[61] Later in the same article it reports that he "travels in circles of fashionable androgyny."[62] John Lombardi interviews an unnamed executive from the Robert Stigwood Organization (RSO) in 1975, who states that the company "markets gayness, but the product it markets is a lot less gay than the Stigwood Organization is. We know the secret of broadening gayness so that it sells to straights. And that's really what you're after, isn't it? How gayness is penetrating the straight marketplace in ways straights can't identify. . . . we've helped put gays out there as a market like women and blacks, but you can't say that yet."[63]

Through different yet related strategies, both *Gallipoli* and *The Road Warrior* become successful gay/straight crossover vehicles. Each capitalizes on the hybridization of Gibson's star persona, facilitating a variety of positions of spectatorial access to its melodramatic narratives of desire and loss. That Gibson does not portray an overtly gay character in either film becomes integral to the crossover strategy, demonstrating that indirect appeals to a variety of target audiences that includes gays are often just as (or more) effective than any direct representations of self-acknowledged homosexual characters. Certainly, the transition of hybridity from star image in publicity text to narrative poses the problem of how to sustain a sense of the star persona's depth without specifying or solidifying any single aspect of "subjecthood" into a definition of the character's identity—that is, without specifying aspects of character that might alienate some audiences. Both films resolve this problem by universalizing the nature of the protagonist's crisis within the narrative through the melodramatic mode: in *Gallipoli*, as a melodrama of loss and the failed attempt to unite its protagonists; in *The Road Warrior*, as a melodrama of the gradual emergence of character depth.

The window of access to gay and straight readings of Peter Weir's *Gallipoli* is the buddy film, a genre popularized in 1970s Hollywood cinema. The film concerns the parallel paths of two runners, Archie Hamilton (Mark Lee) and Frank Dunne (Gibson), in the Australian outback during the first years of World War I. Preparing for a track competition that will take him miles from home at the beginning of the film, the deeply patriotic Archie uses his participation in the competitive sport as a pretense to enlist in the army. He attempts to do so immediately after winning first prize in the track meet, but his mates reveal to the army officials that Archie is underage, and he is found ineligible. He is then joined by Frank, a singularly unpatriotic drifter from Perth who has come in second in the race. Having no immediate commitments, Frank suggests to Archie that they travel together to Perth, where Archie's anonymity might provide him a better chance of successfully enlisting as a soldier. On their journey through the barren outback their friendship intensifies, and by the time that they reach the city, Frank has decided to enlist in the Lighthorse Brigade with Archie in order to remain close to his companion. The Brigade accepts Archie but turns down Frank because he cannot ride a horse. Having nothing better to do, Frank enlists as an infantryman with his fellow mates, and he is later reunited with Archie when the troops are sent off to Egypt. After Archie convinces his superiors to admit Frank to the Brigade because of his running abilities, the reunited friends soon find themselves transported to the battlefront, where machine-gun-armed Turkish soldiers overpower and outnumber the more poorly equipped Australian soldiers. Volunteering Frank for the position of runner to save his life on the day of battle, the film ends with Archie and his fellow soldiers leaping over the trenches to be slaughtered by the Turks, as Frank screams in agony over his inability to prevent his friend's senseless death.

Robin Wood identifies five recurring attributes in films conforming to the buddy film subgenre: (1) a "journey" in which cities serve as points of arrival and departure; (2) a "marginalization" of female characters; (3) the absence of any identifiable "home" where the male protagonists could be said to belong; (4) a "male love story" that subverts the classical Hollywood cinema's narrative trajectory toward a union of the heterosexual couple and the integration of the nuclear family; and (5) the death of at least one of the two protagonists, which precludes any possibility that the relationship will be "consummated."[64] This fifth element becomes integral to containing the subversive homosexual subtext that is activated by the male love story, yet by disavowing "the homosexual nature of the relationship so strenuously, the films actually succeed in drawing attention to its possibility" (229). Although Wood traces the ideological roots of the subgenre to developments specific to 1970s American history, the fact that *Gallipoli* conforms so strikingly to Wood's model suggests one of several ways in which this Australian-made film manages to transcend its very Australianness. For different reasons, both male protagonists are eager to escape the confines of the home: Archie's journey is motivated by patriotic interests, wishing to represent and defend his homeland in a war that has not yet reached its shores; although Frank halfheartedly suggests that he wants to save enough money to open his own bicycle shop, his more aimless wanderings are motivated by a general sense of restlessness. Yet once the protagonists' paths intersect in the competition of a track meet, Frank is easily swayed to tag along with his companion indefinitely.

This sense of aimlessness makes Frank an entirely unanchored figure to which the narrative refrains from ascribing any coherent identity. His domestic environment—his father's home in the city of Perth—figures only marginally in the narrative, as a rest stop for the protagonists before Archie enlists in the Lighthorse Brigade. Aside from identifying him as a runner, the narrative offers no further exposition to characterize its protagonist. Frank's alienation from home is exacerbated by a more universal alienation from the outback where most of the story transpires. He never belongs where he is at any given moment. A waitress at a restaurant in a remote country outpost treats him rudely, suspecting that he is a "city boy," and the elderly men gathered outside his boarding house stare him down intensely as if he were an alien intruder. Still, any suspicions of affected urbanity are counteracted as the city/country dichotomy is subsumed by the Australian/British conflict in the second half of the film. The British officers are caricatures of affected decorum—well-postured, monocled stick-figures who scour derisively at the "crude, undisciplined, and most ill-mannered" as both rural and urban Australian infantrymen mock the poses of superiority that they assume; these very infantrymen are slaughtered by Turks in the trenches in order to ensure the British safe passage to the Turkish shores. Yet even Frank's disdain for the British—who, as his father reminds him, murdered his own grandfather in Ireland—fails to provide him with any patriotic spirit for his "homeland."

Characterized primarily by his alienation from any notion of city or country that might ground him, Frank becomes a "deep" character through his propensity to question the interrelated constructions of patriotism and masculinity that his friend Archie accepts blindly and unconditionally. Provoked by a townsman's comment that "girls run; men box," Archie is driven to refute the implications of this accusation by challenging the man to race him on horseback while Archie runs barefoot. Archie still takes the comment to heart, signing up for a track meet in a village far from home as a pretense for abandoning his home forever to help in the war effort. Frank, however, refuses to perceive this ultimate challenge in the interests of patriotism as a threat to his masculinity, despite his "mate" Snowy's (David Argue) comment that *I'm* not scared to die for my country." And Frank refutes Archie's efforts to persuade him that masculinity can be proven only by patriotism:

ARCHIE: But you gotta be in it.
FRANK: You don't have to if you don't want to.
ARCHIE: You *gotta* be.
FRANK: No, I *don't*. Free country—or haven't you heard?
ARCHIE: I'd be ashamed of myself if I didn't fight.
FRANK: Well, that only proves one thing—that you and I are different.

By constructing a central protagonist with a remarkable ability to "see through" the prevailing categorized definitions of human identity, and by making the national identity of this protagonist opaque and elusive, *Gallipoli* ceases to be *only* about an Australian/English/German war conflict in the early 1900s, but also about themes and topics that inform American sexual politics of the early 1980s: the problems of conforming to a traditionally accepted masculinity, and the problems of love between men. Gay critics such as Simon Watney did not fail to acknowledge the film's homosexual appeal: "In many ways . . . *Gallipoli* goes further [than other contemporary films with self-identified gay male protagonists] in showing sexuality as a system of regulative constraints, with its careful depiction of conflicting values and expectations about masculinity and male behavior."[65] *The Advocate* applauds the film as an "antiwar masterpiece [and] one of the most intensely moving (albeit non-physical) love stories between men ever to grace the screen."[66] Indeed, the film's plot and style accommodate homoerotic readings of Frank and Archie's relationship without specifying the homosexuality of the characters. Women are marginal figures in the narrative, as dancing partners for the men at the Officer's Ball before the soldiers sail off to Alexandria, or as prostitutes who divert the soldiers in Egypt before the men engage in battle.

It is the two men who demonstrate the most devoted commitment to one another, carving "Frank & Archie, 1915" into the stones of an ancient pyramid where they stand alone together, their silhouetted figures immersed in the romantic light of an Egyptian sunset. Their unspoken mutual vow is that they will stay together at any cost. Indeed, the devotion is strong enough for Frank to compromise his own principles. To his mates from Perth, he rather unconvincingly justifies his decision to join the Lighthorse Brigade by explaining that he always intended to do so; the fact is that by joining, he can remain in Archie's presence. The moments in the narrative when their paths do diverge are marked by a series of intimate close-ups, volleying intercuts of bodies reluctantly taking their leave. At one point, a shot from Frank's point-of-view lingers on a scene of Archie disappearing into the crowd, followed by a cut back to the sad-faced, solitary origin of the glance. Later, reunited on the Turkish shores, the two men impulsively strip off their clothes for playful nude bathing with their fellow soldiers, their frolicking interrupted by a stream of bullets that forces them underwater for close to a minute, providing an opportunity for the camera to linger leisurely on hard male bodies in Gibson's (and Lee's) first nude scene.

In its articulation of homoerotic possibilities, *Gallipoli* can certainly be read as a love story between men, but it also manages to transcend any *exclusively* homoerotic appeal through a more universal drama of failed and unarticulated connections between human beings—that is, as a melodrama of human loss. The unrelenting mutual devotion of the protagonists is precisely what enforces the impossibility of their ever remaining together. At the film's ending, in order to stay with Archie, Frank finds himself on the very battleground that he had earlier vowed to avert; offered the opportunity to serve as a runner instead of a fighter on the fateful day of battle, Archie recommends Frank for the runner position in order to save the man who has so loyally followed him. If the two men initially met through the common factor of their record-breaking running speed, it is this same factor of speed that ultimately fails to offer the only means of their mutual salvation.

Steve Neale and Franco Moretti find miscommunications and mistimings to be integral to the production of pathos in the melodramatic mode, enforcing the spectator's sense of helplessness to effect the union of protagonists within the narrative. Death intervenes, with its reminder of the impossibility of reversing time.[67] For Linda Williams, such a union often transpires too late: "In these fantasies the quest for connection is always tinged with the melancholy of loss."[68] The closing sequence of *Gallipoli* comprises an elaborate set of miscommunications and mistimings: after his commanding officer authorizes a cease fire, Frank is commissioned to race back through the trenches at breakneck speed to relay this message to the squad captain in order to prevent the slaughter of the next band of Australian soldiers, which includes Archie. Frank arrives a few crucial moments too late, shrieking and collapsing in agony as the sound of the whistle signals the soldiers' order to advance over the trenches. The race that began as an innocent competition, and has now become a matter of life and death, concludes the film in a haunting freeze-frame of a sprinting Archie pelleted by machine-gun bullets. Archie's death forever secures the impossibility of what Robin Wood describes as the forbidden "consummation" of the relationship between men; at the same time, in the realm of the melodramatic fantasy, the film's ending invites the viewer to speculate upon what might have happened between these two men had the death been averted, "if only" Frank would have arrived in time to save his companion.

The tragedy that might have been averted "if only" there were more time has already unfolded by the beginning of *The Road Warrior*; indeed, the tragedy itself is the subject of the drama that *The Road War-*

rior continues, *Mad Max*, in which Main Force Patrol officer Max Rockatansky fails to prevent the slaughter of his best partner, wife, and child by a ruthless band of outsiders scavenging the barren outback in search of gasoline, the precious "juice" that has become the most valuable commodity in this postapocalyptic world. If *The Road Warrior* continues the narrative of *Mad Max*, it also functions as a sequel to *Gallipoli* in two related ways that involve the concerns of melodrama: first, as a narrative of the effects of unabatable loss on the isolated individual after the melodramatic narrative has been "unsuccessfully" resolved and the hero has nothing left to lose; second, as a narrative that traces the gradual emergence of the authentic and individuated star persona *as a progression of* melodrama. Both of these concerns become integral to maintaining Gibson's accessibility to a wide range of early 1980s audiences as a figure of identification and desire.

If non-narrative star texts had already attempted to secure the fantasy of Gibson's universal accessibility by various constructions of character ambiguity that ensured a variety of positions of access to the star persona, *The Road Warrior* reiterates this same strategy. The producer and director of the Mad Max films conceived the protagonist as a "cross-cultural, mythical hero," and the settings also masked any indications of national specificity in the films. The flat, barren, expansive landscape of *The Road Warrior* is also echoed by Max's characterization. At the beginning of the film, he appears to be largely stripped of identifiable human attributes. As the voiceover narratives suggest, he has become a "burnt-out shell of a man" defined primarily by what he has lost. In no hurry to recapture what he has left behind, he races through remote open spaces in his rusted-out, banged-up V-8 Interceptor without any identifiable destination or goal except to recover the last drops of gasoline from wrecked and abandoned vehicles on the lonely and directionless highway. Unshaven and unwashed, his black leather boots, pants, and jacket with torn-off right sleeve remain the only signs of his former identity as a police officer. His sole companion has become his aptly and generically named "Dog" with whom he shares meals of canned dog food (fig. 22).

This extensive paring away of identifiable human attributes results less in the formation of a "blank slate" or affectless characterization than a man whose insistent attempt to dissociate himself from human emotions and attributes becomes a sign of a deep emotional vulnera-

22   Max and "Dog" roam the barren, postapocalyptic landscape in *The Road Warrior* (1981). Author's personal collection.

bility. Papagallo (Mike Preston), the leader of the community within the gasoline fortress, describes Max as an "animal" because he cannot admit the pain of loss he has suffered; reminded of a past that he would rather forget, Max pushes him away abruptly. Indications of Max's susceptibility to "human" emotion become more resonant as they are largely played out in silence. He maintains an intuitive and intimate connection with his canine companion, communicated by an exchange of glance and gesture: as Max prepares to fire up the Interceptor's turbo charger, the dog gives him a quick look, responding as though he perceives that he must now proceed to a place of safety in the back seat. Intensity of emotional response is also suggested by Max's subtle yet distinct reaction of pleasure when he discovers a musical wind-up toy released from the charred hand of a corpse in an overturned car—the toy offers a momentary recuperation of a sense of humanity in a world where emotions are now better kept hidden. He later surrenders this same toy to the Feral Kid (Emil Minty) as a gift, an offering that recaptures a childhood innocence that Max has irrevocably lost, yet he rejects any more outward appeal to an intimacy with others who might remind him too intently of his past roles of father and husband.

When the Feral Kid clings to the truck cab in an appeal to accompany Max on a journey with his new hero, Max throws the musical toy away from the vehicle to entice the child to retrieve it. Furthermore, the film includes not the slightest hint of the renewal of any heterosexual desire. As Vincent Canby points out, Max "doesn't have much time for women . . . [and] is apparently too busy remembering the unthinkable to have any time for romantic or even sexual thoughts."[69]

If this combination of strength and vulnerability in the emergence of identifiable human attributes gradually renders the protagonist's emotions accessible to the audience as a revelation of depth, the film uses a similar strategy in the representation of Max's body as an object of identification and desire that could play into homosexual desire without soliciting it exclusively. Steve Neale suggests that in mainstream cinema, the rendering of the male body as an object of contemplation threatens to ascribe a too specific homosexual desire to the spectator. Accordingly, such a display must be motivated by a suggestion of the hero's punishment in acts of physical aggression, in conjunction with a "test" of masculinity that invites the heterosexual male spectator's identification, but not desire: "We see male bodies stylized and fragmented in close-ups, but our look is not direct, it is heavily mediated by the looks of the characters involved. And those looks are marked not by desire, but rather by fear, or hatred, or aggression."[70] Neale suggests that instances of an unmediated objectification of the male body result in a "feminization" tolerated primarily in genres such as the musical (18). Curiously, the representation of Max's body conflates these seemingly opposed possibilities: while Max's objectification is clearly linked to punishment and aggression endured at the hands of other males, the mediating "look" at the displayed body is often rather ambiguous.

The sequence in which Max's Interceptor is driven off the highway provides a cogent example. Humungus's followers witness the overturned vehicle, and Max's dog is murdered as he emerges from the wreckage. After the Interceptor explodes in a burst of flames, the followers disperse. A grainy, slow-motion ground-level shot subsequently follows Max from behind as he crawls in agony from the burning wreckage, eventually turning over on his back as the camera hovers over the body of the bleeding and exhausted hero. Here, the display of the battered body occurs long *after* the aggressors have departed from the scene, convinced that the explosion has annihilated its target. The sequence continues with an overhead shot of the wounded victim as the Gyro-Captain (Bruce Spence) transports him to the gasoline fortress by helicopter. Once Max is returned to a place of safety, the sequence progresses with another series of high-angle and overhead tilt shots in an extreme close-up of his naked upper body, and a high-angle shot of his heaving chest as he forces himself into a sitting position, wrenching in pain, the Feral Kid looking on. From the point of the explosion to the end of the sequence, therefore, the "look" at the objectified body is first entirely unmediated, and then mediated only by those who have come to admire the hero. The body is thus offered as object of erotic spectacle even as this eroticization is undercut by a punishment caused, but not perceived, by those who inflict it.

In the opening and closing sequences of the film — slow, low-angle tracking shots advancing and retreating from the battered hero, his eye bloodied and jacket torn — one can infer the source of mediation only retroactively. In both shots, Max looks back at the camera directly, and both are accompanied by a voiceover that is revealed only at the end of the film to constitute the diegetic narration of the Feral Kid, thereby suggesting that the entire narrative comprises his recollection several years into the future. Once again, this look is not linked to aggression; instead, the narration situates the image as wholly accessible to the narrator who perceives Max, advancing and retreating in his own memory, as an idealized figure. Explaining that Max "lives now — only in my dreams," the Feral Kid also enmeshes memory with homoerotic fantasy, regulating his own image of the battered Max in a scene that ensures the hero's continued presence and perpetual accessibility. By such means, the film manages to solicit the "look" of desire at the objectified male body while simultaneously configuring it as a look of identification motivated only by the protagonist's suffering.

This accommodation of homosexual and heterosexual positions of spectatorial access extends to the film's use of "dress codes," and specifically its configuration of black leather as an element of gay culture that has no inherent or exclusive historical associations with homosexuality. As Thomas Harris suggests, the postwar leather phenomenon, which originated in the late 1940s in "straight motorcycle gangs of disaffected youth," was appropriated by emerging gay biker clubs in the 1950s. With Marlon Brando's look in *The Wild One* (1954) as its model, the culture used the motorcycle and the leather jacket as a countercultural antidote to social demands of bourgeois conformity in the 1950s. By the time that the first gay leather bars appeared in the early 1960s, leather had come to signify an aggressive masculinity that many gay men used to separate themselves from associations of homosexuality with effeminacy.[71] Initially conceived as a rebel and outlaw culture, the fringe status of gay leather-S/M culture was compromised in the first years of the gay liberation movement in the early 1970s through the commodification of its artifacts both within and outside of the gay community.[72] By the late 1970s and early 1980s, leather artifacts were being used as countercultural signifiers in the punk and new wave rock phenomena, neither of which maintained any exclusive affiliation with homosexuality. At the same time, however, black leather culture was also being targeted and stereotyped by the mainstream as the realm of a self-obsessed, threatening, and specifically homosexual hypermasculinity. After the release of William Friedkin's controversial film *Cruising* (1980), the dangerous and sadistic leatherman provoked inquiries by the mainstream press regarding the issue of whether gay men were more "naturally" prone to danger, violence, and aggression than straight men.[73]

Directly informed by these developments, *The Road Warrior* distinguishes between the historical significations of black leather while simultaneously attempting to hybridize these same significations. George Miller acknowledges that costume designer Norma Moriceau conducted research in gay magazines as inspiration for Humungus (Kjell Nilsson), explaining that the look of the villain hulk decked out in a facemask, harness, leather neckpiece and wristbands, and studded crotchplate briefs achieved an "almost comical effect."[74] In his exaggeration of the heavily muscled male form accented by the accoutrements of leather-S/M culture, Humungus begins to resemble a comic book construction of villainy. The costumes of the band of followers also signal flat and stereotypical characterizations: Charles Michener's review of the film suggests that "its characters are not people, they're Village People—Punks, Apaches, Lonesome Cowboys and other icons ransacked from the junk heap of today's real West."[75]

While the film may capitalize on the villainization of versions of masculinity that gay culture had recently marketed successfully to mainstream culture, Michener's comment begins to suggest that what the film stereotypes is not homosexuality per se, but the hypermasculine versions of the male body that both gay and mainstream culture had celebrated, but which also do not readily translate to deep characterizations in cinematic narrative. While villainous hypermasculinity becomes shallow in its maniacal and untempered aggression, Max's version of masculinity is softer, and paradoxically more "masculine," because he does not need to draw attention to it. In contrast to the villains, Michener finds in Max an "easy, unswaggering masculinity" that makes him more accessible to audiences.[76] Certainly, the film establishes connections between the villains' and Max's behavior: at one point, Papagallo suggests that as a scavenger of gasoline he is "no different from the animals out there." Max also wears more tight-fitting black leather than any other character in the film, and his garb is in sharp contrast to the lighter colored, airier costumes sported by the humanitarians in the gasoline fortress. Nonetheless, as Sheila Benson observes, "The difference is that the bad guy's leathers are cut away to the waist in the back."[77] Max attains a more liminal status: his leather codes him as a less threatening figure who is as much a rebel and an outsider as the villains, but who has no need to assert his rebellion in displays of antisocial masculine aggression. The version of elemental man embodied by this hero becomes yet more resonant as it is always something more, something deeper, that can be contained by neither emblem nor icon.

The suggestion that the villains are wholly stereotypical characters without depth cannot, however, account for the emotional resonances and instances of human sensitivity that the narrative ascribes to them. While Humungus's costume codes him as an aggressive and sadistic male, he does not lack compassion or the ability to empathize with the pain of human loss. After Wez (Vernon Wells) shrieks in agony and demands revenge for the Feral Kid's murder of his lover, Humungus tells him that "I understand your pain. We've all lost someone we love." Curiously, the "villain's" condolences make him, in at least one way, more "human" than Max, who has also exacted revenge on his aggressors (in *Mad Max*) but who has chosen to isolate himself in his own suffering rather than share it with others. The gay press was highly attentive to such observations. While noting its largely one-dimensional formulations of character, *Advocate* critic Clifton Montgomery nowhere refers to any suggestions of homosexual stereotyping in the film, and he praises *The Road Warrior* for its sensitivity in including a "matter-of-fact portrayal of a gay couple."[78]

In *Gallipoli* and *The Road Warrior* as well as early press articles, structured ambiguities of character and narrative accommodate seemingly inconsistent, and often contradictory, readings of the star persona — as Australian and American, masculinized and feminized, strong and vulnerable, gay and straight — through a "depth" model that depends on the withholding and emergence of identifiable character attributes. What *is* consistent during this period, however, is the composite star image of this discourse: Gibson as natural and elemental man. In the early 1980s, Gibson is consequently always something "more" and "other" than what he appears to be at any given moment; according to the structure of melodrama, the star discourse thereby anticipates future revelations that point to, yet never fully contain, the true nature of the star.

With respect to the construction of gay male subject positions of access to Gibson, the star discourse would never again be quite as accommodating as it had been in the early 1980s. While publicity texts and cinematic narratives supported the persona's universal accessibility early in his career, subsequent transformations of the star persona cumulatively delimit these positions of access in ways that "resolve" Gibson's persona within the progressive melodramatic "narrative" of star texts constituting his career from the mid-1980s to the present. Certain discursive strategies are common to both periods: Gibson's image continues to conform to the depth model, in the construction of an authentic, elemental, and natural man. Through the interaction of ideological shifts in the star texts, changes in mainstream perceptions of homosexuality, and shifts in gay politics, however, Gibson's star persona becomes progressively less accessible to gay readings and fantasy constructions.

Conservative Politics: Gibson as Family Man

The conservative political climate of the Reagan/Bush years, as well as its emphasis on the reintegration of the stable nuclear family, deeply affected mainstream cinema's strategies in the representation of gay characters. Within a year of *The Road Warrior*'s release in the summer of 1982, the press was acknowledging the advent of a "gay new wave" in Hollywood, featuring such representations as the homo-hetero love triangle of Arthur Hiller's *Making Love*, the undercover-cop/gay buddy relationship in James Burrows's *Partners*, and the permutations of gender and sexual "performances" in Blake Edwards's *Victor/Victoria*. By the mid- to late 1980s, however, Vito Russo notes that Hollywood had all but abandoned such attempts to represent gay characters and themes; a second crest of this "new wave" in 1986 comprised exclusively independent productions.[79]

Several explanations for this shift have been offered. First, whether due to the quality of the productions or the reticence of the mainstream public to be lured by gay themes, most of the 1982 films failed to sell as many tickets as anticipated, despite considerable efforts to target both straight and gay audiences. Another influence on this shift, however, was that the "new wave" coincided with a rash of publicity regarding the new "gay cancer" that would come to be known as AIDS: a sexual orientation that had only recently begun to escape the long-term effects of social pathologization was now being repathologized. By 1982, "gay cancer" was making the already highly visible gay community yet more vulnerable to the negative effects of such visibility. *The Advocate*'s annual report of "The State of the Gay Union" at the start of 1982 verifies that along with recent news of the mysterious spread of the "cancer," homosexuals were also confronting a resurgence of antigay violence and hate crimes, the reduction or elimination of federal and local budget allocations to gay community services, and an increasingly influential Moral Majority responsible for inspiring efforts to revoke antisodomy laws and for exerting pressure on the media industries.[80] As Russo reports, the mainstream press was already showing signs of a conservative shift by 1982: a 20/20 segment intimated that the "new wave" films constituted a form of gay propaganda against which the Motion Picture Association of America's rating system provided an inadequate form of protection (302). By the mid-1980s, however, conservative factions were taking more reactionary measures against gay culture, as reflected by William F. Buckley's recommendation that AIDS carriers be tattooed, and Pat Buchanan's suggestion that AIDS was just punishment for offenders of the moral order.

This increasingly conservative culture climate might not have resulted in any demonstrable change in Mel Gibson's "universal" accessibility to American audiences across the lines of sexual orientation. After all, his accessibility to gay audiences was secured through both deliberate and inadvertent window advertising strategies; it was not solicited by self-acknowledged gay characterizations. The non-narrative star texts of the mid- to late 1980s nonetheless gradually construct a more noticeably conservative version of his star persona that stands for the same family values that ultraconservative factions were promoting to counteract a moral indecency that the gay lifestyle epitomized.

Part of this transformation extends as a logical progression of the rising star's career in Hollywood. Before his appearance in his first American-made film in 1984 (Mark Rydell's *The River*), Gibson's image as an exotic hunk figure with remarkable crossover potential did not require the revelation of details of his personal life. Although he was already married with two children by the time that he made *The Road Warrior*, the early texts mention such details only offhandedly. In fact, until he took residence in the United States in the mid-1980s, mainstream star texts kept his private life private. The media portray Gibson's eventual promotion from Australian actor to international superstar as a stressful and uneasy transition. After his highly successful (heterosexual) romantic lead in Peter Weir's *The Year of Living Dangerously* (1983), Gibson's popularity rose so quickly that he was solicited to make a series of four films in less than two years: *The Bounty* (1983), *The River*, *Mrs. Soffel* (1984), and *Mad Max Beyond the Thunderdome* (1985). In a 1985 article proclaiming Gibson "The Sexiest Man Alive," *People* magazine reports that Gibson's star status had begun to take its toll: he was arrested for drunk driving while filming *Mrs. Soffel* in Toronto, and he was becoming infamous for taking jabs at the press for misrepresenting and misquoting him in interviews.[81] Biographer Roland Perry reports that he was frequently drunk and incommunicative on the *Thunderdome* set.[82] After completing *Thunderdome*, Gibson took a long-term hiatus from filmmaking and returned to his new ranch in Australia to spend time with his family. As the star texts of the mid- to late 1980s reveal, Gibson's disenchantment with the trappings of his newfound stardom stemmed from his perceived lack of control over his own image, exacerbated by the media's misperceptions of his "real" identity and the blurring of the boundaries between his public and private life, which he struggled in vain to keep separate.

Curiously, the texts reveal more details of his personal life (including his hatred of the press), even as they support Gibson's right to keep his private life "private," by situating the media industries as a collective aggressor that promotes a disingenuous image of the star, and by positing Gibson's stable family life as a corrective sign of his authenticity.

The structuring of this conflict between the disingenuous and the authentic plays on a depth model that is in many ways consistent with the tactics used to promote an earlier version of Gibson's persona as the embodiment of an elemental masculinity. The locative ambiguities that promoted a universal accessibility are now also used to signal a conflict between inconsonant versions of his image that the press promotes: a 1985 *Rolling Stone* article finds that Gibson's binational heritage has resulted in a "decided cultural ambivalence."[83] Two years later, *Mademoiselle* describes a "dichotomy of roots" that leads to Gibson's observation that "I'm not really at home in either place."[84] In the "Sexiest Man Alive" piece, the locative ambiguities are depicted as an internal conflict: he has become an "outsider" because he is worn out by his work, unhappy with his current film project (*Thunderdome*), and angry with the press for drawing attention to this very unhappiness. The article acknowledges that Gibson's discontent stems from these specific problems, yet it also suggests that "he has always been at odds with his surroundings," thereby making his "outsider" status as much a matter of personal history as the result of media exploitation: Gibson felt that he was "on the outside" as a child in Peekskill because of his family's religious affiliations, and he never fit in with his classmates once the family moved to Australia.[85]

Beginning in the mid-1980s, and continuing throughout his career, the star who feels out of place in Australia and America—and, indeed, in his own body—finds the only place that he can call home to be wherever his family is. The family man is the "real" Mel Gibson, and everything else is a disingenuous construction, a fabrication perpetuated by the film industry and the press. Green reports that "if there is anywhere that Gibson seems at ease, it is in the embrace of his family" that was rapidly expanding throughout the 1980s, ultimately to a total of six children. This emphasis on family life is sufficiently flexible to permit a continuity with many aspects of his early, pre-Hollywood screen image. The father who is only himself in the undisturbed privacy of his own home (be it one of two new ranches in Australia and Montana) becomes the ultimate sign of authenticity. Gibson is a good father because he was always meant to be a father. Indeed, as the sixth of eleven children in a deeply religious family (his father was once a minister), Gibson finds in his own childhood the perfect preparation for this inherited role.

The emphasis on the authenticity of family life requires no radical adjustment to the strategies used to construct Gibson's early image. A masculinity that was initially "unswaggering," and largely unselfconscious, appears even moreso when perceived as a natural byproduct of fatherhood. According to *McCall's* in 1985, Gibson's wife Robyn "jokes that he maintains his muscles by lifting infants."[86] Two years later, *Ladies' Home Journal* reports that this "quiet, down-to-earth family man with clear priorities," who is "hooked on fatherhood. . . . doesn't work on maintaining his good looks and rarely even exercises."[87] If Gibson's sex appeal continues to rely on a vulnerable masculinity, the locus of this vulnerability is merely shifted, now purportedly resulting from his victimization by the media industries that consistently evade the star's rights of privacy by imposing and circulating false images of his life. If Gibson is "bashful and defensive," this is only because "he has found himself squirming in the limelight" where he does not feel at home.[88] If he tends to "shy away from interviews in self-conscious confusion," he does so because the press does not respect his personal "responsibility to be brutally honest."[89]

The positing of fatherhood, family life, and family values as the realm of Gibson's authentic self certainly keeps his image open to further investigations of depth. The real man is always kept hidden and ultimately inaccessible, the private Gibson that can be known yet never fully revealed or contained by investigations into the truth of the persona that the star texts continue to solicit. At the same time, however, the new locus of truth and authenticity in a lifestyle that is specifically (and almost aggressively) heterosexual resolves ambiguities previously kept open in the interests of promoting a universal accessibility that crossed lines of sexual orientation. As a result of his tendency to be "brutally honest" in his interviews, Gibson was actively closing off access to a variety of spectatorial subject positions of fantasy that his former image accommodated: the real man emerging from the star discourse is now blatantly heterosexual. In 1987, he tells *Mademoiselle* that "they [i.e., the press] always concentrate on the dark, silent facade of 'Mad Max' . . . or this 'sexiest man alive' trash. Those are cartoon images. . . . Nobody like that can laugh with his kids. So they leave that part out. Well, that's the part that counts."[90] With such statements, Gibson was beginning to assert his own authority in deciding which aspects of his image would remain susceptible to which reception strategies, and the attributes that once constituted his depth are now deemed to be only flat "cartoon images."

Throughout the late 1980s and early 1990s, then, Gibson's image was undergoing a process of ideological adaptation; he was aligning himself with the same family values that conservative political factions were identifying as a social panacea. By 1987, he was actively using his celebrity status to support ultraconservative candidate Robert Taylor in the Australian federal elections. Biographer James Oram notes that Gibson, described as "so conservative [that] he made Ronald Reagan seem like a pointy-headed Liberal," applauded as Taylor exclaimed during a rally that "our nation today is suffering a massive increase in child abuse, drug abuse, suicide, pornography and the AIDS thing."[91] Around the same time, as Oram reports, Gibson began his "personal dispute" with a Catholic Church that had abandoned the traditions of the Tridentine Mass. He became openly hostile in a television interview when Barbara Walters questioned his and Robyn's decision not to practice birth control (12). The man whom director Mark Rydell had described in 1985 as "very respectful of women" was later quoted as saying that "I think that word, feminist, is bull. Feminism is a term invented by some woman who just got jilted."[92] In a *Playboy* interview in 1995, a puzzled Gibson stated that "I don't know why feminists have it out for me," despite the fact that in the same interview he described a former female business partner as "a cunt" and reiterated his unequivocal condemnation of abortion and birth control practices.[93]

In context, then, his first condemnation of homosexual practices in the December 1991 *El Pais* interview constitutes less an abrupt political leap than a statement consistent with the conservative politics he had already been advocating for several years. What is different about the antigay diatribe, however, is that it is framed as a historical correction, simultaneously acknowledging that the actor has been "read" as gay while attempting to secure such a reading as gross misinterpretation: "What happens is when you're an actor, they stick that label on you. . . .

I go from playing rugby one week to taking dance classes in black leotards the next. Many of the girls I met in school took it for granted that I was gay." [94] While such an explanation certainly does not succeed in closing off the possibility of continuing to read the sign of homosexuality on the body of the star, Gibson's comment in the same article that gays "take it up the ass. . . . This is only for taking a shit" takes a definitive step toward premature melodramatic closure in the realm of fantasy object construction. If the fantasy of Mel Gibson always depended on carefully structured ambiguities that both the silent Mad Max and his real life counterpart in the early 1980s did little to disrupt, Gibson's new ultraconservative outspokenness—the shameless, insistent vocalizing of his political position—is instrumental in his attempt to lower the shades over the window of desire for his gay fans.

Male Anxiety and the Straight Hero

Gibson's new, late-1980s image of ultraconservative advocate for family values finds a convenient narrative mouthpiece in Martin Riggs, the cop/hero of the four highly successful *Lethal Weapon* films (1987–1998). Beginning the series of films after a two-year hiatus from filmmaking (1985–87) that followed *Mad Max Beyond the Thunderdome*, Gibson's portrayal of Riggs in the first *Lethal Weapon* establishes a continuity of characterization by combining earlier characters and films that initially established his popularity in America. Biographer Neil Sinyard finds character continuity in "a dimension of madness in his onscreen persona: from *Mad Max* to *Hamlet* via *Lethal Weapon* is a very logical route. . . . There is even a common cause for this craziness and inner violence. These heroes have been unhinged by the violent destruction of their family lives and by the death of their wives and/or other loved ones." [95] While Martin Riggs certainly owes much to Mad Max, *Lethal Weapon* as a buddy film owes just as much to *Gallipoli:* both films portray an intimate bond between male lead protagonists, foregrounding and intensifying the male-male relationship to a degree where the film's main plot begins to seem incidental. In the *Lethal Weapon* series, the objectified male body is on display even more often than it was in these earlier films. Despite these similarities, however, the series aligns itself with the publicity texts of the late 1980s in an effort to resolve the ambiguities of the earlier persona and signal the birth of a specifically heterosexualized image of Gibson.

The star's move from panaccessible object of desire to conservative and heterosexual family man correlates with a transformation in the buddy film genre occurring in the late 1980s. If the earlier films in the genre configured the home as consistently absent, Robin Wood perceives the later films as more concerned with the "restoration of the home [which becomes] synonymous with the restoration of the symbolic Father."[96] Riggs eventually does recapture the foundations of a home in the heterosexual union with the Rene Russo character in the series' third installment, and in the first two films he finds a most adequate "substitute" in the family of Roger Murtaugh (Danny Glover), to whose home he returns with his dog for Christmas dinner in the final scene of the first film. Riggs also plays a pivotal role in defending the patriarchal order, rescuing both Murtaugh and his kidnapped daughter Rianne (Traci Wolfe) from the clutches of villainous heroin dealers. Indeed, the film suggests that another father's willingness to have his daughter killed to protect his own drug-dealing interests is the most unforgivable evil of all.

Riggs upholds patriarchy on the national as well as the domestic front in the film. The villains' crimes in the Mad Max films were at least motivated by a survival instinct largely undifferentiated from Max's, as both parties sought out the gasoline necessary to keep themselves mobile in the deserted wasteland. In *Lethal Weapon*, however, the crime is a form of unmitigated greed designed as especially repulsive within the 1980s conservative political climate: "[The villains] represent enemies because they are drug dealers, one of the most fully drawn domestic evils created in the Reagan mythology, a narrative in which evil drug dealers were ruining the fabric of the nation through attacking the family. . . ."[97] To make matters worse, as Susan Jeffords highlights, the villains' loyalties are doubly misguided. Having organized their drug-dealing operation while allegedly serving their country in the Vietnam War, they now place their allegiance to the corrupt leader McAlister (Mitchel Ryan) above their responsibility to uphold national interests (56).

If *Lethal Weapon* clearly distinguishes between heroes and villains on the basis of domestic and national allegiances to a "law" that *The Road*

Warrior leaves more ambiguous (and that *Gallipoli* yet more radically doubts the point of upholding), it no less rigorously, if more problematically, attempts to resolve the ambiguities of what constitutes an acceptable version of masculinity. Here once again, it is indebted to the earlier films. Riggs is an expert shooter and fighter, a "lethal weapon" who is yet rendered vulnerable to reminders of his own emotional loss: he jabs a revolver into his mouth early in the first film, ready to pull the trigger and breaking down into tears as he holds his dead wife's picture. This vulnerability is initially secured in an unsolicited objectification of the male body. The camera first reveals an entirely naked Martin (with only his back side visible) getting out of bed with a cigarette in his mouth as he moves to the refrigerator to grab a beer. The two subsequent and laboriously protracted "exposures" of the stripped male body are, however, clearly motivated by another male villain's aggression. In the first, Martin is naked from waist up, suspended from a hook as one of McAlister's henchmen tortures him by dousing his body with water and prodding him with an electrical current.[98] The second instance occurs at the close of the film, when he valiantly strips off his shirt to engage in a brutal fighting match with the already arrested final villain (Gary Busey) as Murtaugh and fellow police officers cheer Riggs on. Each of these last two instances is thus clearly motivated by the presence of a male aggressor, and each is configured as a test of masculinity that, according to Neale's paradigm, justifies the male display by associating it with punishment and violence, thereby securing the heterosexuality of viewing subject and object viewed. In each case, Martin passes the test. He never gives in (fig. 23).

Cynthia Fuchs adds that the violence serves to "displace [the film's] homoerotic subtext" generated by the intimate relationship between Riggs and Murtaugh, and that the displacement is itself evidence of a "masculine body anxiety" that is ultimately homophobic.[99] Tania Modleski finds that the *Lethal Weapon* series demonstrates a "fascination *and* aversion" to the homoeroticism that the films consistently activate, as male anxiety is displaced by transforming the body into a machine.[100] The film often hedges dangerously close to conflating homosocial and homosexual bonding in the depiction of this "male couple," and a comparison of the treatment of the male couple in *Gallipoli* and the *Lethal Weapon* films reveals a relative lack of such anxiety in the earlier film — a lack that ultimately made Gibson's character more

23   The exposed, (in)vulnerable body: Gibson as Martin Riggs in *Lethal Weapon* (1987). Author's personal collection.

accessible as an object of homosexual desire. In *Gallipoli*, the bond between Frank and Archie is strong and deep, but neither character ver-
bally acknowledges its sexual potential. Rather, it transpires through
what is never articulated, and Archie's death ensures the perpetuation of desire as a possibility that will never be, but might have been,
realized. Conversely, *Lethal Weapon* uses excessive verbalization of the
potential sexual bond between Roger and Martin to diffuse the possibility of a homosexual desire that is ultimately more threatening because both of the heroes survive—through *four* films. In the first film,
after Roger grabs Martin's body to protect him from an explosion,
Roger retorts (in jest), "What are you—a fag?" At the end of the second film, Roger cradles Martin's wounded body after his narrow escape from death; as the couple awaits rescuers, in a tightly framed
medium close-up Martin suggests, "Hey, Rog—did anyone ever tell
you—you really are a beautiful man?" When they both chuckle at this
comment, Martin adds, "Give us a kiss before they come." Under the
guise of playful banter between devoted buddies and partners, Gibson
was talking about homosexual desire onscreen long before he began to
denounce it to the press.

Gay Empowerment: Outing and the Responsibilities of Representation

These attempts to acknowledge a homosexual subtext by disavowing
it, and to protest the incontestable heterosexuality of the star who
portrayed these fictional characters, were perfectly consonant with
Gibson's new image as advocate of family values. Still, a survey of the
critical responses of the mainstream press reveals that the "deflections"
of homosexuality were not entirely successful for all readers. David
Ansen draws the film's masculine body anxiety to the surface, suggesting that "'my pistol is bigger than your pistol' is the true theme" in
a narrative packed with "overwrought macho displays." [101] *The Village
Voice* bypasses *Lethal Weapon 2*'s (1989) attempt to displace homosexuality by suggesting that the film offers "a positive image of interracial
male love," [102] and *Newsweek* concurs that here "the real love story . . .
is between the cops" and argues that "the filmmakers don't even try to
create a full-scale female character." [103]

The gay press had been drawing its readers' attention to homophobic characterizations and film narratives in mainstream cinema for

24 Homophobia without homoeroticism: Marianne Graves (Goldie Hawn) and Rick Jarmin (Gibson) in *Bird on a Wire* (1990). Courtesy Photofest.

quite some time, most emphatically in the widely publicized backlash against *Cruising* and the release of Vito Russo's *The Celluloid Closet* (1981), which noted Hollywood's reluctance to offer positive or even matter-of-fact gay characterizations. Still, as Vito Russo suggests in a 1990 *Advocate* article, many still-closeted gay men were not enraged by the stereotyped gay characterizations and homophobic mockery in films such as *Bird on a Wire* (1990): "Most gays don't even notice it, and most critics (many of whom have gay friends) don't condemn it." [104] In the film, Gibson portrays a man once again attempting to escape from his own identity, or in this case the identities he has been forced to assume in the Witness Protection program, having ratted on drug dealers who have now discerned his whereabouts (fig. 24). On the run with his ex-wife (Goldie Hawn), he revisits the salon where he developed the reputation as the "Michelangelo" of coiffure by his flamboyant and stereotypically gay cohorts. As Gibson approaches his ex-boss, he lapses into a mincing, camped up, limp-wristed gay stereotype, as Goldie snickers discreetly in the background. *The New York Native* acknowledges the stereotype with a "homophobia alert," finding the hairdresser sequence to be out of context in the film, and asserting that "surely something really ought to be done about this sort of thing"; however, the piece devotes just as much coverage to the unsightly body hair on Gibson's buttocks that "[bears] no resemblance to the one known and loved from *Lethal Weapon.*"[105]

This complacency was about to change. By 1992, *Christopher Street* writer Bob Satuloff included *Bird on a Wire* with *Cruising* in its list of "The Ten Most Homophobic Movies" of all time, and found himself cheering on the villains after the hairdresser sequence.[106] Gibson's first directorial effort, *The Man Without a Face* (1992), provoked even stronger reactions. Unlike Isabelle Holland's source novel, which overtly acknowledges the homoerotic relationship between tutor Justin McLeod and his pupil, the film version transforms accusations of homosexuality into false rumor and gossip against which McLeod (Gibson) must defend himself. Gays picketed the film's premiere outside the Chinese Theater, and the mainstream press began to echo the gay community's concerns over Gibson's homophobia, documenting the gay community's backlash in its film reviews, and providing space for Gibson and his press agent to respond to the allegations that he deliberately obscured the story's gay subtext. Ansen commented that "the film would have been a lot more challenging if it had remained faithful to its source. . . . [but] Gibson elects to play it safe."[107] *The Seattle Times* used the film adaptation as an example of a "time-honored Hollywood practice" of "straightening" gay characterizations in an attempt to keep homosexuality off the screen.[108]

The press's increasing attentiveness to the inauthenticity of "straightened" and homophobic characterizations, as well as gays' empowerment to influence changes in the representation of gay characters in mainstream cinema, is largely the result of outing strategies that gay activists have used to expose closeted public figures perceived as hypocritical. Although the practice received little attention in the mainstream press before a *Time* magazine cover story in May of 1990, outing strategies were developed much earlier than this, largely in reaction to the political conservatism of the Reagan and Bush years. Outing was initially sanctioned against closeted political figures, as well as other closeted gays with the financial clout to influence policy decisions. Many gays believed that these groups were hampering the advancement of AIDS medical research in the wake of funding cutbacks by refusing to publicly acknowledge their own homosexuality.[109] Outing was equally a response to the efforts of influential right-wing organizations to stifle gay civil rights legislation, as reflected in the 1986 Supreme Court decision in Bowers vs. Hardwick, which allowed states to uphold longstanding sodomy laws (144).

In the effort to counteract the silencing of gay voices and to halt the astronomically growing body count of lives lost to the AIDS virus, ACT UP (AIDS Coalition to Unleash Power) was formed in 1987 to combat public indifference both within and outside the gay community. Re-acting to the failure of the minority "equal rights" politics of tolerance that gays had adopted since the mid-1970s, ACT UP advocated the more radical tactics of the late-1960s sexual revolution. Using "confron-tation, guerilla theater, sit-ins, and non-violent civil disobedience," members of ACT UP (and its offshoot organization formed in 1990, Queer Nation) asserted themselves as a visible and vocal gay presence to be reckoned with.[110]

By the late 1980s, in an attempt to counteract the right wing's in-creasing power to influence the media and entertainment industries, gay supporters of outing also deemed affluent and closeted celebrity figures as fair game—especially, as in the case of Jodie Foster, when they earned large sums by producing or appearing in films that in-cluded stereotypical gay representations. The private sex lives of many closeted media celebrities were revealed by Michelangelo Signorile in the pages of the short-lived *OutWeek* (1989–1991), and many other out-ings resulted from the filtering of information through clearinghouses for international gay news via the American gay press, the tabloids, and eventually, the mainstream press: "While homosexuality was still scandalous, it was now—thanks in no small part to the visibility pro-duced by the burgeoning queer activism of the previous years—mov-ing from being unprintably scandalous to acceptably scandalous." [111] Richard Chamberlain's 1989 outing, for example, was prompted by the Outlines News Service, a gay clearinghouse managed by Rex Wock-ner, who located a story about Chamberlain's gay lover in a French newspaper, and offered the information to the gay *Bay Area Reporter*, from which it was picked up by the tabloids. Although the mainstream press was reluctant to participate in the outing, Signorile recounts that "queer activists saw that they could make Hollywood quake" and that the most effective "way to attack Hollywood was to rip down its facade and expose its duplicity" (300). The strategy succeeded, and by the early 1990s "producers and agents were predicting financial ruin and pleading with queers to stop this madness. And power brokers were asking their friends to write letters to *OutWeek* to defend them" (304).

The December 1991 *El Pais* interview with Mel Gibson appeared at a historical moment when gays were witnessing an unprecedented empowerment through the threat of exposing both gay *and* homophobic celebrity figures as weak and hypocritical. As Signorile documents, in the early 1990s gay activists threatened to disrupt the Academy Awards ceremonies and rallied against homophobic characterizations in films such as *JFK*, *The Silence of the Lambs*, and *Basic Instinct.* Their voices were heard, and Hollywood was forced to respond: in the years that followed, Hollywood stars have voiced their support for AIDS research, more studio heads and marketing executives have begun to attend gay benefits, and many studios have become more attentive to the political responsibilities inherent in the characterizations they offer to the public. In Gibson's case, the rapid dissemination of the news about the Spanish newspaper interview throughout America demonstrates this new gay empowerment. Once Rex Wockner discovered the interview, he immediately translated it and leaked the information through his Outlines News Service. Columnist Liz Smith picked up the story the following month, and news of the interview quickly circulated through the gay weeklies and monthlies before finding its way into the mainstream press in conjunction with the even more widely disseminated news of Gibson's "Sissy of the Year" award.[112] The pressures of the gay community now claim a historical resonance that they once lacked: in subsequent interviews and news stories, the star has been frequently called on to respond to the allegations of homophobia. Additionally, the Gay and Lesbian Alliance Against Defamation (GLAAD), with which the film studios have more actively cooperated since the events of the early 1990s, documents and disseminates a historical record of Gibson's homophobic remarks and characterizations that grows longer with each new transgression. Most recently, GLAAD has focused its efforts on criticizing the stereotypical portrayal of gay characters in *Braveheart* (1995), and the organization has described the murder of Edward II's lover Philip as an act of "gay bashing." [113] The protests have been widely publicized on the CNN and E! networks, as well as in *USA Today* and several local newspapers across the country.[114]

While gay activists have never formally threatened to expose Gibson as a homosexual, their actions have attempted to out him as a homophobe, to force him to acknowledge and be held accountable for the political implications of the representations he offers to his public. Replaying a public/private dichotomy that has been crucial to his construction as a deep star since the start of his career, however, Gibson has resituated this outing in the context of right to privacy issues. Here, politics has become a personal matter devoid of social implications. Despite the fact that his status as a celebrity figure offers him privileged opportunities to disseminate his conservative values to the public, he maintains that his political views are personal opinions—ones he is being victimized for expressing by radical gays who would deny Gibson the right to his private life, in the same way that the media industry has consistently victimized him by constructing a false public image that bears no relevance to the real, private family man—a victimization that reiterates Justin McLeod's self-defense in *The Man Without a Face*. Indeed, Gibson responds to the gay community by rendering himself immune to outside influences, pleading ignorance and bewilderment that anyone might challenge his right to his own opinions. At the same time, Gibson is aggressive in his refusal to capitulate: "I'll apologize when hell freezes over," he said in the 1995 *Playboy* interview, portraying himself as the victim of attacks on his personal freedom by a group of "people just looking for attention" and unduly harrassing him in the process: "I don't want anyone writing to me or coming to my house. I don't want any of that shit. Suffice it say that I've been chased by automobiles doing dangerous things on the freeway. I'm not even comfortable with you printing this because there are certain organizations that like to breathe down my neck. I don't give a fuck what they say as long as they keep it to themselves." [115]

Through the discourse of outing, however, gay activists have foregrounded the importance of disrupting the convenient polarization of public and private that Gibson advocates for both himself and his "oppressors." Rather than granting celebrities immunity to political responsibilities on the basis of their status as private citizens, they are held even more accountable for their expressions of opinions that can never be *just* personal matters. As Signorile suggests, privacy issues may have applied in the 1950s when "outing meant ruin," but in the 1990s privacy promotes fear, self-hatred, and hypocrisy. [116] In this context, by failing to acknowledge his own homophobia or at least own up to the social implications of his personal beliefs, Gibson is increasingly perceived as no more respectable than any other closeted public figure.

This embracing of political responsibility in the spirit of the new gay activism helps to explain how, for many gays, the melodrama of emergence of the true self has been resolved in the career of Mel Gibson. In an era that thrived economically on a high degree of crossover between gay and straight culture, the structured ambiguities in Gibson's films and non-narrative star texts made him accessible to both gays and straights in the early 1980s because these ambiguities accommodated such a diverse set of subject positions in which to situate the persona as a fantasy figure. Indeed, the fantasy of Mel Gibson depended on the notion that he was always in the process of disclosing the secret of a true self that was never fully revealed, but that also never failed to indicate that the star was both authentic and sincere. In the late 1980s and 1990s, the emergence of Gibson as an advocate of family values aligned with a conservative ideology that literally threatens the lives of gay men has been countered by the proponents of a more radical, visible, and vocal gay activism claiming its own power to influence media representations. In this historical context, Gibson's insistence on maintaining his privacy now suggests that he still has something more to reveal about himself, but it also implies that he has something to hide: a homophobia that renders the star's depth disingenuous and hypocritical. Indeed, his very resistence to the disclosure of this secret constitutes its own revelation.

In relation to James Dean, the development of Mel Gibson's persona demonstrates a dramatic shift in the locus of responsibility for the management of acting talent, and in the relation of such management to a subculture's perception and negotiation of the actor's authenticity. In the 1950s, the studios attempted to construct this authenticity through the synergistic relationship between publicity, promotion, film roles, and critical and journalistic reception. Gibson's alienation from a large section of his gay male audience and his subsequent attempts to make amends by inviting gay and lesbian filmmakers to the set of *Conspiracy Theory* show the extent to which the actor, as well as the press agents who manage his public pronouncements, is assessed by his willingness to negotiate his star image with the audiences that receive it. As we move to the 1990s in the next chapter, we will witness a shift yet more dramatic, in which an actor's perceived authenticity, as well as his continued popularity across sexual orientations, requires that the star more actively and strategically invite his audiences to *participate* in this negotiation.

CHAPTER FOUR

Keanu Reeves and the

Fantasy of Pansexuality

*J*ust weeks after serial killer Andrew Cunanan committed suicide outside a Miami Beach resort hotel in July of 1997, the
moderator of a Keanu Reeves fan website [alt.fan.keanu-reeves.
moderated] reported to her newsgroup that producer Dino De
Laurentis had recently offered Keanu Reeves the lead role in a film version of the serial killer's life—an offer that Reeves declined. "Would
this be a good role for Keanu?" asks the moderator, generating over a
dozen responses from a group of fans with detailed knowledge of the
star's history, as well as a strong sense of the actor's possible concerns
on this issue.[1] One participant responds affirmatively that "Keanu is
a good choice for Cunanan. The K-Man has said evil characters are
the most interesting."[2] Responding to a contributor's suggestion that
Keanu's persona would not be irrevocably linked with Cunanan if he
decided to accept the role, another fan adamantly disagrees, arguing
that the star personas of actors such as Tony Curtis, Anthony Hopkins,
Mark Harmon, and Anthony Perkins have failed to shed their association with the serial killers they have portrayed: "If the murderer makes
a strong enough impression on us, I think we will always associate him
with the actor who played the role."[3] A third participant in the debate
believes that Cunanan would not be a good choice for Keanu, remind-

ing readers that "Cunanan killed 2? Or 3? men who were supposedly gay and Keanu has a large gay following."[4]

These three responses cogently articulate issues that have arisen in the history of Keanu Reeves's image construction. The first references the issue of the star's range, his desire to accept challenging roles without much concern for the potential effect on a consistent star image that he has blatantly rejected. The second response is especially perceptive in light of Reeves's career, given that the actor has struggled (and, some would argue, continues to struggle) to dissociate himself from what several critics have described as the airhead image he captured so effectively in his first highly successful starring role of Ted in *Bill and Ted's Excellent Adventure* (1989). Once again addressing the matter of consistency of star image, the third response rightly acknowledges the potential dilemma inherent in Reeves's portrayal of a historical figure who kills gay men. Here the issue is not only that Reeves's gay following can be traced back to his prefilm career when, at the age of twenty, he appeared as a homosexual character in the play *Wolfboy* in Toronto in 1984, or that this following increased when he agreed to play a male hustler in openly gay director Gus Van Sant's *My Own Private Idaho* (1991). Reeves's own sexual orientation has also been a matter of public inquiry, largely initiated by his own design in a 1990 article for *Interview* magazine. Asked to settle once and for all the matter of whether or not he is gay, Reeves equivocated by stating, "No. . . . But ya never know."[5] Shortly after the release of *Speed* (1994), rumors began to circulate in both the mainstream and gay press that Reeves and millionaire producer David Geffen had secretly married in Paris.

While both parties have refuted the marriage rumors, speculations on the truth of the star's sexuality have continued to circulate publicly in the mainstream and gay press, in online newsgroups, and in World Wide Web pages devoted to the actor. Indeed, much of the fascination with the figure of Keanu Reeves in star texts concerns the mystery of a sexuality that has resisted any attempts at being finally settled. At the same time that many gay males have appropriated Reeves as a sexual ally, he continues to maintain a devoted following of straight spectators. In the arena of reception strategies, then, Reeves has much in common with the postmortem construction of James Dean's persona, as well as the early version of Mel Gibson's persona, maintaining an accessibility to audiences across the lines of sexual orientation. Unlike Dean, however, Reeves is not dead, and he actively participates in the construction of his persona in ways that suggest that the appeal to both gay and straight audiences is quite strategic. Unlike Gibson, Reeves has not responded with indignation or defensiveness to the sexual inquiry conducted by the press; instead, he appears to be quite accepting of public attempts to appropriate him as either gay or straight. Instead of burdening himself with the matter of sexual self-definition, however, he has more often preferred to question the efficacy of labels and the positing of any stable sexual identity. The discursive strategies maintaining what might be described as the star's "panaccessibility" and its reception are the concerns of the present chapter.

The Marketing of Homosexuality in the 1990s

While the formation of watchdog organizations such as the Gay and Lesbian Alliance Against Defamation (GLAAD), in conjunction with gay activist groups such as ACT UP and Queer Nation, exerted considerable pressure on Hollywood studios to avoid homophobic representations and themes in the late 1980s, most of the positive cinematic treatments of gays were confined to the realm of independent productions. The Advocate notes in 1991 that activist groups were successful in their efforts to force studios and talent agencies to adopt policy statements of nondiscrimination, yet the same article acknowledges that established Hollywood stars continued to be reticent to play openly gay roles, and studios were still reluctant to finance films with gay themes and characters.[6] Indeed, when Gus Van Sant solicited River Phoenix and Keanu Reeves for the roles of male hustlers in My Own Private Idaho in 1990, both actors were advised not to take the roles because of the potential effect on their careers. "Just being in the film, it becomes an issue politically," Van Sant suggested.[7] Indeed, the film's publicists refused to have Idaho premiere at a 1991 gay/lesbian film festival in Los Angeles. Publicist Mickey Cottrell explained that "the distributor doesn't want the film positioned as a gay film. . . . Then many people would be frightened away. It's better to have the critics say how wonderful it is in dealing with gay characters."[8] Yet the situation was slowly changing: The Advocate suggests that the financial success of the independently produced Longtime Companion (1990) indicated to studios that the AIDS crisis, which had largely contributed to the virtual obliteration of gay-themed projects in Hollywood for several years, might provide palatable subject matter for new productions: "Indeed, some maintain that Hollywood would give up lunches at the fashionable Sunset Boulevard haunt Le Dome for a marketable AIDS story."[9]

Such a story arrived with *Philadelphia*, which has grossed over $200 million worldwide since its release in December of 1993, bringing an Academy Award for Best Actor to Tom Hanks in the process. Many sectors of the gay press denounced the film for playing its gay representations too "safe," but the film's success clearly demonstrated that "the right stars could sell tickets whether they were playing gay or not."[10] Dennis O'Connor, vice president for distribution and marketing for Strand Releasing, argues that the subsequent successful run of the Australian independent film *Priscilla, Queen of the Desert* (1995) was at least equally influential in capturing Hollywood's attention: "When a movie like *Priscilla* makes $15 million, that's not only gay money. . . . Larger companies have seen the success we've had with movies, and they've tried to do the same thing."[11] Indeed, the release of *Jeffrey, Lie Down With Dogs*, and *The Incredible Adventures of Two Girls in Love* in 1995 and 1996 marked a sudden resurgence of gay-themed films, some of which targeted the gay community exclusively, and others of which required separate marketing campaigns for gay and straight audiences. These developments were significant enough for *Entertainment Weekly* to devote a series of articles in the September 1995 issue to "The Gay '90s," arguing that in this "new" era, the eroticization of the male body, previously "confined to art and pornography," is now integral to the marketing strategies of a variety of mainstream films, even those without overt gay themes: "Chris O'Donnell's batsuit [for *Batman Forever*] features a strikingly commodious codpiece; and are we wrong, or does the Riddler have a little *crush* on Bruce Wayne? *Batman Forever* is, in fact, emblematic of the new, mutual inclusiveness—the *give* and *take* and *take back*—of gay and straight audiences."[12]

Although "The Gay '90s" pieces suggest that such phenomena are entirely new to American culture, the parallels between this version of crossover and earlier versions of the late 1970s and early 1980s are unmistakeable. In both cases, studios become cognizant of the profit potential in the targeting of gay audiences, and in both cases the eroticized male body is packaged for both gay and mainstream consumption as an object of identification and desire. While the earlier crossover did little to specify a demographic target market in mainstream culture, however, the new gay crossover is more emphatic in acknowledging the attraction of alternative subcultural identities to disenchanted American youth: "In an era when Americans, especially young ones, are more taken by the cool detachment of cyberspace than with either political party, their own economic futures, whoever happens to be President, and the entire news media, 'independent' or 'alternative' *anything* begins to look a lot more attractive. And the dry, smart outsider mentality represented by much of gay culture seems an interesting stance from which to view the world" (28).

Androgyny, Bisexuality, and Inbetweenness

One emblem of this gay "outsider mentality" that the article finds especially attractive to youth culture is a sexuality that defies definition and strategically avoids all labels. During the same year that this piece appears, feature articles in several other popular weekly magazines note a similar predilection within youth culture. *Newsweek* reports a "new sexual fluidity" popular on campus and in high schools, one student noting that "we just refuse to label ourselves as any of the five food groups." [13] Related descriptions of youth's attraction to an uncategorizable sexuality embodied by contemporary celebrity figures appear in *Harper's Bazaar* and *Vogue*, yet the terms used to describe this ambiguous sexual phenomenon vary.[14] Jess Cagle prefers the term "androgyny," suggesting that "androgyny chic has ushered in a new brand of movie star: Johnny Depp, Leonardo DiCaprio, and Keanu Reeves would all once have been sissies." He proceeds to list other film and music stars who "use sexual ambiguity as a marketing tool—enigmas wrapped in mysteries, they're all things to all persuasions."[15] Whether it is accurate to deem such a sexually ambiguous identity "androgynous" is, however, a perplexing matter, given the inherent problematic of stabilizing a state of "inbetweenness" that deliberately defies categorization. Lexicons only complicate the issue: for example, *The American Heritage College Dictionary* defines "androgyny" as "having both female and male characteristics; hermaphroditic," but also as "being neither distinguishably masculine nor feminine; unisex." [16] The male figures that Cagle includes under the heading of "androgyny chic" certainly do not conform to an image of rugged masculinity, yet when he describes them as "enigmas wrapped in mysteries" who can be "all things to all persuasions," he appears to refer as much to the ways in which these star images are received as to how the images themselves are constructed.

In the discourse of inbetween sexuality so widely popularized in the mid-1990s, and deemed so attractive to American youth, androgyny is often conflated with the equally ambiguous term "bisexuality"—the term preferred by *Newsweek*, *Vogue*, and *Harper's Bazaar*—to designate the status of outsider, and to describe three related phenomena: (1) a constructed sexual image that defies categorization according to the polarities of masculine and feminine; (2) an individual's sexual attraction to both men and women; and (3) an individual's capacity to solicit an attraction from both men and women. In the 1990s, the meaning of this prevalent bisexuality has been rigorously debated in both the academic and popular press. Although *Newsweek*'s cover article is entitled "Bisexuality Emerges as a New Sexual Identity," the article concludes that it is no such identity at all, "less a root than a construction—different in each individual—of passions and actions we are accustomed to calling heterosexual or homosexual." [17] *Harper's Bazaar* describes the bisexual phenomenon as "a desire that doesn't recognize borders," but argues that bisexuality involves a deliberate "transgression" rather than a "blurring" of such borders.[18]

How, then, does one begin to sort through the myriad and often conflicting set of definitions of ambiguous, plural sexuality that youth culture has embraced, and that the popular press has linked to the appeal of several male Hollywood stars? In her seminal work *Vice Versa: Bisexuality and the Eroticism of Everyday Life*, Marjorie Garber provides a possible "solution" to the terminology problem by suggesting that bisexuality is an inherent condition of stardom in the context of fantasy relations. "All great stars are bisexual in the performative mode," she argues, because the goal of star/spectator relations is to mobilize the spectator's identification and desire in fantasy, and to address the desires of a maximum number of spectators, both masculine and feminine; however, "bisexuality" here refers not only or specifically to the star's identity or to the set of already committed sexual acts that constitute the star's history. It suggests, rather (and also), a hypothetical construction, a foregrounding of the inherent *capacity* of the star to desire, and to be desired by, both men and women. Garber relates bisexuality to the concept of gender crossover "in 'object' as well as 'subject.'" As such, her definition of bisexuality in stardom references both the production and reception of the star image: "Whether it is actualized in sexual relationships or remains on the level of elusive attraction, this heightened performative state, this state of being simultaneously all-desiring and all desired, incarnates in the celebrity the two, sometimes apparently conflicting, definitions of bisexuality: having two genders in one body, and being sexually attracted to members of 'both' sexes." [19]

Garber does not suggest that such mobilizations of bisexual desire are specific to the contemporary historical period; rather, she examines a broad range of literary and cinematic narratives across history in which bisexuality operates as an inherent, but often unarticulated, principle. Still, her discussion of subject/object relations of star and spectators in the realm of fantasy seems especially pertinent to the study of celebrity figures at the current historical moment when, in a discourse of ambiguity that posits the absence of stable gender or sexual identities, terms such as "androgyny" and "bisexuality" are used overtly and strategically to designate states of liminality, boundary blurring, and sexual transgression that youth culture embraces, and that star figures are purported to address strategically.

The Discourses of Inbetweenness, Ambiguity,
and Authenticity in Reeves's Star Persona

Both narrative and non-narrative star texts construct a sexual persona of Keanu Reeves as a figure that inhabits a state of inbetweenness, as a youth and as an adult, that addresses a wide variety of subject positions of sexual access. In different contexts, Reeves has been described as either androgynous or bisexual, but he has also been described as either and both heterosexual and homosexual. Star texts both individually and progressively participate in the construction of a celebrity persona whose mystery is perpetually preserved through an ability to address each of these labels even as he manages to avoid stably inhabiting any of them.

That Reeves was chosen to play the James Dean role of Jim Stark from *Rebel Without a Cause* in the 1991 music video of Paula Abdul's

"Rush, Rush" is not so surprising in light of the film roles that he had elected by this time. In *River's Edge* (1986), *Permanent Record* (1988), and *The Prince of Pennsylvania* (1988), he develops the early onscreen persona of the confused and troubled adolescent alienated from both family and community—a role that was instrumental to Dean's popularization of the rebel hero. The nuclear family is in a state of crisis or discord in each film because of absent and/or ineffectual father figures, and home is a place of disarray where human connections are most often strained and violence threatens to erupt at any moment. Each film functions as a melodrama of redemption as the Reeves character reiterates Dean's role, bearing the burden of reinstilling moral order to corrupt domestic and social environments. In *River's Edge*, Matt's (Reeves) father has fled from the home, replaced by a loafing live-in boyfriend who sponges off of his mother and cannot be bothered to assist in the care of the children. Chris's (Reeves) father in *Permanent Record* is perpetually away on business trips. In *The Prince of Pennsylvania* the father becomes a tyrannical figure who beats his wife and forces Rupert (Reeves) to take a "respectable" job with him in a coal mine. Rupert rebels against authority figures and rules that appear insensible to him. He makes arrangements to kidnap his father and collect sufficient ransom so that his mother can leave him for the man that she loves. When his efforts fail, Rupert leaves home for good and takes to the road. In *Permanent Record*, Chris defies the high school administration that refuses to permit him and his friends to pay final tribute to a classmate who has unexplainably committed suicide.

Reeves is consistently alienated and disconnected from his own peer group as well as his family. In *Prince*, Rupert appears to have no friends at all, except for the older woman (Bonnie Bedelia) who owns the restaurant that he manages, and with whom he has a brief sexual encounter before she ultimately abandons him for a ruthless and manipulative police officer. In *River's Edge*, Matt risks ostracization when he decides to reveal to the police that one of his friends has brutally murdered his girlfriend for no other reason than that she "talked shit" to him. In the process, like Jim Stark in *Rebel* and Cal Trask in *East of Eden*, Reeves's characters provide the only hope for any moral and ethical redemption in these melodramas, accepting responsibility for crimes they did not commit, for lives they could never have saved.

Extrapolating from this early onscreen persona, biographers and reporters in the popular press frequently articulate the parallels between the images and lives of Dean and Reeves as rebel figures. Both actors were unreliable, unpredictable, and self-absorbed in their early careers: a biographical piece in *Maclean's* explains that in Reeves's early work for Canadian television and his first films after moving to Hollywood, "Reeves would show up late on the set and not take direction. Eventually, Reeves's agents sat him down for a talk."[20] Keanu's preferred mode of transportation (and most longstanding companion) is his motorcycle—another biography explains that "it would take a very special woman to lure Keanu away from his bikes: 'Sure, I have no shortage of offers, but I prefer to channel my passions into bikes because they're cool, fast and less trouble.'"[21] Like Dean, he is often depicted as a daredevil and thrill-seeker, speeding down Hollywood's winding roads with his lights off late at night. A recent piece on "Hollywood's Hottest Hunks" notes that in the late 1980s "Reeves wowed paparazzi with his James-Dean-like entrances on his bike, but his tendency to crash continues to worry his fans"; indeed, these worries have been justified by the long lateral abdominal scar that the star bears as a result of one serious accident.[22]

Beginning with the early star texts and continuing throughout Reeves's career, the Dean/Reeves connections are elaborated as melodramatic fantasies of origin. The texts note the parallel consequences of early separation from the father figure, attempting to explain the star's current state of unanchoredness and dislocation by returning to incidents of his childhood. While Winton Dean arranged for his son to be raised by relatives in Indiana after his mother's death, Reeves's childhood history has resulted in a more longstanding resentment: Sam Reeves (currently imprisoned for possession of narcotics) abandoned his family altogether when Keanu was very young, and Keanu rarely mentions his father in press interviews: "Keanu would avoid repairing [the relationship] even after he was famous, when Sam gave interviews to the press stating his desire to get back in touch with his adult son."[23] A 1995 piece suggests that his parents' troubled relationship has embittered him to the institution of marriage: "Reeves blames the bad vibes on his folks' breakup when he was a mere tot. 'I have seen nothing to recommend marriage. The only woman I see regularly is my sister Kim.'"[24] The popular press makes frequent connections between the absence of the father figure and the fact that Dean's life was itself nomadic and dislocated. Like Dean, and like the characters in his own early films, the star has no place to call "home."

This sense of dislocation and lack of belonging often activates his fans and co-stars to assume the role of an absent parental figure so that they may shield the vulnerable actor from harm. A recent *Mademoiselle* piece describes the locative ambiguities of the star persona in terms of a "Vulnerable Puppy Syndrome": "Everything we read about Reeves contributes to an urge to protect him: his fatherless upbringing (he never saw his half-Chinese, half-Hawaiian father after age 13); his rootless childhood (the family moved five times, about as many times as Reeves changed high schools); his homeless lifestyle (he lives in hotels, out of a suitcase)." [25] "There's an innocence and openness about him, a vulnerability," Chris Nickson suggests. "People, fans, those who've worked with him all feel an urge to protect him from life." [26] John Malkovich, who appeared with Reeves in *Dangerous Liaisons* (1988), echoes these sentiments, noting that Keanu is "the archetypal troubled young American. He's like your younger brother, someone you should be helping out in some way. He doesn't invite it. I don't think he would like it much. But if you're older, you feel you should protect him" (59). Much in the same way that Dean's persona often activated his fans' maternal instincts, Nickson argues that "the temptation is to mother [Keanu] as much as to make love to him" (192).

In *People* magazine's 1995 cover story listing Reeves as one of "The 50 Most Beautiful People in the World," photographer David Hlynsky suggests that "Keanu has James Dean [sic] charisma, that troubled youth/pent-up sexuality quality." [27] While this is certainly a flattering assessment, it is also slightly peculiar given that Reeves was already thirty-one years old by the time that the article appeared. At age twenty-four, Dean was already testing the limits of credibility by portraying troubled teenagers in *East of Eden* and *Rebel Without a Cause*, but his premature death during the same year that these films appeared helps to explain why he has been immortalized as an emblem of confused and alienated youth; had he lived, his age transformations in the posthumously released *Giant* and his next scheduled performance as Rocky Graziano in *Somebody Up There Likes Me* might quickly have effected, and even necessitated, a correlative transformation of his image. Reeves was required to sustain the alienated youth image for much longer. With few exceptions, he was playing characters who were

25   The classic dude:
Keanu Reeves as Ted
"Theodore" Logan in *Bill
and Ted's Excellent Adventure*
(1989). Author's personal
collection.

at least a decade younger than he throughout much of the first seven
years of his film career. The troubled adolescent label followed him
not only because he carried his age so well on his face, but also because of what critics have described as the almost too perfect fit between the actor's image and his "dude" role as the shaggy-haired Ted
"Theodore" Logan in *Bill and Ted's Excellent Adventure* (fig. 25) and its
sequel *Bill and Ted's Bogus Journey* (1991). The films were so popular
that they inspired product lines of breakfast cereals and Bill and Ted
dolls, as well as a cartoon series (with Keanu and co-star Alex Winter
doing the voices), all of which contributed cumulatively to the effect of
both immortalizing and immobilizing Reeves in the role. As one critic
notes, the Ted role and "so many of [the early] roles played on a sense
of cluelessness that the public (and critics) were beginning to think of
Keanu Reeves as an airhead."[28]

James Dean's premature death allowed critics to take note of the
broad range of his acting abilities by inviting critical speculation on
how much more Dean might have developed, and revealed of himself,
had he survived the fatal car crash. By such means, Dean's onscreen
and offscreen personae became enmeshed in a melodrama of potential,

yet never to be realized, emergence and redemption. Certainly the fact that Dean had actually completed only two troubled adolescent roles helped to facilitate such speculations on his potential range and depth; for Reeves, however, a more extended repetition of adolescent parts made the image association more difficult to question or transcend.

Yet in the "narrative" of Reeves's career development, a correlative transformation does occur. Through the operations of the melodramatic mode, this transformation marks an emergence of the authentic and individuated actor who now redeems himself by demonstrating that the narrow scope of his past film roles, and not the limitations of his acting abilities, have impeded revelations of his range and depth. For some critics, the transformation begins as early as *My Own Private Idaho* (1991). Until this point, attention to Reeves as an actor was primarily confined to the pages of *Teen* magazine, but his association with *Idaho* deemed him worthy of more widespread public attention, not primarily because of the quality of his performance as male hustler Scott Favor (although both *Newsweek* and *National Review* were favorable in their assessments of the star here), but because of the perceived risk of accepting the part at all.[29] David Denby concurs that "for River Phoenix [who plays the role of Mike] and Keanu Reeves, rising stars with young teenage audiences, the movie must be an enormous risk. They've taken on roles impossible to sell on the talk shows. What's remarkable is how fully they give themselves to their parts."[30]

Ironically, however, most critics signal the emergence and arrival of Keanu Reeves as a serious actor three years later, in a role with its own set of potentially stereotypical associations and established genre constraints—as action hero Jack Traven in *Speed* (1994). If critical praise for Dean's performance in *Giant* was often a function of the extent to which he managed to surpass or transcend the constraints of what was perceived as outworn family melodrama, some critics attributed Reeves's distinctiveness in *Speed* to his abilities to infuse vitality and depth into the role of an action hero, to overcome the constraints of a potentially two-dimensional, cardboard characterization in a genre that had become a Hollywood staple by the mid-1990s. As the stereotyped character is individuated, Reeves emerges as a more authentic and skilled performer: "Though a man of action, [Reeves] manages to look intermittently thoughtful: not slack-jawed and cow-eyed like Sly Stallone, or terminally obnoxious like Steven Seagal."[31]

Consonant with a melodramatic emergence of character that also informed Mel Gibson's performance in *The Road Warrior*, the means of accomplishing such a transcendence, of producing a figure of considerable depth and individuality, is a softening of the stereotypical hard-man action hero, and a subtle, "minimalist" acting style that permits and requires spectators to infer the actor's withheld emotion rather than offering them a too overt demonstration of affect: "Reeves gives a smashing performance as an action hero. Short-haired and bullet-headed, he offers a little personality—but not too much. There's a fascination in such minimalist acting. What will the hero respond to? Reeves, warming up here and there, convinces us that Jack . . . is not only a selfless cop with fabulous physical instincts but a good man."[32] Biographer Chris Nickson is no less enthusiastic about Reeves's ability to "tweak . . . the action movie hero stereotype," and he observes that the secret to the actor's success in the role is the juxtaposition of heroism with the attributes of ordinariness, resulting in the creation of the "hero as a 90s man." Here, the overt signs of "hard" masculinity that previous actors have brought to the action hero type are revealed to be excessive and overdetermined, whereas Reeves individuates the type by imbuing Jack with personal attributes that result in the hero's accessibility: "He wasn't excessively macho. Quite the opposite. The bluff exterior concealed a personal shyness and a dry sense of humor. . . . Jack was very human, a bit of an outsider."[33]

If up to this point Keanu Reeves had become virtually synonymous with "Ted Logan" in the popular press—a sign of the "real" and narrowly limited place of the star—with *Speed*, the Ted role is revealed to be a construction. Reeves has now clearly redeemed and authenticated himself in a demonstration of his potential that suggests how much more remains to be revealed about the star's acting abilities. *Rolling Stone* declares that "we'll be able to hear [Reeves's] name in the future without silently mouthing the word *dude*."[34] In a *Newsweek* review appropriately entitled "Goodbye, Airhead," David Ansen announces that "in neither role [referring to Jack Traven and Reeves's previous role as Prince Siddhartha in *Little Buddha*] is there a trace of Ted. What is unmistakably Keanu is that breathy earnestness when he plays intense."[35]

Reeves transcends his stereotypical associations with Ted Logan by breathing life into a generic action hero through minimalist underacting, and in the process he is perceived to be emerging as a more authentic actor because of his very malleability, his ability to drastically alter his persona according to the demands of each new role, revealing slightly more of "himself" in the process. Crucial to this melodrama of self-emergence is the juxtaposition of his roles in *Little Buddha* (1993) and *Speed*, films released only several months apart. Critics are divided on the issue of which film evidences Reeves's more convincing or successful role, but most of them are impressed by the startling oppositions between the two parts. The most noteworthy change is registered on the actor's body. Reeves prepared for his role of Prince Siddhartha by prolonged fasting, resulting in a meager and almost emaciated figure with long, flowing hair; for *Speed*, as *People* magazine describes, "he . . . pumped iron for two months at Gold's Gym to add manly umpf to his formerly lanky frame," gained back some of the weight he had lost, and tapered his hair to a buzz cut (fig. 26).[36] While Stanley Kauffmann finds Reeves more convincing in the former role, he adds that "the best way to get some pleasure out of *Speed* . . . is to see *Little Buddha* first."[37] John Simon finds Reeves more dynamic as Jack Traven, but is singularly impressed by the actor's drastic and startling "transmigration" from Buddhist monk to Los Angeles police officer.[38] Other critics find in this image/body transformation a demonstration of the actor's untapped potential and suitability for roles that seem entirely antithetical to his former image. After appearing in *Speed*, Reeves turned down a lucrative offer to co-star with Al Pacino and Robert DeNiro in *Heat*, preferring the opportunity to portray the lead role in *Hamlet* for $2,000 per week at a theater in Winnipeg. While many critics were initially skeptical about this prospect, *Maclean's* praises "the ingenious lilt to his voice, the blank sense of disconnection that he projects and his valiant efforts to overcome it—those qualities make him a more suitable casting choice for Hamlet than he might at first seem."[39]

Star texts and fan discourse often attribute the mystery and fascination of Reeves's persona to its opacity, its propensity to change unexpectedly, and its ability to exceed any single image or description. "If any one male film actor sums up his generation, it is Keanu," Nickson suggests. "He's a chameleon, literally changing physically with each role."[40] His very malleability, the suggestion that he is always about to shift from one identity to the next, paradoxically indicates the presence of something constant and authentic. "It's that word image. . .", Keanu protested to *Out* magazine. "I guess I'm not trying to conjure

26   Buff Keanu with buzz cut in *Speed* (1994). Author's personal collection.

up any image."[41] Ironically, such protestations enhance his authenticity through a refusal to take any constructed image too seriously. For example, Reeves offers subjective, scientific, and modest reactions to the course taught on his films by Prof. Stephen Prima at the Art Center College of Design in Pasadena: "My understanding of it is that [Professor Prima is] using an artist as a jumping-off point or a sort of strobe light on popular culture . . . and I'm flattered he used me as that jumping-off point."[42] Beyond Reeves's opacity is a humility that also contributes to his authenticity.

While several press articles comment on Reeves's physical preparation for the Jack Traven role, the association of this active, goal-oriented behavior with the demands of image construction serves to deflect any suspicions of narcissism. The actor comments that "I like my body . . . and I know what it feels like when I'm in good shape—but I don't want to work at it all the time. Sometimes I do but if I'm not feeling as cool then I get into my whole other worlds and going to the gym is not at the top of my list."[43] Reeves's decision not to reconstruct his muscular body or his action hero image for a repeat performance in *Speed 2* (despite an offer of more than $7 million) attests to the sincerity of his statement. Liz Smith reports that Reeves "doesn't feel like spending months at Gold's Gym again, pumping up, eating properly, obsessing over his abs and lats etc. (Keanu has a tendency to gain weight between films). . . . He'd rather do what he enjoys, what fulfills him."[44] Such decisions often entice both the popular press and Reeves's fans to note the star's sincerity and authenticity. In a letter to the editors of *Vanity Fair*, a fan writes that "it's a rare individual today who listens to himself and does that which is true to what he hears. He is not wild—I say he is real."[45]

The paradoxical nature of Reeves's depth often centers on the eyes as a site of vulnerability, receptivity and invitation (fig. 27). "There's a hint of sadness in his eyes," comments *Speed* co-star Sandra Bullock.[46] Director Jan De Bont suggests that Reeves's "eyes are very open to the world," and that "you can read emotion into them. There's nothing going on behind the eyes of most action heroes."[47] For many of the devoted fans in one of the web newsgroups devoted to the actor [alt.fan.keanu-reeves], Reeves's eyes provide access to an impenetrable mystery, to the secret of the star's fascination. "I keep thinking about how [sic] 'changeable' nature of his eyes," comments one contributor.

27   Sadness in the eyes of the action hero: Reeves in *Speed*. Author's personal collection.

"Just the eyes alone fascinate me."[48] In a heated debate over the range of Reeves's acting skills, the same fan offers the following account with indirect reference to the star's role in the techno-thriller *Johnny Mnemonic* (1995): "I don't know how to distinguish acting from performing, Keanu's aside. I DO know that his eyes, his looks—this man does NOT need morphing software, he's got the morph deep inside his DNA. I think a.lot [sic] about how he looks. Our Keanu's appearance is not the average face or look."[49]

The nature (or construction) of Reeves's depth is such that what the actor does not reveal about himself only signals what *might* be revealed or disclosed with sufficient probing or investigation, in a perpetuation of the melodramatic narrative of emergence. Like James Dean and Mel Gibson before him, the star is often depicted as a private figure, offering the press little information about his personal life. As titles such as "In Search of Keanu" suggest, interviewers are confounded by the problems of grasping or defining his persona. A recent *Premiere* article entitled "Yearning for Keanu" elucidates these difficulties of access.[50] Reeves consistently dodges the reporter's attempt to interview him on the set of *Feeling Minnesota* (1996) so that the reporter must resort to relying on the testimony of Reeves's co-stars for information about him. Even when Reeves finally permits an interview, his self-descriptions are fumbled and opaque, but just as critical descriptions of Reeves as a "blank slate" yield to revelations of his range and adaptability to a wide spectrum of roles, critics often register the star's difficulties of articulate (and articulated) self-expression as signs of his depth and emotional authenticity. Dennis Cooper, who interviewed Reeves for *Interview* magazine in 1990, secures the star's depth by describing the articulation issue as a struggle that also applies to the actor's onscreen roles: "Most actors just manufacture emotion and expect audiences to match it. With [Reeves's] characters, it's their inability to produce that's the key. They're often, if not perpetually, distressed, spooked, weirded-out by the world. They're always fighting with their contexts." [51]

Reeves's minimalism, understatement, and emotional inexpressibility become the very attributes required for the actor's emergence as an ethereal and transcendent figure. In discussions of his role of Prince Siddhartha in Bernardo Bertolucci's *Little Buddha*, a discourse of ungraspable "essence" transforms the actor's blank-slate persona into an emblem of spiritual harmony, revelation, and enlightenment. Correlating with the demands of the melodramatic mode, the actor is figured as the ultimate repository of meaning, an "essence" that is perceived as yet more significant and authentic because it can never be fully grasped. Contributing to what might be described oxymoronically as the star's "deep emptiness," Reeves is uncharacteristically forthcoming and accommodating in interviews when asked to comment on his physical and psychological preparations for the role: "I read some Rinpoche and I read up on Siddhartha and some commentaries, and I was just practicing some very basic meditation for a while just to see what it would do to me, and studying bodhisattva vows, and stuff like that. Mostly thinking about the four noble truths and positing no self—no ego, the fourfold path." [52] Even before his appearance in the Bertolucci film, the popular press constructed the star as an emblem of the essential whose ethereal nature makes him yet more universally accessible: indeed, in 1990, he was purported "to embody the sensitive soul of all disenfranchised youth." [53] A nineteen-year-old fan explains that "I feel I could step into his soul, just slide in." [54] The subsequent associations of his persona with Buddhism facilitate discursive constructions of the star as an even more harmonic, spiritually enlightened figure, "deep" specifically because he has renounced and emptied himself of connections to the material world.

The attempt to correlate the actor's life with the Buddhist figure reaches its apex in a web site entitled "The Society for Keanu Consciousness." Here, Keanu Reeves takes residence in Keanumandu, a "virtual temple" in which the star's pronouncements through his character portrayals constitute world revelations that the moderator "Lama Jahvah" interprets for the enlightenment of devoted "acolytes."[55] Through elaborate and ingenious acts of textual poaching, the figure of Buddha becomes the logical culmination of a star persona whose propensity to serve as "this century's premier symbol of enlightenment and peace" is revealed to have been evident from the start of his career, dating back to Ted's Socratic speculations in *Bill and Ted's Excellent Adventure*, which form the basis of a "Tao of No (or the No Way)." What critics had often described as the star's "airhead" image is transformed into the magical state of an emptiness that connotes purity and essence, suggested in the index page's epigram by Ted's pronouncement to Bill: "Ah, here it is, So-crates . . . 'The only true wisdom is in knowing that you know nothing.' That's us, dude!" Reeves's role as a messenger who has disposed of his brain so that his head can function as a polygigabyte data storage unit in *Johnny Mnemonic* provided the perfect setting for several critics to correlate the star's blank-slate acting style with the vacuousness of Johnny's character.[56] In the realm of Keanumandu, however, the emptying of Johnny's head becomes the requisite condition for Buddhist spiritual harmony, offering acolytes a model of Keanu's teachings on meditation, described as "Mind Expansion Techniques" (fig. 28).

Buddhist spirituality serves as the perfect vehicle for negotiating the hyperbolic constructions of Reeves's ambiguous and unresolved persona. Positing plenitude through emptiness, the spiritual discourse of this website extrapolates from other ambiguities and oxymorons used to define an enigmatic persona who is somehow much more "present" in his absence, more "here" when he is elsewhere. The Society's website builds its idolization of the star figure on his opaque relation to the concept of "place," an ability to be simultaneously everywhere and nowhere that is correlated with the biographical facts of his heritage. The historical description of Keanumandu explains that

28　The spiritually harmonious blank slate, transferring data in *Johnny Mnemonic* (1995). Courtesy Photofest.

One thousand years ago, in a tiny Nepalese village, a tiny group of monks huddled anxiously around a tiny shaman from whose deep trance would issue the identity of their newly reincarnated lama. But an additional revelation shone into that early morning so far away: the shaman told the little band of holy ascetics that one day a child would be born in Beirut, who would unite his lineage both east and west, and whose image would be miraculously multiplied in light onto the walls of thousands of temples worldwide.[57]

At the same time that this broad-range synthesis of Eastern and Western cultures describes the birth of the child Keanu as mankind's savior, it also announces the birth of the new star Keanu whose image will come to be worshipped in the "temples" of movie theaters world-wide. Alluding to both Buddhism and Christianity, uniting East and West, this description correlates sacred doctrine with star biography in a way that helps to explain how the "secret" of Keanu Reeves's star-dom is intimately linked to his ability to traverse and transcend spatial boundaries.

Reeves's star texts regularly describe this figure that "unites . . . both east and west" in terms of locative ambiguities, accentuating a paradox of place that confounds the notion of stable identity even as it constructs the star as a universally accessible figure. As noted earlier, aspects of Reeves's childhood have left him unanchored to a paternal figure, and he is always approaching or receding from a series of locations without belonging to any of them. His family moved frequently when he was a child, and he still has no place to call home. A discourse of inbetweenness associated with spatial transcendence also informs descriptions of the star's heritage: if he does not fit into a definable category on the basis of domestic ties and allegiances, he is also dislocated in terms of nation, race, and ethnicity. Reeves was born in Beirut, and raised in Australia and Canada; his father is half-Hawaiian and half-Chinese, and his mother is British. The descriptions of Reeves in the popular press preserve this multiethnic heritage even as they erase it, constructing the star according to the terms of an indeterminate "panethnicity." Bernardo Bertolucci chose Reeves for the role of Siddhartha because the actor "has a beauty . . . that's not Eastern or Western." [58] Carrie Rickey suggests that "his voice is breathy and geographically non-specific." [59] Similar to the way in which American publicity texts of Mel Gibson fetishized the star's Australian otherness, press articles on Reeves often locate the source of the star's appeal in the exotic. With Reeves, however, the absence of any "Americanness," compounded by the sheer number of potential ethnic and national allegiances, more often invites negotiations of these ambiguities as an indefinable "extrahuman" exoticism, one that exists in the realm of the spiritual or ethereal. Keanu "is practically everything-but-American. There is something almost otherworldly about him that makes it easy for his most dedicated fans to fantasize about him." [60] Several biographical pieces relate that Reeves's press agent urged the actor to "de-ethnicize" his first name by changing it to "K.C." when he first arrived in Hollywood. [61] Yet the press often refers to the restored original name as a means of regulating an unspecified, undeniably appealing otherness through recourse to the essential. *The Independent* remarks that Reeves is "fashionably ethnic-looking (but not too ethnic-looking, his name means 'cool breeze over the mountains')." [62]

In Reeves's case, the discourse of essence dovetails nicely with the discourse of inbetweenness. As an inbetween figure, Reeves is defined by his ambiguities and paradoxes, by multiple and often conflicting possibilities of identity that exist in a state of tension. The construction of Reeves as an ultimately indefinable and ungraspable essential figure retains these multiple possibilities of identity definition while simultaneously positing a means by which they might be, yet never are, fully resolved, thereby maintaining his universal appeal and the continued interest of his fans to discover more about the star. In the process, both discourses strategically construct a variety of positions of spectatorial access to the star persona. In the realm of ethnicity and national heritage, Reeves can be seen as aligned with a wide spectrum of potential identities, functioning as an ethnic or national "melting pot" in which the actual components of the admixture are less important or distinctive than the fact that they are indistinguishably *combined.*

Moreover, the textual constructions of Reeves's sexuality only serve to accentuate and expand the permutations and combinations of possible star identities, as well as spectatorial positions of access, by emphasizing the notion of a perpetually unstable multiplicity that any essentialist description of the star fails to contain. If the 1990s discourse of ambiguous inbetweenness and transcendent emotional authenticity incorporates a set of often conflicting terms to describe a sexuality that evades labels and both blurs and transgresses boundaries, the star texts' descriptions of Reeves's sexuality reflect the full terminological spectrum currently in use in American culture. The indefiniteness of identity and the terminology used to describe it apply equally to the constitution of the star's gendered identity and the genders of the fans to whom the star is deemed receptive. Commenting on the former, *Premiere* magazine establishes a connection between gender ambiguities and behavioral contradictions: "More than most of us, Keanu Reeves is a mass of ambiguities: He's masculine and feminine; decisive and waffling; focused and goofy; crisp and turgid." [63] *The Independent* suggests that these ambiguities connote an indeterminacy of gender that permits his female fans both to desire him and to identify with him, sometimes even simultaneously: "Then there is his curious hyper-modern unisex quality. Reeves is, well, evolved. In interview he talks with an open-spirited, complex positivity that could easily come from either gender. Women don't just want him—they think they could be like him." [64]

Admirers and fans of Keanu Reeves often constitute the star's unisex identity as androgyny: David Hlynsky, who shot the now-famous homoerotic photograph of Reeves embracing a male co-star in *Wolf-boy*, suggests that "he's a beautiful man in an androgynous way. Make that any which way at all."[65] In a lively discussion on the issue of whether Reeves or Patrick Swayze is more well-suited to the portrayal of a cross-dresser, a contributor to the aforementioned Reeves newsgroup notes: "Swayze is not what I'd call convincingly androgynous under normal circumstances, but I think Keanu has a beautiful sort of androgyny within that slightly exotic visage. When I saw Keanu in "Little Buddha" the first thought I had was 'My God, he could be a beautiful woman.'"[66]

Many of the star texts more directly correlate the ambiguous determinations of identity with the range of Reeves's potential appeal to fans. Some assessments hinge on the fact that, even in its most "buff" or beefed-up form in films such as *Speed* and *Point Break* (1991), the star's body bulk is never overly imposing, alienating, or distancing. Director Jan De Bont suggests that "he's absolutely attractive to both men and women. . . . To women, because he has great eyes and his face is honest. For men because he's not over the top with biceps like crazy. . . . He's more accessible."[67] While preserving to some extent a dichotomy between identification and object choice, in which women desire the star while men want to be like him, biographer Chris Nickson admits that Reeves "has an appeal to both sexes" because he shows his vulnerability and "seems approachable, not on any kind of pedestal. . . . He has something of the regular guy in him."[68] In her enthusiastic assessment of Reeves's appeal, Carrie Rickey connects ambiguities of ethnicity and sexuality directly readable on the star's face: "The actor's enigmatic face suggests a computer-generated composite of every known race and gender. His affect is pansexual and so is his appeal. At the trill of his name—say key-AH-noo—fans female and male heave libidinal sighs."[69]

Cumulatively, these descriptions suggest a virtually unlimited range of possibilities of constructing the gender, sexuality, and ethnicity of Keanu Reeves—a range that conversely applies to the multiple positions of access that his indeterminate persona accommodates. Even the term "bisexual" occasionally arises in the star discourse, often referencing the fact that Reeves's character Scott Favor is shown having sex with both men and women in *My Own Private Idaho*.[70] Rickey's term "pansexual" seems the most appropriate descriptor to apply to the myriad constructions of identity and reception that Reeves's star discourse evidences. Derived from the Greek word for "all," *pan* retains an integral component of the discourses of inbetweenness and essence as they relate to authenticity: the concept of an unfixed, unstable identity perpetually in the process of reformulating itself as something else, yet also retaining, accumulating, and harmonizing the traces of each "something else" that it addresses. For many, it is this notion of harmony that becomes the most resonant component of the star's appeal, applying equally to what the star projects and to what he invites his admirers to receive. Responding to Acolyte Michael's inquiry regarding whether or not it is "odd" that Reeves appeals to both men and women, Lama Jahvah explains that in Keanumandu, gender divisions are often transcended: here, "enlightenment most often strikes those who know a most triumphant and non-bogus thing when they see one. . . . They have recognized that Keanu is unlike other actors, and that his career is like a veil drawn over a thing of great beauty—lift the veil, and illumination strikes the yearning soul."[71] Speculating on the commonalities of many of these website contributions, one writer finds that they "have a distinctive air about them . . . inquisitive . . . tending toward the analytical, introspective even. . . . alt.fan.keanu-reeves posts have a potliteness [*sic*] about them . . . a sort of patient forbearance, an odd, almost courtly formality. . . . hmmm . . . wonder what we all have in common that would influence us in this direction. . . ."[72]

Gay Appropriations of the Star Image

The construction of Reeves as a spiritually enlightened and enlightening figure constitutes one way that fans secure the star's meaning and significance as an emblem of truth and authenticity in the melodramatic mode. The appropriation of the star persona by self-identified gay fans, spectators, and critics, however, depends no less heavily on the operations of melodrama and fantasy. The melodramatic mode situates Reeves as an emblem of significance that accommodates individual "authentications" of the star persona, making him receptive to gay spectators' specific and various investments of truth and meaning. Fantasy offers these spectators the promise of momentarily stabilizing the malleable star persona in scenarios activating the dynamics of desire.

The use of "handles" and code names in internet newsgroups enables contributors to disguise their own gender identities; consequently, when these contributors participate in discussions concerning such matters as which of Reeves's body parts in which screen roles made the most significant impression on them, it is sometimes impossible to discern whether one is witnessing expressions of gay or straight desire.[73] In light of Reeves's pansexual appeal, such ambiguities of online identity are perfectly appropriate. Yet many of the contributors to Reeves's fansites do identify themselves as gay, and in the two years in which I followed the proceedings of one such newsgroup's discussions, I rarely witnessed instances in which contributors were ridiculed, harassed, or belittled for such an admission. More often, in fact, contributors are challenged or questioned if their entrics evidence narrowmindedness or conservative perspectives on issues of gender and sexuality. In one case, a self-identified gay male challenged a contributor who asked which partner assumed "the woman role" in the rumored relationship between Keanu Reeves and David Geffen: "What precisely is the 'woman role' supposed to be, and how on earth could it apply to a relationship between men?"[74]

This contributor's question marks an egalitarian politics, one that questions the efficacy of maintaining culturally established definitions of "appropriate" roles of gender and sexuality—a politics that Reeves himself consistently reiterates. In a cover article for the "Straight Issue" of *Out* magazine in 1995, interviewer Tim Allis poses the hypothetical question, "What would be the best thing about being straight, aside from the sex?" Reeves responds, "But wouldn't whatever that *thing* is be the best thing for being gay as well? There are no lines. I mean it's *humans*, man. I mean . . . what would I say? . . . We can go to different bathrooms in a restaurant!"[75]

In making such statements, Reeves aligns his persona with other textual constructions of the star as a figure who attempts to be accessible to all, and who is entirely comfortable with the diverse ways in which his image is appropriated. *W* magazine explains that "Keanu himself is non-plussed by the idea that he appeals to both the sexes. 'You mean most actors don't?' he asks."[76] Reeves's equivocal response to *Interview* magazine when asked to "settle" the matter of his sexual orientation invites the speculation that the sexual diversity of his fans is echoed by a similar lack of fixity in his own sexual self-definition.

Although many fans are fully cognizant of the ways in which the in-stability of the star image strategically ensures panaccessibility, this awareness does not prevent them from appropriating the star as they wish in deployments of identification and desire. In the newsgroup, one fan who prefers to consider Reeves to be "straight" points out that the actor is "not stupid. He may be straight, but if he leaves room for question it gives more inscentive [*sic*] for gays to buy his films and music in the hope that he is gay. Same with straights. This way every-one can fantasize about him."[77] In response to this evaluation, another fan suggests that whether or not the actor's ambiguities are strategic, his avoidance of labels and categorical definitions reinforces his au-thenticity: "Just being non-hostile towards gay people would probably have the same effect. . . . I'm convinced he's straight and like to think of him that way also. . . . But it's just as useless a category as 'gay' is, I guess. I mean, if you take into account all the grey areas of sexual interest, 'homosexual' and 'heterosexual' are not so much descriptions as they [are] labels that one might attach to a person for convenience. It's like eve[r]yone is supposed to line up and cho[o]se a side or some-thing."[78]

At the same time, one might wonder how the actor's embrace of a sexuality that blurs the boundaries between straight and gay might be read in the context of 1990s gay identity politics—a politics that often interprets protestations of "indeterminate" sexual orientation, espe-cially by celebrity figures, as a markedly apolitical undecidedness anti-thetical to lesbian and gay platforms, and that conveniently permits the "sexually undecided" to take recourse in the social privileges of heterosexuality.[79] Curiously, suggestions that Reeves is "hiding some-thing" from himself or from the public by maintaining ambiguities of sexuality are conspicuously absent in the star texts and fan discourse. This absence results from the fact that, unlike Mel Gibson, Reeves openly acknowledges and addresses the matter of his gay following, and never expresses even the slightest hint of hostility at the pros-pect of being appropriated as gay. "Reminded that some gay men think he's sexy," explains Tim Allis of *Out* magazine, "Reeves laughs again, maybe a little embarrassed. 'That's cool,' he says. 'That's cool.'"[80] Even though his agent issued a statement that the actor is "straight" after the rumors of the David Geffen marriage circulated through the press, Reeves himself does not use the Geffen incident as an occasion

to close off access to his persona by gay spectators; instead, he reiterates a more "politically correct" stance that shows his respect for sexual
diversity. Shortly after the Geffen incident, Reeves explains, "Well, I
mean, there's nothing wrong with being gay, so to deny it is to make
a judgment. And why make a big deal of it? If someone doesn't want
to hire me because they think I'm gay, well, then I have to deal with it,
I guess. Or if people were picketing a theatre. But otherwise, it's just
gossip, isn't it?"[81]

Through the indeterminacy of his sexual identity and his accommodation of the same-sex desire of his fans, Reeves's persona is also
situated within a heated debate between essentialist and social con-
structionist factions within 1990s queer theory and politics. If essen-
tialism suggests that sexuality is a stable category of identity, social
constructionism posits the production of instability as a crucial political strategy for disrupting boundaries between "heterosexual" and
"homosexual" identity and desire. As noted earlier, Teresa deLauretis
finds that the positing of any stability of identity denies the specificity
of the constitution of individual subjecthood, "not only her or his psychic or fantasmatic configuration, the places or positions that she or
he may be able to assume in the structure of desire, but also the ways in
which she or he is located in social relations of sexuality, race, gender,
etc., the place she or he may assume as subject in the social."[82] Recent work by Judith Butler emphasizes the preferability of constituting
identity as unstable rather than striving for a coherent identity that is
always necessarily exclusionary and thus susceptible to the power of
the opposing structure that attempts to repudiate it.[83]

If the construction of Reeves's sexuality is consistently ambiguous,
he is also situated as an inbetween figure in relation to this debate.
Star texts often implicate the star as striving for an essence deemed
integral to the construction of his panaccessibility, yet the essence to
which he is purported to aspire becomes a function of his resistance
to any specific categorical definition. Indeed, his persona becomes im-
plicated in an interrogation of the efficacy of positing any stable categories of identity, and through such interrogation, he is perceived as
more authentic and true to himself. Similarly, in refusing to confirm
or dispute his inclusion within a category of homosexual identity, he
accommodates multiple perceptions of what it means to "be" gay, to
"look" and "act" like a gay man. By transgressing the boundaries of

sexual identity, Reeves's persona also evades any stereotypical formulation of what gay men "are" or what they "want." Serially, he can embody the images of "beefed-up" hunk, alienated rebel, and even new age and much less buff spiritualist, without ever being defined exclusively as any of these images. By denying his own specificity according to categories of identity, he accommodates and sustains individual constructions of his persona according to the subject's constitution of individual subjecthood, opening up new spaces for the deployment of desire.

In the star texts authored by gay men, for the purposes of appropriation in fantasy, asserting the incontestable identity of the star as homosexual is consistently less crucial than maintaining the possibility that he *might be* constructed as gay, and yet more importantly, that he is potentially *receptive* to gay desire, in a manifestation of the melodramatic "if only" construct. Accordingly, the sexual ambiguities of the star persona offer the pleasure of facilitating negotiations of the persona as gay, and the act and process of constructing the receptive fantasy figure become integral to the production of such pleasure. The construction of such a possibility of receptivity structures Allis's approach to his interview with Reeves for *Out*. Arguing at the start of the piece that "Reeves can seem all things to all people," he proceeds by a strategy of indirection, posing hypothetical questions ("What would be the best thing about being straight?"), and citing numerous references to the ways in which gay fans have appropriated his image, to ensure that among the options, one *specific* manifestation of the star's pansexuality is homosexuality. If Reeves is situated as an emblem of significance in a melodrama of emergence for his fans, here he is shown to emerge as a gay or gay-receptive figure. The World Wide Web pages of *KeanuNet* emphasize the integral role of ambiguity in facilitating gay negotiations of the star persona in fantasy. Among the pages of this on-line biographical document is one entitled "Is Keanu Gay?" Published shortly after the appearance of the *Vanity Fair* article, the 1995 version of the page offers the following response: "If Keanu is a fantasy figure for you, imagine that he prefers YOU. The truth is really not so important, is it?"[84]

Discussing the gay appropriation of images of male Hollywood stars, gay critic Bob Satuloff writes that "in order for a film actor to register in the public mind as being sexy, he needs to give off the

illusion of accessibility."[85] That Reeves has offered such an accessibility to gay males is incontrovertible and well documented in the star
texts. The appeal is linked first to his selection of roles, beginning
with his appearance as a homosexual character in the play *Wolfboy* in
1984. Nickson explains that "the play became a cult hit in [Toronto],
resonating strongly with the gay community in the early days of AIDS
deaths. With its success, Keanu acquired his first gay following. . . ."[86]
Reeves explains that in one of the publicity photos, "I had my eyes
closed and this guy is almost kissing me with this like *grin*? So the first
couple of performances we had leather boys comin' out. You know,
caps and the whole deal."[87] During his interview with Reeves, Dennis
Cooper explains (much to the actor's fascination) that "this gay-and-
lesbian anarchist group called the New Lavender Panthers" invented
a punk rock dance called "The Keanu Stomp," modelled on Reeves's
lumbering gait as he trudges across rows of abandoned cars in the
opening sequence of *The Prince of Pennsylvania*.[88] In an essay entitled
"My Own Private Keanu," Paul Burston notes that Keanu is "very, very
popular with gay men. When Greg Gorman persuaded him to pose
naked for a photo session, the evidence found its way on to the walls
of homosexual abodes the world over," and Burston proceeds to cite
gay references to the star in such works as Armistead Maupin's *Maybe
the Moon* and Dennis Cooper's *Frisk*.[89] More recently, Reeves has been
listed as one of "Our Favorite Boys" in the "Idols" page of the World
Wide Web's *Queer Planet*.[90]

Many of the gay press's explanations of Keanu's appeal to gay men
are not so different from the evaluations in the mainstream press, extrapolating gay accessibility from panaccessibility through discussions
of the actor's depth, receptivity, and vulnerability. Allis is drawn to the
actor because he is "not just another in a long line of macho swash-
bucklers."[91] *Advocate* editor Jeff Yarbrough suggests that Reeves "has
an interesting sexuality, an unthreatening sexuality," and that "it is the
blankness and calm of Reeves' beatific face . . . that allows people to
project their fantasies onto him, big time."[92] Several accounts locate
the source of vulnerability and expressiveness at the site of the eye as
source of the inner soul. John Patrick's analysis of the star in his *Best of
the Superstars* series begins with Michael Gregg Michaud's elaborate
account of his gay desire for the star: "I love his almond-shaped eyes,
their vacant look. . . . When he acts sad, or shy, which he does so well,

when he acts lost and detached, which is probably natural, that's when I love him most, really."[93]

Queer Appropriations in Film Narrative

If such factors as depth, receptivity, and vulnerability become equally important to straight and gay spectators in securing the star's authenticity and accessibility, many of Reeves's film roles invite negotiations of his persona that foreground differences in the ways that viewers interpret the star's sexuality in relation to their own. Many critics and fans cite three films as most integral to the construction of Reeves's persona as either potentially gay or gay-responsive, incorporating the reception strategies of self-identified gay critics and fans. The first two films, *Point Break* and *Speed*, position Reeves in narratives that extend the discourses of inbetweenness, essence, and authenticity, securing a panaccessibility that accommodates gay-responsive constructions of his persona, even though his character in each film also develops an intimate relationship with a female character. The third film, *My Own Private Idaho*, requires more elaborate negotiations of character and narrative, even though the film offers the only instance in which Reeves portrays a character who has sex with men.

While the operations of the melodramatic mode play out differently in three films, in each case melodrama is central to many gay spectators' access to the star persona in fantasy relations of identification and desire. *Point Break* is structured as a melodrama of the emergence of the authentic self, emphasizing the actor's attempt to aspire to a state of spiritual essence that is also a feature of the non-narrative star texts. In accordance with the melodramatic fantasy of origin, the film promises a connection and reunion of male protagonists that is ultimately rendered impossible to realize. *Speed* also offers its protagonist tentative and similarly failed connections to another male figure, as well as a social community, while simultaneously functioning as a melodrama of redemption, an opportunity for the protagonist to correct past mistakes by rectifying the moral order in the world of the narrative. Structured most literally as melodramatic fantasy, *My Own Private Idaho* situates Reeves as a figure who holds the promise of securing an intimate bond with his male companion, yet who also elects to close off the realization of this connection. For many gay spectators, however, the film permits the construction and stabilization of scenarios of homosexual desire in spite of their eventual disruption within the narrative.

Kathryn Bigelow's *Point Break* (1991) concerns the efforts of FBI agent Johnny Utah (Reeves) to infiltrate a close-knit community of California surfers who finance their international surfing expeditions by robbing banks, assuming the disguises of former U.S. presidents. Attempting to become a member of the surfing community, Johnny solicits the aid of surfing instructor Tyler (Lori Petty), gaining her trust by pretending that they share a common element of personal history: the death of their parents by car accident. Tyler introduces Johnny to Bodhi (Patrick Swayze), an experienced surfer for whom the sport has taken on spiritual resonances that his followers share in a cultist devotion to their leader; indeed, during one torchlit beach party, one of the surfers confesses that "surfing is better than sex." By the time that Johnny begins to suspect that Bodhi is also the mastermind of the "Ex-Presidents" gang, Johnny has already begun a romantic relationship with Tyler. In the meantime, however, Johnny has also developed an at least equal passion for surfing, as well as a distinctive fascination with Bodhi, who has saved his life from another group of thug surfers entirely out of tune with the spiritual dimension of the sport.

Operating as a buddy film and recalling the structure of *Gallipoli*, *Point Break* organizes an elaborate series of arrivals and poignant departures in which the two central male protagonists struggle to maintain their intimate connection against all odds. Similar to *Gallipoli*, the bond is established in *Point Break* through a number of tests of masculinity, loyalty, and friendship, positing a homosocial relationship that never overtly acknowledges its homosexual undercurrent. A college football star whose career was prematurely curtailed by a knee injury, Johnny proves himself a veritable athlete by demonstrating his passing and tackling skills to Bodhi and his surfer cohorts in rough games at the beach; after only brief hesitation, Johnny later jumps from a skydiving plane with other members of the group to experience the "killer rush" of a freefall (fig. 29).

By the time that he incontestably verifies Bodhi's involvement in criminal activities, Johnny's loyalty to the man who has enlightened him to the transcendent nature of risk-taking has already threatened to override his professional obligations as an officer of the law. Johnny intentionally fumbles an attempt to shoot Bodhi in a long chase scene after one of the bank robberies. After a volley of eyeline match shots between the FBI agent and the Ronald Reagan-masked criminal accentuates his hesitation, Johnny fires his gun into the open air, groaning with frustration. After a sociopathic accomplice of Bodhi's subsequently kidnaps Tyler, Bodhi coerces Johnny to participate in a bank robbery to protect her. Even when Bodhi's spiritual enlightenment has notably transformed into greed and a marked propensity for betrayal, Johnny remains loyal, intentionally botching two additional attempts to incarcerate him. The final showdown unfolds on a South Australian beach during a storm whose path Bodhi has followed in the hopes of experiencing the ultimate wave. Having instinctively discerned the whereabouts of his nemesis, and now unexplainedly unaccompanied by the earlier rescued Tyler, Johnny permits Bodhi to end his life by merging with an approaching tidal wave, rather than deliver him into the hands of justice. In the final shot of the film, with the battle won, Johnny tosses his badge onto the sand and walks away.

Point Break extends the discourse of inbetweenness from Reeves's teen-oriented roles, continuing a melodrama of self-emergence without ever fully resolving it. Johnny is a rebel whose strategy of mastering the mystique of the surf to catch criminals is clearly perceived as an unorthodox method by his FBI cohorts—most notably by his immediate superior, who castigates the ex-football star for circumventing standard procedures, describing the overly eager Johnny as "young, dumb, and full of cum." And, also similar to Reeves's earlier film roles, Johnny is a loner figure who belongs nowhere—not with his fellow legal officers, yet no more with the band of surfers since he is introduced to their community under false pretenses (fig. 30). Indeed, his lack of belonging motivates a central narrative conflict: a recent transplant to the city of Los Angeles, Johnny ends up feeling much more at home and accepted by the surfing community than by the judicial system whose standards he is obligated to apply against this community. When he loses focus on these obligations, both his partner Angelo (Gary Busey) and another police officer are killed as a result. Still, Johnny never fully reconciles himself to the role of either legal officer or impulsive risk taker: his circumvention of proper police procedures by letting Bodhi die by his own means, as well as the discarding of his

29   Bodhi (Patrick Swayze) tests the loyalty of Johnny Utah (Reeves) in *Point Break* (1991). Courtesy Photofest.

30   Johnny Utah succumbs to the lure of the surf (or the surfer?) in *Point Break*. Author's personal collection.

own badge, suggest that he will not continue with the FBI. Having witnessed the fatal end of lives motivated too exclusively by the pursuit of euphoria, however, he also appears to have relinquished thrill-seeking once and for all. Like Matt in *River's Edge* and Rupert in *The Prince of Pennsylvania*, at the end Johnny Utah's path is left undetermined, his divided loyalties leaving him alienated and unconnected to anyone.

Correlating with the unresolved melodramatic narrative of emergence is a failed attempt at transcendence and an unsuccessful search for a pure state of being, figured as a return to origin. *Point Break* configures this search in personal terms, with Johnny attempting to attain some sense of purpose in his life after his knee injury prematurely curtails the pursuit of his goal to play football professionally. It is perhaps for this reason that he is drawn to Bodhi so strongly, finding himself momentarily willing to disavow the surfer's means of survival because the ends are so enticing. By making personal redemption and spirituality accessible to Johnny through the crest of a wave, Bodhi offers him an example of a life lived on its own terms—an example that Johnny appears not have been aware that he was seeking until Bodhi reminds him.

The lure of the surf lies mostly in its promise of a sensation that defies and exceeds verbal description within the melodrama of emergence; unspeakable and unspoken, it is a pure state attainable and shared only by a select group who recognize each other intuitively. The narrative consistently represents the ecstasy of surfing pleasure in sexual terms. It is not coincidental that one group member uses a sexual analogy to approximate the pleasure of the wave (though even he admits that the analogy is insufficient), or that Johnny can communicate only by emitting orgasmic groans when he becomes proficient enough at the sport to know what Bodhi has been raving about. The surf becomes an emblem and repository of spiritual meaning and significance for the two protagonists, one that permits sexual pleasure to be displaced onto the ecstatic pleasure of sport. Consonant with the operations of melodrama, their bond becomes infinitely deeper and more authentic because words fail to describe or even approximate its intensity. This ultimate inexpressibility only serves to accommodate and accentuate the sexual implications of the bond that develops from the first time that Johnny sees Bodhi in action: a shot of Johnny entranced and transfixed by the surfer is followed by an extended point-of-view shot of Bodhi, the object of his gaze, riding the crest of a wave in slow motion as the music swells on the soundtrack.

The film was a box-office failure, receiving primarily negative reviews in both the mainstream press and the few gay journals that devoted any attention to it at all. Significantly, however, the gay press articles emphasize how little negotiation is required to configure the relationship between Johnny and Bodhi as a homosexual bond. Accommodated by melodrama's emphasis on the inexpressible, critics authenticate their own desire to witness the connection of the ill-fated protagonists, "correcting" the heterosexual pretense of the relationship between Johnny and Bodhi by stabilizing it as a scene of homosexual desire. In an article explaining how extensively the male body is permitted to be on display in Hollywood cinema as long as the heterosexuality of its heroes is maintained, Bob Satuloff describes the film as "little more than a collage of action sequences punctuated by smoldering-eyed interludes of Swayze and Keanu Reeves cruising the living daylights out of each other."[94] In a longer review of the film for the *New York Native*, Satuloff notes that "from the moment they meet, Bodhi and Utah give the appearance of working overtime keeping their tongues in their mouths. . . . In this world of guy-to-guy camaraderie, the line between bonding and blow jobs becomes perilously thin."[95] Paul Burston concurs that the characters' heterosexuality is unconvincing:

> Keanu [plays] . . . an undercover cop assigned to penetrate the surfer's ring—though for much of the film he looks as though he'd much rather be penetrated by the gang leader, played by Patrick Swayze. . . .Bigelow was rewarded with the best adult performance Keanu has given—and the most easily appropriated in gay terms. A sperm-fest of surf, sweat and male bonding rituals, *Point Break* was to homoerotica what Bigelow's earlier *Blue Steel* was to dykey androgyny. Despite the fact that homosexual acts never fully enter the picture, it remains the queerest thing that Keanu has committed himself to.[96]

If the connections between spiritual and sexual transcendence make Reeves's character in *Point Break* readily accessible to the appropriation of many gay male viewers, the constructed ambiguities of inbetweenness are both reinforced and recontextualized through elements of plot and character in *Speed*, a narrative even more well-suited to the action hero genre so popular in 1990s mainstream film.[97] The narrative concerns the efforts of Los Angeles police officers Jack Traven (Reeves) and his partner Harry (Jeff Daniels) to combat the operations of ex-cop terrorist Howard Payne (Dennis Hopper), who demands ransom in exchange for the release of citizens whose lives he endangers through a series of bomb threats. In the first sequence of the film, after Howard traps a group of workers in the elevator of a high-rise office complex, Jack and Harry successfully subvert his threat by securing an anchoring hook to the top of the elevator shaft. After the passengers are released, however, Howard captures Harry, forcing Jack to shoot his partner in the leg to divert the villain. With the subsequent explosion of a bomb offscreen, it appears momentarily that Howard has been killed, and Jack and Harry are valorized as heroes for their efforts. After Jack subsequently witnesses the bus explosion that causes the death of its driver, Jack receives a call from the miraculously resurrected Howard, who warns him that another bus on the streets has been armed with a bomb that will explode after the vehicle decreases its speed below fifty miles per hour. With the wounded Harry no longer able to accompany him, Jack boards the bus alone. Eventually the passengers alight successfully, with considerable help from passenger Annie (Sandra Bullock). Confined to the speeding bus, however, Jack is unable to avert the death of Harry and other fellow officers when their entry into Howard's home triggers a powerful explosive device. In the final sequence of the film, Howard covers Annie in a suit of dynamite in a subway car, warning Jack that he will trigger the explosives. Ultimately, a struggle that ensues atop the car leads to Howard's death, and at the end of the film the speeding vehicle emerges to ground level with both Jack and Annie finally safe from harm.

Paul Burston finds in Reeves's portrayal of Jack Traven "the best facsimile yet of all that gay men desire: an action man with gripping hands and eager, come-fuck-me eyes. Sadly we don't get to see much of his body. He never gets around to taking his shirt off."[98] This reticence to reveal and disclose, however, serves as part of a greater strategy in which the lure of the hero's sexual appeal becomes stronger, more universally accessible, and ultimately more negotiable in the realm of fantasy, by what it withholds from view. As in *Point Break*, this strategy ultimately involves the operations of the melodramatic mode. The narrative of *Speed* constitutes a melodrama of the hero's redemption, emphasizing how his handling of current crises offers a means of correcting past mistakes that have resulted in lives lost. *Speed* also offers the promise of reunion and connection between its male protagonist buddies, a connection whose possibility is eventually curtailed by Harry's death. As with Mel Gibson's Max in *The Road Warrior*, the hero of *Speed* becomes accessible and emotionally resonant specifically because his own affective responses are so severely understated. Accordingly, the spectator's inference of emotion promises the emergence of the authentic and individuated hero. As Jack's emotions are downplayed, the range of the character's potential affective responses is broadened and subtly accentuated, and in the process, Jack transcends the limitations of the action hero stereotype. Certainly he demonstrates the strength, agility, and resourcefulness that have come to be associated with the heroic figure of this genre; however, these attributes are consistently tempered by a physical and emotional vulnerability that adds resonance, depth, and authenticity to the characterization. His vulnerability makes him accessible as a figure of both identification and desire: it activates the spectator's need to relate to him and to protect him from harm, yet it also constitutes him as an object whose body is on display (fig. 31).

The ravaged, strained, and always fully clothed body of the hero is frequently sexually objectified. Jack's vulnerability is conveyed not only by frequent high-angle and overhead shots that emphasize his helplessness, but also through plot elements that require the hero's body to undergo elaborate gymnastic contortions. Jack is suspended upside-down, then lowered and raised, by cable in an elevator shaft as he attempts to latch a hook to the top of a fallen car to rescue its terrified passengers. The hero is placed in positions that emphasize his passivity and vulnerability. An explosion propels him through the air and against a wall. Groaning as rubble falls around his helpless body, he sinks to the floor in slow motion with legs spread open. The scene in which he is transported by mechanic's dolly underneath the bus in an attempt to disassemble a bomb is marked by crosscutting between low-angle shots of Annie looking down at him from the driver's seat, and overhead shots of the helpless hero from Annie's point of view. Once he is underneath the bus, the shot composition changes to a series of

31 High-angle shots emphasize the buff hero's vulnerability in *Speed*. Author's personal collection.

close-ups of the hero's body in severely cramped quarters. The dolly is propelled out of control, and ground-level shots show Jack frantically groping for any part of the underside of the bus that might provide a supportive, steadying anchor. The mise-en-scène of one extreme close-up features Jack's left bicep flexing and straining in the foreground right, while in the background left his legs and feet dangle off the now wildly swerving dolly. After the dolly permanently veers away from his body a few shots later, another ground-level shot offers a more dramatic fragmentation of body parts, revealing only a clenched torso and pair of legs that strain desperately to avoid scraping against the pavement.

The most emphatic revelations of vulnerability are conveyed by the uncharacteristically expressive intensity of Jack's reactions to his own helplessness as he confronts the villain, Howard Payne. After Howard telephones Jack to inform him that his partner Harry has been killed, the hero emits a slow, agonized, low-pitched groan; his head and back slumped over in despair, he suddenly erupts into a wild, convulsive state, gripping and shaking the handrail of the bus as the camera lingers on his straining arm muscles. After Annie manages to calm Jack down, he resignedly informs her, "We're gonna die." Yet it is this very vulnerability that ultimately places Jack in a position of power both to defeat the villain and save his own life. In the closing moments of the final struggle between the two men on the roof of a speeding subway car, Howard manages to pin Jack underneath him, beating him senseless with a steel bomb trigger, and boasting that he has outsmarted and outmaneuvered him. Jack's supine, submissive, and seemingly helpless position ironically becomes a position of safety. In a desperate effort, he succeeds in raising the head of his aggressor ever so slightly, just enough for it to be lopped off by a safety light mounted to the subway tunnel ceiling.

Vulnerability is also a function of locative ambiguities that extend from the star's publicity discourses to the film narrative: both establish the hero as alone and socially unconnected, suggesting an alienation resulting from an unspecified loss. In the realm of melodrama, this vulnerability invites viewers to rectify his alienation and unanchoredness by anticipating the promise of reconnection. The hero's lack of personal history accentuates this need for reconnection by inviting viewers to fill in expository gaps that the narrative leaves open. A man without a past, Jack harbors a despair defined by various absences. While one may assume that he belongs to a family and has a home, the narrative reveals no such domestic space. Despite the social connections afforded him as a police officer, he remains unconnected, unfixed. The day after receiving a medal of honor for his rescue of the elevator passengers, when a local merchant comments that he must have celebrated his success the night before, Jack responds, "It can't have been too great—I woke up alone."

The narrative offers Jack a provisional connection to others, counterbalancing his alienation through a temporary and functional alliance with a community, an alliance that is also integral to the construction of the star as a universal fantasy figure. In *Speed*, human survival depends on the organized efforts of the community to withstand threats imposed on it by the outside world. Community is confined within tight, containable, public spaces—an elevator car, a bus, a subway car—vulnerable to the forces that attempt to disband it. It is the action hero who comes to assume responsibility for establishing and maintaining the community as a cohesive entity by encouraging cooperation, dispelling dissent, and establishing trust. Before Jack arrives on the scene, community membership on the bus is distinguished only by common disadvantage: in a city plagued with traffic problems brought about to some extent by those who travel alone in cars, the group of bus passengers comprises those who cannot afford private vehicles, those like Annie whose driving privileges have been revoked, and those like the tourist, Stephens (Alan Ruck), who cannot find their way. The common disadvantage uniting them in this public space of mass transit establishes a spirit of mutual tolerance more than unity of purpose, and while some passengers know each other by name, their interaction is fleeting and tentative, lasting only as long as it takes to reach their respective stops.

In an effort to establish its political correctness, *Speed* is insistent in emphasizing the diversity of the community by representing differences in age, race, ethnicity, gender, and domestic situation. Such differences appear to be tolerated until Jack makes the passengers aware of the bomb that threatens them. From this point forward, when the goal of the passengers is no longer to reach a specific destination, but to remain alive, differences among the community members become a source of conflict, and their cooperative effort is consistently in danger of being vitiated. Jack is initially greeted with suspicion and distrust, since he appears to them as a "madman" who unwelcomely disrupts their daily routine, and also because his identity as a police officer places him in a position of power and privilege. The disruption becomes life-threatening when one passenger, Ray (Daniel Villareal), suspects that Jack will arrest him. The passenger panics and inadvertently shoots the bus driver, consequently risking the other passengers' lives.

Jack's mission is to organize cooperative activity according to rules that Howard, the "real" madman, has established: the bus must not decrease its speed below fifty miles per hour, and no passenger is permitted to alight. His mission is complicated because he must impose order without posing himself as a threat, but also neutralize the stratification of the community by establishing his trustworthiness and inspiring the passengers to trust one another. The first goal requires him to prove that under the present circumstances, his role of police officer is secondary to his role as fellow human being who is willing to risk his life to save theirs. He accomplishes this as soon as he boards the bus: after Ray pulls out his gun when Jack displays his police badge, Jack responds reflexively by pulling out his own gun, but then he makes a plea to the frightened passenger: "I don't know you, man. I'm not here for you. Let's not do this. . . . Listen! I'm putting my gun away, okay? Okay? Now, listen. I don't care about your crime. Whatever you did, I'm sure that you're sorry. So it's cool now. It's over. I'm not a cop right now. We're just two cool guys hanging out."

To achieve the second goal he must serve as mediator of conflicts that erupt as tension mounts within the enclosed space. When one passenger exclaims that he cannot die because he has a family to support, an unmarried male passenger reacts vehemently that his own life is no more expendable because he is single. Conflicts also arise between Ortiz (Carlos Carrasco) and Stephens, the tourist who is in one sense an "outsider" since he uses mass transportation by choice rather than out of necessity. Jack gradually guides the community to celebrate mutual accomplishments, and to identify and resolve differences. They attribute this resolution not only to Jack's organizing presence, but to their own resourcefulness.

While Jack's participation in these community efforts certainly serves the immediate needs of the bus passengers, it also provides the hero with an opportunity to correct his past mistakes; accordingly, *Speed* also functions as a universal melodrama of a hero's redemption of loss. If Howard's terrorist "games" compromise moral order by threatening the lives of innocent passengers, Jack is required to restore order by securing their safety. Indeed, his rescuing of the bus passengers constitutes an act of atonement for his inability to prevent the explosion of the first bus, which resulted in the death of its driver. His responsibilities become more urgent with Harry's death, for which he also holds himself responsible: by shooting his partner in the leg, Jack has relinquished his ability to protect him.

Combined with Jack's role as advocate of a diversely defined community, the universality of the problem of loss in this melodrama of emergence and redemption retains the hero as a figure whose qualities support spectators' efforts to negotiate the identity of the star according to their own desires. This universal accessibility is not without deterrents, however, and perhaps the strongest of these are the markings or hints of the hero's heterosexuality, as evidenced by his relationship with Annie. As in *Point Break*, however, heterosexuality itself remains a negotiable element within the narrative of *Speed*. Although the film concludes with the promise of Jack and Annie's romantic involvement, it is a promise that blooms only after his partner Harry is killed. Up to this point, the film stresses an evolving homosocial intimacy and the promise of an ultimately failed connection between the male partners. This "couple" is constructed as two aspects of an identifiable whole: Harry possesses technical knowledge and psychological insight, while Jack demonstrates a complementary physical agility and fearlessness. Together they are able to confound Howard's scheme and save the passengers in the fallen elevator. Savoring their accomplishment immediately afterward at the elevator shaft, Jack inquires, "Was it good for you?" "It was great for me," responds Harry. When he shoots Harry in the leg in order to confuse Howard, he loses not only his partner's active engagement, but also his own ability to perform his duties effectively. Rendered impotent, he can now communicate with Harry only by phone, yet this separation of partners only strengthens the bond between the characters, and in the realm of the melodramatic "if only," Harry's subsequent death accentuates the possibility that they *might* have been reunited (fig. 32).

Unfolding as melodramas of emergence and redemption, both *Point*

32 Jack Traven's (Reeves) phones partner Harry (Jeff Daniels) in *Speed*. Author's personal collection.

Break and *Speed* readily accommodate viewers' attempts to negotiate and authenticate the star persona as potentially gay or gay-receptive. Ironically, however, Scott Favor in *My Own Private Idaho*—the only Reeves character who has sex with both men and women—is seemingly much less accommodating. Of the three films, *My Own Private Idaho* is certainly the most rigorously structured as a melodramatic fantasy of origin, even though the subject of this fantasy is not the Reeves character, but his companion Mike (River Phoenix). More than the other two films, *Idaho* emplots homosexual desire in its structuring of the possibility of the connection and reunion of its central protagonists. At the same time, its narrative more definitively resolves the melodramatic "if only" by emphasizing the impossibility of this connection. As a melodrama of redemption, the narrative appears to suggest the duplicity of the Reeves character, rather than promoting his authenticity, yet the reception strategies that many gay critics and spectators use in the film demonstrate an intricate process of negotiation whereby

Reeves is deemed even more receptive to homosexual desire, in spite of melodramatic resolutions within the narrative.

The gay press eagerly anticipated the film's release (just four months after *Point Break*), not only because its director was openly gay, but also because it offered the promise of witnessing well-known Hollywood actors portraying gay men. As Michael Bronski explains in an article for *Gay Community News*, "It is no surprise . . . that the hearts and cocks of gay men everywhere were stirred when it was announced that cute, well-built teen heartthrobs River Phoenix and Keanu Reeves were going to play male hustlers in Van Sant's latest." [99] If the actors' decision to appear in the film was in itself perceived as audacious in 1991, it also appears that much of the prerelease hype centered on speculations as to whether or not the actors would kiss or have sex.

That such anticipations structured many gay men's responses to the film *before* its release becomes evident in press accounts of the film's premiere, as well as film reviews in gay publications. *L. A. Weekly* confirms that the audience at the benefit premiere was largely gay, yet the only mention of the film's content is that **"Keanu Reeves** *doesn't* kiss **River Phoenix"** (boldface and italics in original).[100] Many critics were perplexed by the positioning of *Idaho* as a gay film at all, given Van Sant's overt denial that he was attempting to represent gay political or cultural interests. Bronski explains that "any new images of gay sexuality are welcome in a culture that increasingly promotes queer invisibility, but whether queer audiences will take to Van Sant's vision of gay alienation—as well as his own alienation from gay life—remains to be seen." [101]

The positioning of Reeves's character of Scott Favor within the narrative subverts the authenticity and accessibility that the actor's two action-adventure films so rigorously maintain. At the beginning of the film, Scott appears to be in a position of inbetweenness that echoes the actor's early roles of alienated teen rebels. The son of the wealthy mayor of Portland, Oregon, Scott seems more at home in the world of street hustlers and male prostitutes in which his friend Mike (River Phoenix) struggles for survival. As was the case with Rupert in *The Prince of Pennsylvania*, Scott deliberately strives not to live according to standards of respectability that his father establishes for him. In the first half of the film, he wears a leather jacket on his motorcycle rides

33   Street hustlers Scott Favor (Reeves) and Mike (River Phoenix) cruise the streets of Portland in *My Own Private Idaho* (1991). Author's personal collection.

with Mike (fig. 33). He delights in arranging for the Portland police to discover him and Mike in bed together in the room of a gutted hotel, eagerly anticipating his father's ire. Soon enough, however, his rebellion is revealed to be only a ruse, a strategy to make his antici- pated transformation to respectable citizen seem more wondrous to his father. In an aside to the audience he reveals that "I will change when everybody expects it the least," vowing to leave behind his street life, as well as the friends who have grown to love and trust him. Scott even calculates the exact moment of the transformation: his forthcom- ing twenty-first birthday, at which time he will become eligible for his seriously ill father's inheritance.

Long before his startling transformation of character at the end of the film, Scott has already begun to disrupt the character's panacces- sibility. The bond between the male protagonists is established early, with Scott serving as a figure of comfort for his narcoleptic compan- ion. When Mike loses consciousness in front of a rich client's home, Scott wraps him in his coat to keep him warm, assuring his friend that he will be much safer sleeping on the lawn in an affluent section of town than on the streets of the city center. Mike frequently confides in

Scott, demonstrating his devotion to his friend, yet in the celebrated "campfire scene," Mike's direct invocation of homosexual love serves only to close off the possibility of its realization:

SCOTT: I only have sex with a guy for money.

MIKE: Yeah, I know.

SCOTT: Two guys can't love each other.

MIKE: Yeah—well, I don't know. I mean, for me—I could love someone, even if I wasn't paid for it. I love you, and you don't pay me.

SCOTT: Mike—

MIKE: I really want to kiss you, man. I love you. You know that.

Scott is certainly not repulsed by the confession: the scene ends as he cradles his friend's head in a gesture of comfort. Several scenes later, however, when the protagonists find themselves in a farmhouse outside of Rome (where Mike believes his mother has resettled), Scott suddenly and inexplicably falls in love with Carmella (Chiara Caselli), a woman he has met the same day. Rather abruptly, he begins to treat Mike with indifference, subjecting his male companion to the groans of late-night lovemaking, and ignoring Mike at the breakfast table as his and Carmella's transfixed, interlocked gazes clearly signal that the intruder's presence is unwelcome.

Rather than promoting his ultimate redemption, the closing scenes of the film present Scott's double betrayal of love and trust. If Jack Traven's panaccessibility in *Speed* is accentuated by his allegiance and attentiveness to the needs of the diverse community on the bus, Scott entirely divorces himself from his (now "past") affiliations with the street hustlers. Having inherited his fortune after his father's death, he now executes his intention to cast off all ties to his former life by assuming the "respectable" role that his father always wanted for him. Dressed in a smart business suit with his new wife Carmella by his side in a fashionable Portland restaurant as the hustlers look on, Scott shuns the greeting of his former friend Bob Pigeon (William Richert), pretends never to have known him, and orders Bob off the premises. The double funeral in the following scene links Scott's exclusivity of sexual object-choice to the class stratification that Scott outwardly upholds: as the subdued, solemn services for his father take place in one section of the cemetery, the boisterous proceedings of the nearby hustlers

mourning Bob's death (from a broken heart) elicit only a brief, disaffected glance from Scott, who equally averts his gaze from Mike's.

Given Scott's clear renunciation of homosexual love and his rejection of gay characters who declare their love for him, one might
suspect that the characterization would challenge, or at least have an
adverse effect on, the actor's accessibility to gay admirers, especially
since the narrative negatively resolves the melodrama of reunion and
reconnection. The fact that press reports indicate exactly the reverse
provides important clues to the matter of how Reeves's sexuality is
negotiated. Burston concurs that it is difficult to read Scott's homosexual activity in the film as anything but a business arrangement, yet
he is not surprised that the role did not change many gay men's images
of the star: "Gay men being the contradictory creatures that they are,
this was the performance which resulted in legions of queens fantasizing about their own private Keanu." [102]

Still, Burston's assessment is insufficient as an explanation. Many
press accounts acknowledge Scott's cruelty as evidence of a successful
and convincing character portrayal, while simultaneously downplaying or rejecting any association of character with actor. The negative
or unsuccessful resolution of melodrama within the narrative is sup-
planted by a melodrama of the emergence of a deep and authentic star
persona *outside* of the narrative boundaries—that is, in the context of
Reeves's development as an actor. He is perceived as a deeper and more
accomplished performer as a result of the role, and his authenticity as
an actor takes precedence over the disingenuousness of the character
he portrays. The *Philadelphia Gay News* explains that "Reeves buries the
air and sense of the uppity deep inside his character and only unleashes
it when necessary and most effective. And when he does, it is totally
disarming, shocking and, in a necessary way, repulsive." [103] The *San
Francisco Sentinel* stresses only that his convincing portrayal of Scott
finally puts the image of Ted to rest.[104] The fact that Reeves and Phoenix agreed to be in the film at all overrides the implications of either
characterization, and the figure of Reeves that emerges is stabilized as
a more specifically gay or gay-receptive persona. As *The Advocate* maintains, Reeves "has played a gay character and worked for an openly
gay director. . . . so in the minds of at least 90% of the gay men in
America, he's one of us," and columnist Bruce Vilanch later proposes
the construction of the star as potentially gay offers "an elaborate way

of making him more attainable and easier to fantasize about."[105] Other reports postulate that the *Idaho* role only supported his appropriation by gay viewers who were already aware of the precedent established by his appearance in *Wolfboy*.[106]

Repeatedly, the matter of the onscreen and offscreen intimacy of Reeves and Phoenix keeps open the possibility of a homosexual connection between the two figures. Biographies stress the deep friendship that developed between the actors, suggesting that their commitment to the project was a mutual pact. Phoenix explains, "We said 'OK, I'll do it if you do it. I won't do it if you won't.' We shook hands, that was it."[107] Phoenix is often cited as one of the few close personal friends of the very private Reeves, and the actors' offscreen bond becomes crucial to securing the onscreen intimacy between Mike and Scott. If critics clearly convey that Scott's "repulsive" attributes have no relation to Reeves's own character (except that he conveys these attributes so effectively as an actor), the emotional intensity of their relationship in the film requires that the attributes of actors and characters be *reconnected* as extensions of one another. Nickson suggests that many gay viewers "quite vocally believed that Keanu and Pheonix [*sic*] had to be gay because it was the only way they could have achieved so much depth in their performances."[108]

The notion that Reeves's character rejects homosexuality appears to be less salient than the fact that he and Phoenix appear together in *scenes* of rejection with which many viewers, both straight and gay, can identify and empathize—scenes intimately related to the melodramatic fantasy of the origin of self, manifested in the desire to attain a state of impossible connectedness. Similar to many of Dean's 1950s melodramas, as well as the star discourse circulated after the actor's death, *My Own Private Idaho* is structured quite literally as a search for the mother, the anticipation of the return to an original state of connectedness and unity.[109] Indeed, the two protagonists leave Portland on a long journey from Idaho to Rome to locate Mike's mother, who appears only as a flickering, fleeting image in Mike's narcoleptic consciousness. When he does see this image, she is always holding him and comforting him, telling him not to worry. While he never finds the body that can make the image "real" to him, he does find in Scott a potential source of comfort, one that ultimately proves to be just as elusive, and just as unattainable, as a maternal figure.

The desire for reconnection to this source of comfort is nowhere stronger than in the campfire scene, in which the object of the search is momentarily transformed from Mike's mother to Scott. If the scene is structured as a fantasy, the positions of identification and desire seem firmly fixed: the camera focuses more intently on Mike than Scott, the confessor's struggles intensified by his inability to witness the re-actions of the object of his desire who has receded to the background of the frame. The scene functions as a microcosm of the larger, more futile search for the maternal figure: Mike needs a verbal affirmation of his love for Scott in the same way that he needs to see his mother in order to affirm the validity of his memory of her. Ultimately, confes-sions and searches yield the same result: a reminder of what is lost, of what can never be recaptured. Indeed, Scott's gesture of comfort by offering to hold Mike in his arms at the end of the scene only exacer-bates the sense of loss, given that the source of comfort is so quickly revoked once Scott finds a more "suitable" companion in Carmella.

Certainly the film provides no moment of catharsis in which rejec-tions, missed encounters, or transcontinental searches for elusive and unattainable objects are redeemed by ultimate reunions or reaffirma-tions. Once Scott finds Carmella, Mike loses him forever, and after Mike discovers that his mother has abandoned her most recent resi-dence outside of Rome without leaving any trace of a forwarding ad-dress, the search appears to have been curtailed. The ending of the film finds Mike alone on the same desolate Idaho highway where the narrative began, collapsed after another narcoleptic episode as uniden-tified figures in a truck stop to rob him and pick him up. In sharp con-trast to Scott's character resolution through the socially stabilizing and heterosexually sanctioned institution of marriage, however, this ulti-mate resolution of the film's larger narrative works against stabilization and any notion of a coherent ending. As Robert Lang elucidates in his discussion of queer road movies, *Idaho*'s final scene anticipates a sub-sequent, yet undisclosed, narrative that perpetuates "the underlying fantasy of most road movies that are on some level about cruising, hus-tling, or hitch-hiking: that the next encounter will be the one that will take the protagonist 'home.'"[110]

Accordingly, the ultimate futility of Mike's search enhances the resonance of those moments in which the possibility of reconnection is sustained in the realm of the "if only"—those moments that *are* sta-

bilized in the scenes of the melodramatic fantasy. For many gay viewers, the campfire scene affords one such moment of stabilization. Referring to the manifestation of Mike's desire in this scene, *Advocate*
reviewer David Ehrenstein comments that "hustlers may exist in the
margins of the gay world, but the love that Mike feels for Scott is central to us all." [111] Viewers' investment of affect is not, however, limited
to Mike, the figure of identification within the scene of melodramatic
fantasy; it also applies to the object Scott, whose function as the one
who rejects homoerotic advances makes him no less crucial a participant in the scene of desire or the fantasies that the scene enables. The
fact of Scott's presence and participation in the scene becomes sufficient to retain his accessibility. Allis identifies the campfire scene as
crucial to an understanding of "why [Reeves] has caught the eye of
many gay men": "By campfire light, he broke River Phoenix's heart.
And ours." [112] In describing the campfire scene as "the tenderest gay
love scene of the year, even if one of the characters (and both of the
actors) is straight," the *San Francisco Sentinel* demonstrates that the
homoerotic dynamics generated by the scene of desire are themselves
sufficient to sustain possibilities of access, despite the sexual "identities" of both actors and the characters they portray.[113]

The mobilization of an unrequited desire for Scott/Reeves in the
campfire scene of *My Own Private Idaho* does not in itself suggest any
inherent interchangeability of spectators' identification and object-
choice. Accounts of the scene are consistent in signalling that an access
to desire of Scott/Reeves is enabled by an identification with Mike/
Phoenix in his failed attempt to unite with an object already lost. Still,
this lack of interchangeability does not discount the notion that the
interdependence of identification and object-choice is integral to maintaining the structure of the fantasy as a scene of desire—a scene in
which both Mike and Scott participate and that the viewer also constructs. By deploying the logic of the "if only," the (here unattainable)
goal of the fantasy is to stabilize the potential for the desire to be maintained by stabilizing the scene itself, despite its eventual outcome. In
Reeves's case, the possibility of such stabilization depends as much
on the fantasy dynamic as on other already established conditions of
the star persona's "history"—his willingness to appear in a film by an
openly gay director, his prior appearance in *Wolfboy* as a gay character, the ambiguities of the star persona constructed in publicity texts,

and the actor's acceptance and sanctioning of his appropriation by gay audiences.

Rumor, Gossip, and Fantasy

With the appearance of weeklies, journals, and other critical and social forums targeting gay audiences, as well as recently emerging online technologies such as Web pages, chat lines, and newsgroups, the circulation of rumors and gossip about the sexuality of celebrity figures offers another form of empowerment to the gay community. If watchdog organizations such as GLAAD have exerted power in regulating the stereotypical representations of gays in Hollywood film, rumor and gossip discourses empower gays to appropriate Hollywood celebrity figures through the constructions of their own fantasy scenarios that also interrogate the boundaries between public and private. Indeed, rumor and gossip offer a place for the production and expression of images and fantasy scenarios that would never be accommodated on the screens of the local cineplex.

Rumor and gossip texts extend the public negotiation of Keanu Reeves's sexual persona beyond the domains of publicity texts and cinematic narratives in which the star appears, yet they rely on the same ambiguities instrumental in constructing the star's panaccessibility. The versions of the star persona produced by rumor and gossip also present another manifestation of the logic of the melodramatic "if only," using "wishful thinking" to maintain the possibility that largely unverifiable accounts of the actor's offscreen activities *might be* true, and in the process reasserting the extent to which the construction of the star persona accommodates gay appropriation.

The construction of Reeves as a "private" star who adamantly withholds his offscreen activities from public view enhances the range of possibilities for such appropriation. One biographical piece asserts that "of all of Hollywood's leading men, Keanu Reeves is one of the most private. Think of it: how many times have you seen photographs of him out on the town with glamorous dates? He tends to avoid any high-profile events, and his silence for so long as gay rumors swirled around him led many of his fans to decide they were true."[114] While the studios in the 1950s issued press releases to enforce the notion that James Dean's resistance to being settled with one woman in a monogamous relationship was only another indication of immanent eligibility to female fans, the tabloid press of the 1990s assumes the former function of the studio. As discussed earlier, Reeves is often depicted as resistant to the institution of marriage because of his parents' failed relationship, yet he is just as often associated with the practice of "hyperdating" female celebrity figures. For example, a 1995 piece for the *Star* entitled "Keanu Reeves' Hot Secret Dates with Cheers Beauty" documents sightings of Reeves with Jackie Swanson, Amanda de Cadenet, and Nicole Thompson.[115] More often than not, however, the tabloids' protestations of the star's incontestable heterosexuality result in the reactivation of speculations that the star cannot be defined as exclusively straight. Another *Star* piece that begins by asserting (erroneously) that Reeves explained "I love women!" in his *Out* interview continues by reviving accounts of his gay following since the production of *Wolfboy* and introducing yet another rumor to contest the star's heterosexuality: "Last month, Reeves was angered by a Canadian magazine's report that he was having an affair with a male dancer in Winnipeg, where he was starring in a stage production of *Hamlet.*"[116]

Yet a crucial difference emerges between tabloid speculations on Dean's sexuality in the late 1950s and Reeves's sexuality in the 1990s. In the contemporary period, the appearance of "dish" columns in gay weeklies, monthlies, and annuals across the country readily participate in a reciprocal exchange of speculations on the offscreen activities of star figures. The existence of these publications is well known outside of the gay community. *Entertainment Weekly* acknowledges that "dozens of underground gay publications dish about closeted celebs with impunity" and explains that press agents now monitor these publications "which have fast become required stops on publicity campaigns."[117] Gay writer John Patrick annually publishes a volume entitled *The Best of the Superstars: The Year in Sex*, comprising his own assessments of the indeterminate sexuality of male Hollywood stars. In a 1996 piece entitled "Wishful Rumors: Keanu Reeves, Etc.," he explains that "Keanu has never had any high profile romances with women; he took his sister to the Oscars. I mean, honey, what's a girl to think?"[118]

The gay "dish" columns often maintain that they can provide more reliable and privileged insights into star sexuality because they obtain their information through a network of underground, subcultural connections that are off limits to the more mainstream tabloids. In his biweekly "Filth" column for *Gay Chicago Magazine*, for example, Billy Masters reports that "more and more people come forward every week with their own Keanu stories," the latest of which involves two gay men who report that Reeves propositions men in gay bars by exploiting his pansexual appeal: "I'm not homosexual. I'm not heterosexual. I just like sex. Come home with me." [119] Another column attempts to explain Bernardo Bertolucci's "unlikely" casting of Reeves in *Little Buddha* by proposing the following solicitation: "Bertolucci . . . was not at all interested—that is, until Keanu went to visit him personally at his suite in the Waldorf Astoria in New York City. After two hours, our sources report 'a rumpled Keanu emerged with a big grin on his face, and the part.' Go figure!" [120]

Many of the rumors initiated by the mainstream tabloid press provide the groundwork for more extensive negotiation in elaborate fantasy scenarios in gay-oriented publications and on-line information services. The foremost is the rumor that in early 1995 Reeves secretly married David Geffen, who has protested that "I know where [the rumor] comes from. . . . It's *gay people!*" [121] As John Patrick explains, however, the marriage rumor first appeared in the *New York Post*, which reported a sighting of Reeves shopping at Barney's with Geffen's credit card. It subsequently circulated to the Italian tabloid *Corriere Della Sera*, then to the *Hollywood Reporter*, and then back to the *Post* before ultimately appearing in Bruce Vilanch's column in *The Advocate*.[122] Aligned with a publication that has openly expressed its disdain for outing practices, Vilanch reprimands his gay audience for maintaining the validity of such rumors, arguing that by doing so "we are playing into the number one fear of the straight community—that all we really want is a piece of them." [123] Although Vilanch protests unapprovingly that gay men are merely "stroking [their] own fantasy furnace" through such rumors, others such as David Ehrenstein perceive the "open secret" of such rumors as a logical and empowering expression of curiosity regarding the lifestyle of successful, self-identified gay figures such as Geffen: "If David Geffen is 'out,' and rich beyond one's wildest dreams, then he can have anyone he wants—say, Keanu Reeves. After all, hadn't Keanu played a male hustler in a film by an openly gay writer-director?" [124]

Other gay authors stress that any imposed restrictions on fantasy constructs of Hollywood stars constitute an unhealthy form of self-censorship. "It's a rumor, yes, but ugly it's not," argues Justin Zane of the *Bay Area Reporter.* "We can't think of anything more sexually arousing than two attractive, powerful faggots getting it on in the face of adversity. Memo to Geffen: if you're not having an affair with Reeves, you should seriously consider starting one." [125] In his online column "So . . . Hollywood," A. J. Benza adds that "you're allowed a little FANTASIZING about what it would be like to just be out with . . . our version of unconfirmed truth once and for all." Benza then proceeds to imagine a postwedding scenario that stabilizes fantasy in the realm of the "if only": "David looks so much happier. . . . And God knows I haven't seen Keanu this thrilled since he worked with his ex-boyfriend River Phoenix in My Own Private Idaho [*sic*]. Who knew that ride they took on the Harley would really be a metaphor for their romance riding off into the sunset?" [126]

While some gay men's fantasies of the "if only" limit themselves to constructions of scenarios under which "unauthorized" sexual desire finds a safe place, other accounts are much more explicit in their descriptions and visualizations of sexual acts in which Reeves might engage. For example, Larry Perovic's online fantasy narrative "Keanu's Hot Hollywood Adventure" places the actor in "Hot Holes, a LaBrea gay bar" that he and other stars frequent to indulge in "hot gay action." [127] In the dimly lit bar, Reeves surveys Burt Reynolds fellating a teenager while Reynolds is spanked by a "400-pound bearded fairy," as well as Jonathan Taylor Thomas with a "10-inch cock hanging out of his pants," before Reeves finds his gaze reciprocated by Dan Aykroyd. After Reeves and Aykroyd retire to an even darker back room, Perovic graphically describes an extended scenario in which the two well-endowed actors engage in a session of rough oral and anal sex before Aykroyd urinates and defecates on Reeves (much to Keanu's delight).

Clearly, the fantasy plays on accounts of the star persona's vulnerability that mainstream press reports highlight to maintain his pan-accessibility. Here, Reeves often assumes a "submissive" position in which he receives the bodily fluids of his partner: at one point, Perovic narrates that Reeves "closed his eyes as Dan's hot piss splattered all over his chest, washing away the glistening droplets of cum that had accumulated over his abdominal scar (where they had to operate after he had a motorcycle accident)." In his fantasy narrative, however, Perovic consistently emphasizes matters of reciprocality and interchangeability of the "top" and "bottom" roles, not only in the sexual acts themselves, but also in the way that Reeves initially controls the situation by soliciting Aykroyd to return his gaze when the two partners initially meet in the more public area of the bar. Perovic also stresses the matter of the actors' mutual consent: while Aykroyd is more aggressive throughout, he secures Reeves's permission before the scene turns toward the scatological.

Indeed, the matter of consent and license frames the entire fantasy scenario, extending from the interplay between the two actors to the relationship between author and text. At the end of the narrative, Perovic explains that "they held each other, savoring their erotic connection and their own consensual pleasure. And if their pleasure seems bizarre or incomprehensible to us, who are we to judge?" In the author's warning that precedes the unfolding of the narrative itself, Perovic stresses that what follows is a "WORK OF FICTION" and not an account of what he purports to have observed transpiring between Reeves and Aykroyd. Here, however, the caveat functions to uphold the author's own license to imagine, describe, and circulate the workings of his private fantasy to the public: "The story is entirely a product of my imagination and bears no resemblance whatsoever to reality, save for the fact that people with these names ACTUALLY EXIST and are FREE, as citizens of the greatest nation on earth, to perform acts like these with each other IF THEY WERE TO CHOOSE TO DO SO."

Perovic's fantasy recalls the activity of Slash fiction authors who empower themselves, as Henry Jenkins notes, by accommodating their own pleasure in the construction of same-sex scenarios between male characters of many television series.[128] Perovic's work is also consonant with Constance Penley's observation that positions of identification and desire often remain unfixed in Slash narratives of *Star Trek*.[129] Such accounts of how a fan of Keanu Reeves claims license to appropriate the star in scenes of desire of his own choice demonstrate how the boundaries between public and private, personal and political, and fact and fiction are both blurred and transgressed in the network of fantasy. Here and elsewhere, the private and personal appropriations of the star persona become more widely accessible through printed "dish" columns and recent computer technologies over which no censoring agency has yet to assume a position of regulation or control. Private fantasies become political statements demonstrating that the workings of the individual imagination are capable of exceeding whichever restrictions the Hollywood film industry may impose on the representations of its characters in film narratives in the contemporary period. Ultimately, the fantasies of Perovic and other fans also indicate the extent to which gay appropriations of a Hollywood star rely, for their authorization, on an already established network of star texts that maintain an ambiguous construction of the star persona's sexuality. In the form of an inbetween figure in his early films, as well as an authentic figure later purported to aspire to a state of transcendence, Reeves consistently embraces a fashionable, indefinable sexuality that renders him susceptible and receptive to an optimum number of manifestations of the melodramatic "if only." In the process, his resultant panaccessibility confounds attempts to formulate any single version of the star persona as definitive since individual stabilizations of Reeves's identity always anticipate subsequent transformations within and outside the realm of any one specific fantasy.

With private worlds of fantasy made public through the Internet, we witness a form of the crossover phenomenon about which gay men in the 1950s might only have dreamed. Rather than needing to resort to piecemeal assembly of accessible figures of identification to remind the disenfranchised subject that he is not alone in the world, self-identified gay men in the contemporary period are now provided not only with star figures who address their own desires without disavowing such address, but also with the license, means, and forums for exchanging such fantasies with each other, and for making these fantasies accessible to all. Current technologies ultimately afford self-identified straight and gay individuals, as well as those who elect not to specify or define their sexual orientation, a common place for sharing, debating, and negotiating their versions and perceptions of popular cultural icons.

*B*y demonstrating how a "universal" psychical construct enables disenfranchised spectators to find a place in a society
that does not always accommodate or directly address their
needs and desires, and that often ignores their political concerns, this
book responds to continuing debates regarding the interrelation of
narrative modes, fantasy operations, and the social practices of individual spectators and spectatorial "communities." That the spectatorial negotiation of star sexuality constitutes an act of social resistance
is most clearly demonstrated in the contemporary historical period, in
which members of a specific subculture have found ways to become
more visible to one another, and also to mainstream culture, through
the development and widespread circulation of their own publications
and discourses, and through the still largely unregulated new media
technologies of the Internet. Gay men have secured their efficacy as
social "agents" by developing and sharing narratives and scenarios that
mainstream culture does not formally authorize.

In queer theory and star studies, this work opens up further ave-
nues of investigation of the instability of star/spectator relations across
time. As we have seen, it is not only the construction of star personas
that changes, but also the personal, social, and political concerns of

disenfranchised spectators and spectatorial communities who negotiate these constructions. Further studies correlating these two vectors
of historical change are especially important at this moment, when
mainstream stars are more openly acknowledging their gay followings,
and when empowered gay spectators hold stars accountable for their
pronouncements. It would be enlightening to examine figures such
as John Travolta, Richard Gere, and Tom Cruise in future studies,
since both mainstream and gay publications have scrutinized the private lives of each of these figures and interrogated their sexual orientations. Travolta would be an especially pertinent figure to study, since
his persona has undergone a series of dramatic "reconstructions" since
he appeared in the crossover vehicle *Saturday Night Fever* in 1977.

Studies that emphasize historical changes in both star personas and
spectators are now afforded a new dimension, as more established
actors elect to appear as self-identified gay characters in Hollywood
films, such as *In and Out*, that are not targeted exclusively or specifically to the gay community. Tom Selleck, who portrays the openly
gay tabloid journalist in *In and Out*, would provide a fascinating case
for a historical study that examines the relationship between homosexual character portrayals and an actor's sexual identity. In the 1970s,
Selleck, like Mel Gibson, was identified as one of the breed of hunk
actors whose sexual objectification was authorized by the mainstream
press and linked to the growing influence of "gay culture" on the mainstream. In 1991, Selleck successfully sued one of the mainstream tabloids for attempting to "out" him, yet in interviews he has emphasized
that the protestations of his self-acknowledged heterosexuality do not
constitute homophobia, and that he harbors no resentment toward the
gay community. In a recent interview for *The Advocate*, Selleck stressed
that he has been attempting to convey the message that "it's not antigay
to say that you're not gay."[1]

Finally, with the rapid proliferation of websites, on-line newsgroups, and chat rooms that provide forums for both straight and
gay spectators to negotiate star personas and to construct their own
private versions of public celebrity figures, future studies of star/
spectator relations can more extensively interrogate the boundaries
between straight and gay sexualities, and between the realms of the
public and the private. Such studies anticipate additional, valuable in-

sights into the ways in which reception practices afford possibilities of resistance to normative constructions of socially assigned roles of human sexuality. At the same time, these studies will further illuminate the complexity of historically specific relationships between sameness and difference, and between self and other.

Notes

Introduction

1 Andrew Ross, "Uses of Camp," in *No Respect: Intellectuals and Popular Culture* (New York: Routledge, 1989), 139.
2 Richard Dyer, *Heavenly Bodies: Film Stars and Society* (London: BFI Press, 1986); Janet Staiger, *Interpreting Films. Studies in the Historical Reception of American Cinema* (Princeton: Princeton University Press, 1992).
3 Ross, "Uses of Camp," 158.
4 Stuart Hall, "Encoding/Decoding," in *Culture, Media, Language: Working Papers in Cultural Studies*, ed. Stuart Hall, Dorothy Hobson, Andrew Loew, and Paul Willis (London: Hutchinson, 1980).
5 Elizabeth Cowie, *Representing the Woman: Cinema and Psychoanalysis* (Minnesota: University of Minnesota Press, 1997), 133.
6 Christine Gledhill, "Signs of Melodrama," in *Stardom: Industry of Desire*, ed. Christine Gledhill (New York: Routledge, 1991), 212.
7 Dyer, *Stars*, 50.
8 Linda Williams, "Film Bodies: Gender, Genre, and Excess," *Film Quarterly* (Summer 1991): 2–13.
9 Ibid., 11–12.
10 Steve Neale, "Melodrama and Tears," *Screen* 27, no. 6 (November/December 1986): 19.
11 Mary Desjardins, "Meeting Two Queens: Feminist Filmmaking, Fan Cul-

ture, Identity Politics, and the Melodramatic Fantasy," *Film Quarterly* 48, no. 3 (Spring 1994): 26–33.

12 Sigmund Freud, "Group Psychology and the Analysis of the Ego," in *The Complete Psychological Works of Sigmund Freud*, trans. James Strachey (London: The Hogarth Press, 1955), 18:106.

13 See especially the illuminating chapter on Sheila McLaughlin's *She Must Be Seeing Things*, in Teresa deLauretis, *The Practice of Love: Lesbian Sexuality and Perverse Desire* (Bloomington: Indiana University Press, 1994).

14 Thomas Waugh, *Hard to Imagine: Gay Male Eroticism in Photography and Film from Their Beginnings to Stonewall* (New York: Columbia University Press, 1996), 4–45.

15 In this respect, my findings differ from those of Jackie Stacey, who notes a blurring of identification and desire in her work on female spectators of Hollywood actresses in the 1940s. See her illuminating discussion in "Feminine Fascinations: A Question of Identification?" *Star Gazing: Hollywood Cinema and Female Spectatorship* (New York: Routledge, 1994), 126–75.

16 Alexander Doty, *Making Things Perfectly Queer: Interpreting Mass Culture* (Minneapolis: University of Minnesota Press, 1993), xi.

ONE *James Dean and the Fantasy of Rebellion*

1 John d'Emilio, *Making Trouble: Essays on Gay History, Politics, and the University* (New York: Routledge, 1992), 85.

2 Sam Astrachan, "The New Lost Generation," *New Republic*, 4 February 1957, 17. As David Hofstede notes in *James Dean: A Bio-Bibliography* (Westport, CT: Greenwood Press, 1996), Astrachan's article elicited a considerable backlash from Dean's fans, who expressed their criticisms in letters published in the February 18 issue of *New Republic*.

3 Janet Staiger, *Interpreting Films: Studies in the Historical Reception of American Cinema* (Princeton, NJ: Princeton University Press, 1992), 75.

4 Michel Foucault, *The History of Sexuality, Volume 1: An Introduction* (New York: Vintage Books, 1990), 95.

5 John d'Emilio & Estelle B. Freedman, *Intimate Matters: A History of Sexuality in America* (New York: Harper & Row, 1988), 288.

6 d'Emilio & Freedman, *Intimate Matters*, 288–89. For documentation and testimony on the experiences of gay men and women in the military, see John d'Emilio, *Sexual Politics, Sexual Communities* (Chicago: University of Chicago Press, 1983), 23–39.

7 The findings of the report are summarized and discussed extensively in d'Emilio, *Sexual Politics, Sexual Communities*, 33–39.

8 For a discussion of the debate between advocates of the psychological and cultural origins of homosexuality in the 1950s, see Robert Corber, *In the Name of*

National Security: Hitchcock, Homophobia, and the Political Construction of Gender in Postwar America (Durham, NC: Duke University Press, 1993), 19–59.

9 d'Emilio, *Sexual Politics, Sexual Communities*, 42.

10 Corber, *National Security*, 69.

11 The scapegoating and blackmailing of homosexuals in this period is documented in d'Emilio, *Intimate Matters*, 293. See also d'Emilio, *Sexual Politics, Sexual Communities*, 43–39; and Corber, *National Security*, 6–8.

12 James Gilbert, *A Cycle of Outrage: America's Reaction to the Juvenile Delinquent of the 1950s* (New York: Oxford University Press, 1986), 19–20, 204.

13 Gilbert, *A Cycle of Outrage*, 22–23.

14 The activities of the ccpcd and the Children's Bureau are treated extensively in Gilbert, *A Cycle of Outrage*, 42–62.

15 d'Emilio, *Sexual Politics, Sexual Communities*, 44.

16 U.S. Congress. Senate Committee on Expenditures in Executive Departments, *Employment of Homosexuals and Other Sex Perverts in Government*, 81st Cong., 2d sess., 1950, 3–5; quoted in d'Emilio, *Sexual Politics, Sexual Communities*, 42.

17 Gilbert, *A Cycle of Outrage*, 74–75.

18 Elaine Tyler May, *Homeward Bound: American Families in the Cold War Era* (New York: Basic Books, 1988), 94.

19 Robert J. Moskin, "The American Male: Why Do Women Dominate Him?" *Look*, 4 February 1958, 79. The article is the first of a three-part series on the plight of American men in the 1950s. Barbara Klinger offers a fascinating discussion of two parts of this series in relation to Rock Hudson's masculinity in the 1950s in *Melodrama and Meaning: History, Culture, and the Films of Douglas Sirk* (Bloomington: Indiana University Press, 1994), 104–16.

20 May, *Homeward Bound*, 96. For a pertinent discussion of the male child's dependence on (and control by) female role models, see also Moskin, "The American Male: Why Do Women Dominate Him?" 77–80.

21 For a discussion of the stress that men encounter in maintaining the role of provider and breadwinner, see William Atwood, "The American Male: Why Does He Work So Hard?" *Look*, 4 March 1958, 71–75. Atwood responds to the question of the article's title, "in our matriarchal American society, men feel the need to assert themselves and prove their masculinity by accomplishing things. As they get older, this drive can even become a substitute for loss of potency."

22 May, *Homeward Bound*, 101–102; Barbara Ehrenreich, *The Hearts of Men: American Dreams and the Flight from Commitment* (New York: Anchor Press, 1983), 20.

23 Ehrenreich, *The Hearts of Men*, 24.

24 Moskin, "The American Male: Why Do Women Dominate Him?" 80. The author identifies three of man's sexual defenses against "female domination":

1) "bachelorhood"; 2) "withdrawing from sexual relations"; and 3) "homo-sexuality, which one scientist labels the 'flight from masculinity.'"

25 Gilbert, *A Cycle of Outrage*, 40–41.

26 Corber, *National Security*, 19–25.

27 George B. Leonard Jr., "The American Male: Why Is He Afraid to be Different?" *Look*, 18 February 1958, 100–101.

28 Ehrenreich, *The Hearts of Men*, 22–23.

29 Klinger, *Melodrama and Meaning*, 38–39. For a discussion of marketing and reception of foreign art cinema in the United States in the late 1940s and 1950s, see Staiger, *Interpreting Films*, 178–95.

30 Robert Sklar, *Movie-Made America: A Cultural History of the Movies* (New York: Vintage Books, 1975), 273. For a more extensive discussion of the "Miracle" case, see Richard Corliss, "The Legion of Decency," *Film Comment* 4, no. 4 (Summer 1968): 24–61.

31 Corliss, "The Legion of Decency," 24–61.

32 On the controversy surrounding Wertham's book, see Gilbert, *A Cycle of Outrage*, 91–108. In addition to comics, Wertham also targeted the advertising industry in the incitement of juvenile crime and racism.

33 For a discussion of the Kefauver hearings, see Gilbert, *A Cycle of Outrage*, 143–61.

34 Klinger, *Melodrama and Meaning*, 74–75.

35 U. S. Congress. Senate. *Hearing before the Subcommittee to Investigate Juvenile Delinquency of the Committee of the Judiciary*, 84th Cong., 1st sess., 15 June 1955; excerpted in *Film Culture* 1 (Winter 1955): 14.

36 Gilbert, *A Cycle of Outrage*, 157.

37 Geoffrey M. Shurlock, to J. L. Warner, Burbank, 22 March 1955. Files on *Rebel Without a Cause*, Warner Bros. Archives, Cinema-Television Library, University of Southern California, Los Angeles.

38 "Analysis of Film Content" for *Rebel Without a Cause*. Production Code Files, Special Collections, Margaret Herrick Library, Academy of Motion Picture Arts and Sciences, Los Angeles.

39 Gilbert, *A Cycle of Outrage*, 163.

40 Gilbert, *A Cycle of Outrage*, 128–42. Among others, the author discusses *The Crime Problem* (1955), in which Walter Reckless treated delinquency in the context of class relations. Walter B. Miller's 1959 study is especially interesting in its suggestion that lower-class adolescents join gangs in order to find positive male role models lacking in their "female-oriented family environments."

41 Richard Dyer, "*A Star Is Born* and the Construction of Authenticity," in *Stardom: Industry of Desire*, ed. Christine Gledhill (New York: Routledge, 1991), 134.

42 Corber, *National Security*, 19.

43 Chon Noriega, "'SOMETHING'S MISSING HERE!': Homosexuality and Film Reviews during the Production Code Era, 1934–1962," *Cinema Journal* 30, no. 1 (Fall 1990): 27–29. In this fascinating piece, Noriega also explains that in *Cat on a Hot Tin Roof* (1958), "repressed homosexuality is recast as a heterosexual problem."

44 d'Emilio, *Sexual Politics, Sexual Communities*, 65–66. John d'Emilio supports his description of Mattachine's Marxist practices with reference to papers and speeches written by the original Mattachine Society's founders and members (as well as the Society's Missions and Purposes Statement) in 1951.

45 I am indebted to John d'Emilio's detailed description of the Mattachine Society's activities in *Sexual Politics, Sexual Communities*, 57–91.

46 *Mattachine Review* 1 (1955): 10.

47 For a pertinent example of an anthropological perspective, see Omer C. Stewart, Ph.D., "Homosexuality Among the American Indians and Other Native Peoples of the World," *Mattachine Review* 6, no. 1 (January 1960): 9–12. The article indicates the proliferation of homosexual behavior not only among American Indians and the ancient Greeks, but also among "All primates, and many of the lower animals such as cows, horses and sheep. . . ."

48 A. D., California, "Readers Write," *Mattachine Review* 3 (May–June 1955): 33.

49 *Mattachine Review* 1 (1955): 6.

50 *Mattachine Review* 1 (1955): 10. Many of the letters to the editor in the "Readers Write" column demonstrate an active and often hostile intolerance for homosexuals who adopt the discourse of anti-Americanism. In response to a previous article that compared intolerant individuals to "neo-fascists," "Mr. P. R., Texas" writes that "I do not think Mr. Barr is a communist or a communist sympathizer. If he was he wouldn't be writing in the Review. His choice of political invective, however, is unfortunately close enough to the mumbo-jumbo of the Daily Worker to lay him open to attack by implied guilt of association," *Mattachine Review* 4 (July–August 1955): 34–35.

51 Harry Johnson, "And a Red too . . . .", *One* 1, no. 9 (September 1953): 3.

52 Donald Webster Cory, *The Homosexual Outlook: A Subjective Approach* (London: Peter Nevill, 1953), 36. Originally published as *The Homosexual in America: A Subjective Approach* (New York: Greenberg, 1951).

53 Lyn Pedersen, "The Importance of Being Different," *One* 2, no. 3 (March 1954): 5.

54 Cory, *The Homosexual Outlook*, 11.

55 Arthur B. Krell, "We Need a Great Literature," *One* 2, no. 5 (May 1954): 21.

56 In his illuminating *Homosexuality in Cold War America: Resistance and the Crisis of Masculinity* (Durham, NC: Duke University Press, 1997), Robert Corber convincingly argues that gay postwar American fiction includes numerous ex-

amples of narratives that constructed "a gay male subject-position that was masculine" (140), with protagonists whose active rebellion was constituted by a resistance to the dominant ideological masculine positions of "organization man" and "breadwinner." Krell does not name specific authors in his discussion, and consequently it is difficult to assess how such constructions of masculinity might have been received in the 1950s. It is possible that the ideologically oppositional stance of a novel such as Gore Vidal's *The City and the Pillar*, which Corber treats extensively, might have been subsumed by the fact that the novel ends tragically; if so, this would only serve to delineate more closely the parameters of what authors such as Krell considered as acceptable and unacceptable role models. Corber's fascinating work paves the way for further studies on the intersections of ideology, masculinity, and gay reception studies.

57 Krell, "We Need a Great Literature," 19.

58 Ibid., 20.

59 Ibid., 22.

60 In her treatment of the reception strategies available to gay men in the 1950s, Janet Staiger dispels the notion that all of the characterizations of homosexual characters by writers of gay fiction were negative, self-defeating, or assimilationist. For a discussion of this literature, see *Interpreting Films*, 167–72.

61 Richard Dyer, *Now You See It: Studies on Lesbian and Gay Film* (London: Routledge, 1990), 138.

62 d'Emilio, *Sexual Politics, Sexual Communities*, 179.

63 David Rodowick, "Madness, Authority and Ideology: The Domestic Melodrama of the 1950s," in *Home Is Where the Heart Is: Studies in Melodrama and the Woman's Film*, ed. Christine Gledhill (London: BFI Publishing, 1987), 268–80. Rodowick argues that since the patriarchal figure in domestic melodrama determines social and sexual relations, female sexuality is channeled into "the passive positions which patriarchy has defined for it; that is, heterosexual monogamy and maternity."

64 Geoffrey Nowell-Smith, "Minnelli and Melodrama," in *Home Is Where the Heart Is: Studies in Melodrama and the Woman's Film*, ed. Christine Gledhill (London: BFI Publishing, 1987), 73.

65 Rodowick, "Madness, Authority and Ideology," 271.

66 Ibid., 272.

67 Geoffrey Nowell-Smith notes an intimate connection between the son's desire to determine his own identity and the Freudian "family romance," in which the child returns to the scene of his own conception. See "Minnelli and Melodrama," 72–73.

68 Elma LeCron, Analyst, Synopsis of final script of *Rebel Without a Cause*, 25 September [1957]. Files on *Rebel Without a Cause*, Warner Bros. Archives.,

Cinema-Television Library, University of Southern California, Los Angeles; Final script of *Rebel Without a Cause*, story by Nicholas Ray, 25 March 1955. Files on *Rebel Without a Cause*, Warner Bros. Archives, Cinema-Television Library, University of Southern California, Los Angeles.

69 Peter Biskind, *Seeing is Believing* (New York: Random House, 1983), 201.

70 See David Dalton, *James Dean: The Mutant King* (New York: St. Martin's Press, 1974), 163–65. Dalton explains that Dean and Dick Davalos were invited to explore the tensions between the Trask brothers during test shooting. This exploration resulted in a scene depicting both characters naked from the waist up, and Davalos in bed watching Dean sitting on a chair in the foreground of the frame. As Davalos explains, "Sure the test we did had some homosexual undertones, but no one has ever said it before, though some people reacted wildly to it when they saw the rushes. That's why it was never put into the film."

TWO *Stories without Endings*

1 According to Randall Riese, students at Immaculate Mary High School in Los Angeles formed this first fan club. It was appropriately named the "Immaculate Heart James Dean Appreciation Society." See *The Unabridged James Dean: His Life and Legacy from A to Z* (New York: Random House, 1991), 175.

2 Personal and social alienation also become prominent in one of Dean's last television appearances, in "The Unlighted Road" (CBS's *Schlitz Playhouse of Stars*, May 6, 1955), in which he portrays a hitchhiker who stumbles into a criminal plot in an attempt to find work at a diner, and in his role of an escaped convict in "Life Sentence" (NBC's *Campbell Soundstage*, October 16, 1953).

3 "Moody New Star," *Life*, 7 March 1955, 125.

4 Letter from Warner to Elia "Gadge" Kazan on the casting of *East of Eden*, 10 March 1954. Files on *East of Eden*, Warner Bros. Archives, Cinema-Television Library, University of Southern California, Los Angeles.

5 Riese, *The Unabridged James Dean*, 147–57.

6 Undated, unsigned press Warner Bros. press release on the ordering of photos for fans. Files on *Giant*, Warner Bros. Archives, Cinema-Television Library, University of Southern California, Los Angeles; Joe Halperin, undated Warner Bros. press release on Dean's amicability. Files on *Rebel Without a Cause*, Warner Bros. Archives, Cinema-Television Library, University of Southern California, Los Angeles.

7 "Biography of James Dean," Warner Bros. press release, 28 July 1954, James Dean Files, Margaret Herrick Library, Academy of Motion Picture Arts and Sciences, Los Angeles.

8 "Moody New Star," 125.

9 "New Star Is Born," Warner Bros. press release, February [1955]. James Dean Files, Margaret Herrick Library, Academy of Motion Picture Arts and Sciences, Los Angeles.

10 Among the holdings of the Fairmount Historical Museum is a cardboard construction of the train that brought Dean's mother's body from California to Indiana for her funeral. A caption in the museum indicates that the model train was given to James in response to his request (at age 10) to have a token of his mother's memory.

11 Sidney Skolsky, "Demon Dean," *Photoplay*, July 1955, 78; William Bast, "There Was a Boy . . ." a three-part series published between September and November of 1956 in *Photoplay*. The series consists of excerpts from the first book-length Dean biography, William Bast's *James Dean: A Biography* (New York: Ballantine, 1956).

12 Ted Ashton, Warner Bros. press release on Dean's living quarters at the studio, 23 July 1954. Files on *East of Eden*, Warner Bros. Archives, Cinema-Television Library, University of Southern California, Los Angeles.

13 Ted Ashton, Warner Bros. press release on Dean's living quarters on location for *East of Eden*, 4 June 1954. Files on *East of Eden*, Warner Bros. Archives, Cinema-Television Library, University of Southern California, Los Angeles.

14 Joe Halperin, undated Warner Bros. press release on Dean's search for a new home. Files on *Rebel Without a Cause*, Warner Bros. Archives, Cinema-Television Library, University of Southern California, Los Angeles.

15 Joe Halperin, Warner Bros. press release on Dean's California apartment, 17 May [1955]. Files on *Giant*, Warner Bros. Archives, Cinema-Television Library, University of Southern California, Los Angeles.

16 "Biography of James Dean," 28 July 1954.

17 "Moody New Star," 128.

18 Richard Moore, "Lone Wolf," *Modern Screen*, August 1955, 75.

19 *James Dean Revealed!*, ed. David Dalton (New York: Delta Books, 1991), 51–53.

20 Moore, "Lone Wolf," 76.

21 Barbara Klinger, *Melodrama and Meaning: History, Culture, and the Films of Douglas Sirk* (Bloomington, IN: Indiana University Press, 1994), 72.

22 John McCarten, "Steinbeck, Lay That Bible Down," *New Yorker*, 19 March 1955, 140.

23 "Kazan's Steinbeck," *Newsweek*, 7 March 1955, 90.

24 Bosley Crowther, "The Screen: Delinquency," *The New York Times*, 27 October 1955, 28; Allen M. Widem, "Films: 'Trial' Opens at Loew's Poli; 'Rebel Without a Cause' at Strand," *The Hartford Times*, 2 November 1955, 38.

25 John McCarten, "Southwestern Primitives," *New Yorker*, 20 October 1956, 179. Andrew Sarris reiterates this observation and emphasizes that the style adds little to characterization: "As the film plods through three decades and blue-

gray hair powder is applied, [Elizabeth Taylor's character of Leslie] loses her basically youthful personality without substituting any genuine maturity." See his review of *Giant* in *Film Culture* 2, no. 4 (1956): 23-24.

26 Andrew George Sarris, "East of Eden," *Film Culture* 1, no. 3 (May–June 1955): 24.

27 "East of Eden," *Variety*, 16 February 1955.

28 Klinger explains that the social value of morally suspect films such as Kazan's controversial *Baby Doll* (1956) and the film version of *Peyton Place* (1957) was often upheld by critics through a comparison of film aesthetics to the aesthetics of respectable novelists in the realist literary canon. See discussion in *Melodrama and Meaning*, 74–77.

29 Andrew Sarris, Review of *Giant, Film Culture* 2, no. 4 (1956): 23. Conversely, *Variety* praises the "penetrating realism in a story that pulls no punches" ("Giant," 10 October 1956).

30 Columnist Dorothy Killgallen explains that "parents worried about juvenile delinquency will hit the ceiling when they see the bloody switch-blade scene between teen agers in 'Rebel Without a Cause'" ("Gossip in Gotham," *New York Journal-American*, 11 August 1955, 11). For a discussion of the filming of this scene, Neil Rau, "The Fight Was for Blood—and They Got It," *Los Angeles Examiner*, 22 May 1955, 15.

31 A reviewer for *Newsweek* suggests that the combination and synthesis of modes, styles, and tones is well-suited to the film's intended effect: "Brick-hard realism, sky-high poetry, psychological penetration, and noisy melodrama would seem to be poorly matching parts to make up an effective movie. In this instance, however, a sensitive director and understanding actors have fitted them into a drama that is genuinely distressing as well as exciting" ("A Moving Performance," *Newsweek*, 7 November 1955, 117).

32 Christine Gledhill, "Signs of Melodrama," in *Stardom: Industry of Desire*, ed. Christine Gledhill (New York: Routledge, 1991), 222–24.

33 Steven Cohan, *Masked Men: Masculinity and the Movies in the Fifties* (Bloomington: IN: Indiana University Press, 1997), 224 25.

34 Sarris, Review of *East of Eden*, 24.

35 Review of *East of Eden, Time*, 21 March 1955, 102.

36 Louella Parsons, "Hollywood is Talking About . . ." *Los Angeles Examiner*, 15 May 1955, Section V, p. 9.

37 Lee Rogow, "Essay for Elia," *Saturday Review*, 19 March 1955, 25.

38 Review of *East of Eden, Variety*.

39 Bosley Crowther, "The Screen: 'East of Eden' Has Debut," *The New York Times*, 10 March 1955, 33.

40 Robert Kass, Review of *East of Eden, Catholic World*, April 1955, 60.

41 *Los Angeles Times*, 27 March 1955, Part I-C, p. 3.

42 "Kazan's Steinbeck," 90.

43 Leo Mishkin, "'Rebel Has Share of Merit: Mainly a Monument to Dean," *The Morning Telegraph*, 27 October 1955, 3.

44 Archer, "Generation Without a Cause," *Film Culture* 2, no. 1 (1956): 18.

45 Arthur Knight, Review of *Rebel Without a Cause*, *Saturday Review*, November 1955, 29.

46 McCarten, "Southwestern Primitives," 178–79.

47 Andrew Sarris, Review of *Giant*, 23. The *Time* magazine review also praises the actor's mastery of the Texas accent and "wrangler" mannerisms; see "The New Pictures," *Time*, 22 October 1956, 108. Several Warner Bros. press releases emphasize that Dean naturally "blends in" with the Western settings of Marfa, where the Reata scenes were filmed. An undated studio press release indicates that Dean is learning to rope calves in his spare time off the set; another undated release explains that "with his slouch and western garb Dean was rarely recognized as a film star when he wandered around the town of Marfa. He was just another cowhand" (Ted Ashton, Files on *Giant*, Warner Bros. Archives, Cinema-Television Library, University of Southern California, Los Angeles).

48 Edgar Morin, "The Case of James Dean," *Evergreen Review* 5 (1958): 10.

49 Bosley Crowther, "The Screen: Large Subject," *The New York Times*, 11 October 1956, 51.

50 "The New Pictures," *Time*, 22 October 1956, 108.

51 Hollis Alpert, "It's Dean, Dean, Dean," *Saturday Review*, 13 October 1956, 29. This consistency of character is also confirmed by *Giant* director George Stevens; see Alfred C. Roller, "The James Dean Myth Blows Up," *World Telegram and Sun Saturday Magazine*, 3 November 1956.

52 Robert Hatch, Review of *Giant*, *The Nation*, 20 October 1956, 334.

53 Morin, "The Case of James Dean," 6.

54 Marlene Swaim, St. Louis, "Readers Inc." *Photoplay*, January 1957, 8.

55 Mary Anne Condon, Chicago, "Readers Inc." *Photoplay*, April 1957, 34.

56 "Biography of James Dean," Warner Bros. press release, 6 August 1956, James Dean Files, Margaret Herrick Library, Academy of Motion Picture Arts and Sciences, Los Angeles.

57 "Biography of James Dean," Warner Bros. press release, 13 June 1957, James Dean Files, Margaret Herrick Library, Academy of Motion Picture Arts and Sciences, Los Angeles.

58 "Death Premonition By Dean Recalled," *Los Angeles Times*, 2 October 1955.

59 Jeanne Balch Capen, "The Strange Revival of James Dean," *The American Weekly*, 29 July 1956, 4.

60 Morin, "The Case of James Dean," 10.

61 "In Memory of James Dean," *The Fairmount News*, Special Edition, 7 October 1955.

62 Sam Schaffer, "James Dean—The Ghost Driver of Polonio Pass," *Whisper,* December 1957, 8-11, 57.

63 Morin, "The Case of James Dean," 11-12.

64 Freida Joan Rudnick, New York City, to Jack Warner, New York City, 9 October 1956. Files on *Giant,* Warner Bros. Archives, Cinema-Television Library, University of Southern California, Los Angeles.

65 Evelyn Washburn Nielsen, "The Truth About James Dean," *Chicago Tribune,* 9 September 1956, Sunday Magazine Section, 22-23, 48-49.

66 Alpert, "It's Dean, Dean, Dean," 28-29.

67 George Scullin, "James Dean: The Legend and the Facts," *Look,* 16 October 1956, 120-28. The use of psychiatric discourse in the explanations of the star's public appeal in terms of identificatory processes is a prominent feature of several articles released approximately one year after his death, near the time of *Giant*'s release. See "Dean of the One-Shotters," *Time,* 3 September 1956; "Stars That Won't Dim," *Newsweek,* 18 June 1956, 22; Seymour Korman, "The Last Hours of James Dean," *Chicago Tribune,* 6 February 1956; and Clayton Cole, "The Dean Myth," *Films and Filming* 3, no. 4 (January 1957): 17

68 The first poem, "To James Dean," appears in *Photoplay,* January 1956, 50-51. The letter and follow-up poem, "So Little Time (To James Dean)," appear in *Photoplay,* June 1956, 32.

69 Helen Bower, "Oscars Will Go to East of Eden," *Detroit Free Press,* 11 March 1955, 11; Philip K. Scheuer, "James Dean Cheats Car Death in Bit of Film Irony," *Los Angeles Times,* 30 October 1955, Part IV, p. 2.

70 E. B. Radcliffe, "A Best Ten Study of Pride and Envy," *The Cincinnati Enquirer,* 15 April 1955.

71 Bill Tusher, "The Girls in James Dean's Life," *TV and Movie Screen,* 1955, 68.

72 Steven Cohan convincingly argues that the new, young male actor of the 1950s is often constituted as a "bisexual boy." In his discussion of Montgomery Clift, Cohan asserts that "because his desirability is based in spectacle, Matthew [Clift's character in *Red River*] himself does not act upon desire but excites it in the person who looks at him, thereby soliciting a male gaze just as readily as a female one" (*Masked Men,* 216-17). It is interesting that in a correlative manner, desire around Dean's persona is articulated through the spectacle (and fan discourse on this spectacle) of the actor's vulnerability: his sexual appeal (and, paradoxically, his maturity) stems from fans' desire to act on his need to be comforted.

73 Lou Cameron, "The Triumph and Tragedy of Jimmy Dean," in *James Dean Revealed!,* ed. David Dalton (New York: Delta Books, 1991), 14-45. According to Dalton, the cartoon biography originally appeared in a one-shot magazine entitled *Elvis and Jimmy* (1956). In the same collection, see also Robert DeKolbe, "James Dean Speaks from the Grave," 138-43, in which the psychic Anna M. Van Deusen relays Dean's description of a utopic postmortem

state: "Here, there is no confusion, no unhappiness, no cold, no hunger. . . . And I have my mother with me, whom I lost when I was only seven years old."

74 Cameron, "The Triumph and Tragedy of Jimmy Dean," 31.

75 Some examples: "Friends of Pier Angeli and James Dean are beginning to wonder whether their frequent rides together on the Griffith Park bridle path may not lead them down the bridal path. They spent several hours riding horseback together yesterday on their day off [f]rom 'The Silver Chalice' and 'East of Eden,' respectively" (Ted Ashton, 28 June 1954. Files on *East of Eden*); "Whenever Dean has a free minute . . . he drives over to 'The Silver Chalice' set to be with Pier and vice versa" (Ted Ashton, 24 June 1954. Files on *East of Eden*); "James Dean and Ursula Andress didn't hide their affection for each other as they watched a sneak preview of Jimmy's latest picture, "Rebel Without a Cause," in Westwood over the weekend" (Ted Ashton, 29 September 1955. Files on *Rebel Without a Cause*); Dean "has eyes for British actress Diane Wynters, recent arrival to the States. Dean and Miss Wynters were holding hands at the Villa Capri last night" (Joe Halperin, 20 April 1955. Files on *Rebel Without a Cause*). All of the above press releases are located in the Warner Bros. Archives, Cinema-Television Library, University of Southern California, Los Angeles.

76 Joe Halperin, undated Warner Bros. press release on Rock Hudson, Tab Hunter, and James Dean. Files on *Rebel Without a Cause*, Warner Bros. Archives, Cinema-Television Library, University of Southern California, Los Angeles.

77 Nell Blythe, "Jimmy Dean Fights Back from the Grave," *Movie Life*, June 1956, 26.

78 Nell Blythe, "The Untold Story of the Love Jimmy Lost," *Movie Life*, January 1957, 64.

79 Sam Schaeffer, "James Dean's Black Madonna," *Whisper*, February 1956, 14.

80 Joel Raleigh, "The Girl James Dean Was Going to Marry!" *Lowdown*, May 1957, 16–17, 62–64.

81 Larry Ashenden, "Did Jimmy Dean Leave a Son?" *Rave*, January 1957, 30–35.

82 David Dalton, *James Dean: The Mutant King* (New York: St. Martin's Press, 1974), 163–65.

83 Geoffrey M. Shurlock to J. L. Warner, 22 March 1955. Production Files on *Rebel Without a Cause*, Warner Bros. Archives, Cinema-Television Library, University of Southern California, Los Angeles.

84 Chon Noriega, "'SOMETHING'S MISSING HERE!': Homosexuality in Film Reviews during the Production Code Era, 1934–1962," *Cinema Journal* 30, no. 1 (Fall 1990): 20–41.

85 J. C. Wynn, Review of *Rebel Without a Cause*, *Presbyterian Life*, 26 November 1955, 42.

86 William Bast, *James Dean: A Biography* (New York: Ballantine Books, 1956), 51.

87 Lynne Carter, "I Was A Friend of Jimmy Dean," *Rave*, January 1957, 35.

88 *Rave* published several negative responses to Carter's article in April 1957, at which time she was prompted to defend the accuracy of her assessments as revealed truths that she had learned on a first-hand basis. For Carter's retort, see "I Learned About LOVE From Jimmy Dean," *Rave*, April 1957, 24–27.

89 Donald Webster Cory, *The Homosexual Outlook: A Subjective Approach* (London: Peter Nevill, 1953), 23.

90 While it is neither my intention nor my desire to pinpoint the time in which Dean's popularity began to show signs of wear, it is interesting to note a rather sudden change in the hero's status in two pieces published in the same journal only four months apart in the early 1960s. On September 30, 1960, the *Los Angeles Mirror* reported that "one cult, called 'The James Dean Death Club,' resulted in the auto death of a Los Gatos high school honor student. A member of the club, she ran her car into an oak tree. Santa Clara County deputies called the death suicide. A few months earlier another student killed himself when his car crashed into [a] tree" ("James Dean's Fans Still Write to Him," Part II, p. 2). The January 26, 1961 issue mentions Dean only briefly under the heading of "Department of Fleeting Fame," announcing "the demise of the national Dean cult."

91 Taylor Mead, "The Movies Are a Revolution," *Film Culture* 29 (Summer 1964): 9.

92 Robin Bean, "Dean—Ten Years After," *Films and Filming* 12, no. 1 (October 1965): 13.

93 Douglas McVay, "Rebel Without a Cause," *Films and Filming* (August 1977): 16.

94 Derek Marlowe, "Soliloquy on James Dean's Forty-Fifth Birthday," *New York*, 8 November 1976, 42.

95 Juan A. Suarez, *Bike Boys, Drag Queens, and Superstars: Avant-Garde, Mass Culture, and Gay Identities in the 1960s Underground Cinema* (Bloomington, IN: Indiana University Press, 1996), 173.

96 Vito Russo, *The Celluloid Closet: Homosexuality in the Movies*, 2d ed. (New York: Harper & Row, 1987), 135.

97 Al La Valley, "Out of the Closet and on to the Screen," *American Film* 7, no. 10 (September 1982): 61. Besides Stephen Harvey, the participants in this debate include Richard Dyer, Vito Russo, Robin Wood, Andrew Britton, and Doug Edwards.

98 John d'Emilio, *Sexual Politics, Sexual Communities* (Chicago: University of Chicago Press, 1983), 139.

99 "The Homosexual: Newly Visible, Newly Understood," *Time* 94.18 (31 October 1969): 51, 56–57.

100 d'Emilio, *Sexual Politics, Sexual Communities*, 140.

101 For a detailed discussion of legal challenges in this period, see d'Emilio, *Sexual Politics, Sexual Communities*, 144–47.

102 d'Emilio, *Sexual Politics, Sexual Communities*, 159.

103 In *Sexual Politics, Sexual Communities*, d'Emilio explains, that by this time, Donald Webster Cory had "increasingly propounded the view that homosexuals were disturbed and that cure was desirable" (166–68). Cory threatened to leave the New York Mattachine Society if the "antisickness resolution" was passed. He did leave, and soon afterwards, he abandoned his pseudonym, and became a "sociologist of deviance" for New York University.

104 Cory, *The Homosexual in America*, 157.

105 Donald Von Wiedenman, "NBC to Air 'Portrait' of Dean," *The Advocate*, 25 February 1976, 33, 37–38.

106 John Howlett, *James Dean: A Biography* (New York: Beaufort Books, 1975), 30–33. Howlett also suggests that Dean's dealings with "street-corner hustlers" in Santa Monica is an indication of his "uncertainty and lack of purpose" in the early 1950s.

107 Venable Herndon, *James Dean: A Short Life* (Garden City, NY: Doubleday, 1974), 94–98.

108 Dalton, *James Dean: The Mutant King*, 8. The author discusses Dean's fusion of male and female attributes on pp. 151–52.

109 Cory, *The Homosexual in America*, 159.

110 d'Emilio, *Sexual Politics, Sexual Communities*, 153.

111 John d'Emilio and Estelle B. Freedman, *Intimate Matters: A History of Sexuality in America* (New York: Harper and Row, 1988), 321.

112 Parker Tyler, *Screening the Sexes: Homosexuality in the Movies* (New York: Anchor Books, 1972), 143–44.

113 Jack Babuscio, "James Dean—A Gay Riddle," *Gay News* 79 (1975): 17–18. Royston Ellis's out-of-print and difficult-to-locate *Rebel* was published in London in 1962.

114 Kenneth Anger, *Hollywood Babylon II* (New York: E. P. Dutton, Inc., 1984), 135–47.

115 Von Wiedenman, "NBC to Air 'Portrait of Dean,'" 37.

116 John Gilmore, *The Real James Dean* (New York: Pyramid Books, 1975), 30.

117 John Gilmore, "Author Reveals—'I Had Sex With James Dean!'" *The Hollywood Star Reporter*, [1980], 15–20.

118 My use of the term "therapy" here is influenced by Mimi White's discussion of the therapeutic aspects of confessional narratives in *Tele-Advising: Therapeutic Discourse in American Television* (Chapel Hill: University of North Carolina Press, 1992).

119 Gilmore, *The Real James Dean*, 99–100.

120 Derek Marlowe, "Soliloquy on James Dean's Forty-Fifth Birthday," 46.

121 "The Slow Fade," *Crawdaddy*, March 1978, 49–56.

THREE *Identity Transformations*

1 Army Archerd, "Just for Variety," *Daily Variety*, 29 May 1996, 4.

2 Al Kielwasser, "Braveheart," *GLAAD Reports* July/August 1995 [http://www.glaad.org:80/glaad/9507/braveheart.html], retrieved 14 February 1997.

3 A transcript of portions of the *El Pais* article, as well as the *Good Morning, America* interview, are available in Rex Wockner, "Mel Gibson's Anti-Gay History," *Cyber Queer Lounge*, ed. Tom Hicks [http://www.cyberzine.org/html.GLAIDS/Wockner/gibson.html], retrieved 26 November 1996.

4 Rex Wockner, "Mel Gibson's Anti-Gay History."

5 Herb Caen, "Pocketful of Phlug," *The San Francisco Chronicle*, 22 January 1992, News Section, D1.

6 "Mel Puts His Foot Down," Press Association Newsfile, The Press Association Limited, 24 August 1993.

7 Kielwasser, "Braveheart."

8 "The 1992 Sissy Awards," *The Advocate*, 30 June 1992, 37.

9 John d'Emilio and Estelle B. Freedman, *Intimate Matters: A History of Sexuality in America* (New York: Harper & Row, 1988), 323.

10 David F. Greenberg, *The Construction of Homosexuality* (Chicago: The University of Chicago Press, 1988), 478. See also Neil Miller, *Out of the Past: Gay and Lesbian History from 1869 to the Present* (New York: Vintage Books, 1995), 422–29.

11 Dennis Altman, *The Homosexualization of America, The Americanization of the Homosexual* (New York: St. Martin's Press, 1982), 160.

12 Altman, *The Homosexualization of America*, 35.

13 Lawrence O'Toole, "Gay Style," *Maclean's*, 18 February 1980, 46. O'Toole also traces a rise in the acceptance of heterosexual promiscuity to gay social and sexual formations of the 1970s: "The first flush of liberation that came with the gay escapist sensibility found itself rising into the previously pallored straight face. The gay mass sex watering holes, of which New York's Mineshaft is the last of its kind, were responsible for the grope-in-group straight equivalents such as Plato's Retreat" (47).

14 "How Gay Is Gay?" *Time*, 23 April 1979, 72–78.

15 "Gays on the March," *Time*, 8 September 1975, 32–43. For an insightful account of the increasingly favorable and supportive treatment of gays in the media, see David Gelman, "Gays and the Press," *Newsweek*, 20 October 1975, 93–94. For a caustic condemnation of the reactionary activities against recent social advancements of gays in the wake of Anita Bryant's antigay campaign

of 1978, see Doug Ireland, "The New Homophobia: Open Season on Gays," *The Nation*, 15 September 1979, 207–10.

16 Daniel Harris, *The Rise and Fall of Gay Culture* (New York: Hyperion, 1997). This "aestheticism of maladjustment" is discussed in the first chapter, "The Death of Camp: Gay Men and Hollywood Diva Worship, from Reverence to Ridicule" (8–39).

17 Altman, *The Homosexualization of America*, 18.

18 "How Gay Is Gay?" 76.

19 O'Toole, "Gay Style," 46.

20 "Gays: A Major Force in the Marketplace," *Business Week*, 3 September 1979, 118–120.

21 John Lombardi, "Selling Gay to the Masses," *Village Voice*, 30 June 1975, 10–11. Neil Miller documents the curious coexistence of gay and straight patrons of the Continental Baths—a mostly straight clientele attended the shows, while gay men marched around the premises and its restricted upper floor wearing only bath towels. See *Out of the Past: Gay and Lesbian History from 1869 to the Present* (New York: Vintage Books, 1995), 10–11.

22 Lombardi, "Selling Gay to the Masses," 10.

23 Miller, *Out of the Past*, 427–28.

24 Jamake Highwater, "Dancing in the Seventies, *Horizon*, May 1977, 30–33.

25 Jesse Kornbluth, "Merchandising Disco for the Masses," *The New York Times*, 18 February 1979, Sunday Magazine section, 21.

26 Highwater, "Dancing in the Seventies," 33.

27 Lombardi, "Selling Gay to the Masses," 10.

28 Greenberg, *The Construction of Homosexuality*, 477.

29 Karen Stabiner, "Tapping the Homosexual Market," *The New York Times*, 2 May 1982, Sec. 6, 76.

30 Stabiner, "Tapping the Homosexual Market," 36. According to *Business Week*, "Projections from another Los-Angeles-based study suggest that gays control 19% of spendable income in the U.S." ("Gays: A Major Force in the Market-place," 118).

31 Stabiner, "Tapping the Homosexual Market," 76–80.

32 Altman, *The Homosexualization of America*, 14.

33 Michelangelo Signorile, *Life Outside: The Signorile Report on Gay Men: Sex, Drugs, Muscles, and the Passages of Life* (New York: HarperCollins, 1997), 52–56.

34 Harris offers a fascinating and extensive discussion of physique magazines in the chapter, "A Psychohistory of the Homosexual Body," 86–110.

35 Robert Corber, *Homosexuality in Cold War America: Resistance and the Crisis of Masculinity* (Durham, NC: Duke University Press, 1997), 143–44.

36 Thomas Waugh, *Hard to Imagine: Gay Male Eroticism in Photography and Film from Their Beginnings to Stonewall* (New York: Columbia University Press,

1996). See especially the chapter on physique culture, "Strength and Stealth," 177–283.

37 Lombardi, "Selling Gay to the Masses," 10.

38 Ken Emerson, "The Village People: America's Male Ideal," *Rolling Stone*, 5 October 1978, 27.

39 Stabiner, "Tapping the Homosexual Market," 74.

40 Cliff Jahr, "James Dean Was Dylan and Maybe Garbo Too," *Village Voice*, 6 November 1975, 124.

41 David Ansen, "The Incredible Hunks," *Newsweek*, 23 May 1983, 48.

42 Richard Corliss, "Apocalypse . . . Pow!" *Time*, 10 May 1982, 115.

43 Charles Michener, "'Shane' in Black Leather," *Newsweek*, 31 May 1982, 67.

44 Jim Callo, "Up from Down Under: Heartthrob Mel Gibson Lives Dangerously—But Only in the Movies," *People*, 14 February 1983, 99.

45 *Reuter Library Report*, 18 December 1992.

46 Bob Vilard, "Road Warriors," *Cinefantastique* 12.4 (May–June 1982): 6.

47 "Hollywood Can Wait," *Newsweek*, 31 May 1982, 67.

48 Production files for *Gallipoli* and *The Road Warrior*, Margaret Herrick Library, Academy of Motion Picture Arts and Sciences, Los Angeles. Aside from emphasizing the star's versatility and recognition by his peers, these files provide rather standard biographical traces.

49 Michener, "'Shane' in Black Leather," 70.

50 Brenda Eady, "Unforgettable Faces of Our Time," *People*, 30 April 1994, 102.

51 "Hollywood Can Wait," 67.

52 Ansen, "The Incredible Hunks," 50.

53 Teresa deLauretis, *The Practice of Love: Lesbian Identity and Perverse Desire* (Bloomington: Indiana University Press, 1994), 129.

54 David Ragan, *Mel Gibson* (New York: Dell, 1985), 31. Ragan's description of his first encounter with the actual "star body" is also significant: "as handsome and as engaging as his screen image. Not as tall as expected—5′10″ or so, maybe less. Heavily muscled shoulders and arms. Highly articulate. Vulnerable. Self-contained. Feisty. Shy. Well-mannered. Amusing. Rock steady. Unaffected."

55 Neil Sinyard, *Mel Gibson* (New York: Crescent Books, 1992), 8, 21, 28.

56 Elizabeth Darcy, "Mel Gibson: Superstar . . . Super Dad!" *McCall's*, January 1985, 114.

57 Dan Yakir, "Those Gallipoli Boys," *After Dark*, November 1981, 46.

58 Harris, *The Rise and Fall of Gay Culture*, 64. Harris offers an extensive discussion of the transformation from "high culture" to "low culture" coverage in gay journals from the 1970s to the present in the chapter, "The Invention of the Teflon Magazine: From *After Dark* to *Out*" (64–85).

59 See the article on Christopher Reeve in *After Dark*, December 1980), 13; Susan Shapiro, "Sex Onscreen: Explicit, Yes; Erotic, Rarely," *After Dark*,

July 1980, 41, 46; James D. Teel, "The Puritans Have Landed," *After Dark*, March 1981, 22–23 (which also includes an alluring photo of a bare-chested Gregory Harrison from the made-for-TV film *For Ladies Only*); and the "Editor's Update" in *After Dark*, May 1980 and July 1980; and Vito Russo, "The Celluloid Closet: Silver Screen Sin," *After Dark*, August–September 1981, 40–42.

60 For reports on Stigwood's successful crossover strategies in the 1970s, see Molly Haskell, "J. C. Enterprises, Inc.," *Saturday Review*, 30 October 1971, 65–67, 82; "A Man to Whom the Angels Flock," *Fortune*, June 1977, 44; "Supermogul in the Land of Opportunity," *Forbes*, 10 July 1978, 42; and "The Stigwood Style: Cashing in on Splash," *Business Week*, 24 July 1978, 53–54.

61 Tony Schwartz, "Stigwood's Midas Touch," *Newsweek*, 23 January 1978, 40, 50.

62 David Ansen, "Rock Tycoon," *Newsweek*, 31 July 1978, 40–47.

63 Lombardi, "Selling Gay to the Masses," 10.

64 Robin Wood, "From Buddies to Lovers," *Hollywood from Vietnam to Reagan* (New York: Columbia University Press, 1986), 222–44.

65 Simon Watney, "Hollywood's Homosexual World," *Screen* 23.3-4 (November–December 1982), 122.

66 Clifton Montgomery, "Taxis, Tokens, and Quick Takes at the Movies," *The Advocate*, 21 January 1982, 47.

67 Franco Moretti, "Kindergarten," in *Signs Taken for Wonders* (London: Verson, 1993). Neale discusses Moretti's notion of mistiming in "Melodrama and Tears," *Screen* 27.6 (November–December 1996): 6–22 (see especially 7).

68 Linda Williams, "Film Bodies: Gender, Genre, and Excess," *Film Quarterly* (Summer 1991): 11–12.

69 Vincent Canby, "Post-Nuclear 'Road Warrior'," *The New York Times*, 28 April 1982, C24.

70 Steve Neale, "Masculinity as Spectacle: Reflections on Men in Mainstream Cinema," in *Screening the Sexes: Exploring Masculinities in Hollywood Cinema*, ed. Steven Cohan and Ina Rae Hark (New York: Routledge, 1993), 18.

71 Harris, *The Rise and Fall of Gay Culture*, 179–82. Harris provides an extensive discussion of transformations of the leather S&M community from the 1940s to the present in the chapter entitled "The Death of Kink: Five Stages in the Metamorphosis of the Modern Dungeon" (179–202).

72 For a discussion of leather crossover in the mid-1970s, see Richard Goldstein, "S&M: The Dark Side of Gay Liberation," *Village Voice*, 7 July 1975, 10–13.

73 See especially "The Gay World's Leather Fringe: Do Homosexual Males Consciously Seek Danger?" *Time*, 24 March 1980, 74–75. The piece itemizes and describes many of the activities taking place in leather bars, and it cites Masters and Johnson's observation that "homosexual males have more violent fantasies than heterosexual males."

74 Villard, "Road Warriors," 6. For this reference I am indebted to Christopher

Sharrett, who provides an insightful discussion of the relation between myth and male iconography in the Mad Max films in "Myth, Male Fantasy, and Simulacra in *Mad Max* and *The Road Warrior*," *Journal of Popular Film and Television* 13.2 (Summer 1985): 81–91.

75 Michener, "'Shane' in Black Leather," 70.

76 *Ibid.*

77 Sheila Benson, "Action on a Full Tank in 'Warrior,'" *Los Angeles Times*, 20 May 1982, 8.

78 Clifton Montgomery, "Film Ticket," *The Advocate*, 8 July 1982, 45.

79 Vito Russo, *The Celluloid Closet: Homosexuality in the Movies*, revised edition (New York: Harper & Row, 1987), 301.

80 Larry Bush, "The State of the Gay Union," *The Advocate*, 21 January 1982, 22–29, 74.

81 Michelle Green, "The Dish from Down Under," *People*, 4 February 1985, 70–76.

82 Roland Perry, *Lethal Hero* (London: Oliver Books, 1993), 136.

83 Kurt Loder, "The Heroes of Thunderdome: On the Road with Mad Max," *Rolling Stone*, 29 August 1985, 40–44, 74.

84 Diana Maychick, "Mel Gibson Unbuttoned," *Mademoiselle*, March 1987, 232.

85 Green, "The Dish from Down Under," 70–72.

86 Darcy, "Mel Gibson: Superstar . . . Super Dad!" 79.

87 "Mel Gibson: From Macho Man to Family Man," *Ladies' Home Journal*, August 1987, 72–73.

88 Green, "The Dish from Down Under," 75.

89 Sinyard, *Mel Gibson*, 8.

90 Maychick, "Mel Gibson Unbuttoned," 234.

91 James Oram, *Reluctant Star: The Mel Gibson Story* (London: Fontana, 1991), 120.

92 Darcy, "Mel Gibson: Superstar . . . Super Dad!" 114; Oram, *Reluctant Star*, 12.

93 "Interview with Mel Gibson," *Playboy*, July 1995, 51–56, 68, 136–42.

94 Wockner, "Mel Gibson's Anti-Gay History."

95 Sinyard, *Mel Gibson*, 10.

96 Wood, *Hollywood from Vietnam to Reagan*, 241.

97 Susan Jeffords, *Hard Bodies: Hollywood Masculinity in the Reagan Era* (New Brunswick, NJ: Rutgers University Press, 1994), 55. Notably, in the slightly more ideologically risky *Tequila Sunrise* (1988), Gibson portrays an ex-drug dealer who struggles to convince his friend and lover (Michele Pfeiffer) that he has seen the error of his ways, yet his integrity is ultimately secured when he rescues the lover from the clutches of his ex-employers.

98 In her illuminating analysis of the *Lethal Weapon* series, Tania Modleski notes the racist and nationalist implications of representing this torturer as an Asian man: "in this way the film manages to suggest a defeat of the Asian enemy

we were unable to accomplish twenty years ago." *Feminism without Women: Culture and Criticism in a "Postfeminist" Age* (New York: Routledge, 1991), 143.

99   Cynthia J. Fuchs, "The Buddy Politic," in *Screening the Male: Exploring Masculinities in Hollywood Cinema*, ed. Steven Cohan & Ina Rae Hark (New York: Routledge, 1993), 195–202.

100   Modleski, *Feminism without Women*, 142–44. Modleski also finds in *Lethal Weapon 2* homophobic references to the AIDS crisis, as Murtaugh's fellow police officers tease him about his daughter's appearance in a television commercial for condoms.

101   David Ansen, "Urban Rambo," *Newsweek*, 16 March 1987, 72.

102   Stuart Klawans, "Faster, Copycat! Kill! Kill!" *Village Voice*, 11 July 1989, 72.

103   David Ansen, "Gibson and Glover Return," *Newsweek*, 17 July 1989, 68.

104   Vito Russo, "A Critic Gets 'Bad,' Mad, and Just Plain Fed Up With Bigots and Spineless Gays," *The Advocate*, 5 June 1990, 60.

105   Peter Miller, "Touches of Misogyny, Homophobia, and a Visit to a Film Set," *New York Native*, 28 May 1990, 24.

106   Bob Satuloff, "Homophobia Goes to the Movies," *Christopher Street*, 25 May 1992, 13–17.

107   David Ansen, "Goodbye, Mr. Gibson," *Newsweek*, 30 August 1993, 52.

108   Jeff Cohen and Norman Solomon, "Why the Movie Industry Likes to Play It Straight," *The Seattle Times*, 16 October 1993, A13. See also Monica Yant, "Man Without a Homosexual Face," *Los Angeles Times*, 5 September 1993, Calendar Section, 28, in which *Face* press agent Lisa Callamaro explains that "the thought was: How do we get this movie made? One of those (concerns) was not to scare people off in terms of pedophilia and the gay community. Nobody wanted to offend the gay community, and none of us really felt that the sexuality had anything to do with the basic story."

109   Warren Johansson and William A. Percy, *Outing: Shattering the Conspiracy of Silence* (New York: Harrington Park Press, 1994), 139.

110   Johansson and Percy, *Outing*, 138, 175.

111   Michelangelo Signorile, *Queer in America: Sex, the Media, and the Closets of Power* (New York: Random House, 1993), 291.

112   For documentation of the Sissy Award, see Mark Lundgren, "Macho Mel Gibson is a Big Sissy," *The San Francisco Chronicle*, 15 June 1992, People section, Personals column, D3; see also James Warren, "Bashing Back: Gay and Lesbian Weekly Names Mel Gibson Its Sissy of the Year," *Chicago Tribune*, 25 June 1992, Tempo section, 2. The Chinese Theater protests are documented in the Press Association Newsfile, 24 August 1993.

113   "'Braveheart'—An Exercise in Dishonesty," *GLAAD Reports*, July–August 1995 [http://www.glaad.org:80/glaad/9507/dishonest-history.html], retrieved 14 February 1997.

114   "Los Angeles 'Braveheart' Demonstration Coverage," *GLAAD Reports*, July–

August 1995 [http://www.glaad.org:80/glaad/9507/braveheart-demo.html],
retrieved 14 February 1997.

115 "Interview with Mel Gibson," 140.

116 Johansson and Percy, *Outing*, 186.

FOUR *Keanu Reeves and the Fantasy of Pansexuality*

1 Amethyst [amethyst@nc5.infi.net], "Cunanan role offered to Keanu Reeves
—your opinions?", 1 August 1997, in [alt.fan.keanu-reeves.moderated], retrieved 12 August 1997.

2 Bgrinc, [bgrinc@ral.mindspring.com], "Re: Cunanan role offered to Keanu
Reeves—your opinions?", 1 August 1997, in [alt.fan.keanu-reeves.moderated],
retrieved 12 August 1997.

3 Mysti96501, [mysti96501@aol.com], "Re: Cunanan role offered to Keanu
Reeves—your opinions?", 5 August 1997, in [alt.fan.keanu-reeves.moderated],
retrieved 12 August 1997.

4 Kimbo, [rgreen@juno.com], "Re: Cunanan role offered to Keanu Reeves—
your opinions?", 5 August 1997, in [alt.fan.keanu-reeves.moderated], retrieved 12 August 1997. Reeves has since taken the role of serial killer (but *not*
one who pursues gay victims) in *The Watcher* (2000).

5 Dennis Cooper, "Keanu Reeves," *Interview*, September 1990, 134.

6 James Ryan & G. Luther Whitington, "Homophobia in Hollywood," *The
Advocate*, 26 March 1991, 32–41. The article includes a reprint of a *Variety* advertisement taken out by the Helmsdale Releasing Corporation in an attempt
to secure actors and studio backing for a production of *The Front Runner*, dispelling the myth that "if I play a gay role, I'll never work in this town again"
with a listing of over fifty well-known actors and actresses who have "survived" gay roles.

7 Steve Warren, "Van Sant Won't Gussy Up to His Own Private Art," *San Francisco Sentinel*, 10 October 1991, 39.

8 David Fox, "Gay Film Fest Loses Out on Four Films," *Los Angeles Times*,
9 July 1991.

9 Ryan and Whitington, "Homophobia in Hollywood," 40.

10 Jess Cagle, "America Sees Shades of Gay," *Entertainment Weekly*, 8 September
1995, 26.

11 Rene Rodriguez, "Hollywood is Catching Up with Gay Movies," *Austin-
American Statesman*, 18 August 1995, p. E5.

12 Cagle, "America Sees Shades of Gay," 22.

13 John Leland, "Bisexuality Emerges as a New Sexual Identity," *Newsweek*,
17 July 1995, 46.

14 Lynn Darling, "Bisexuality," *Harper's Bazaar*, June 1995, 136–38, 170, 172;
Robert S. Boynton, "Going Both Ways," *Vogue*, June 1995, 132, 143.

15 Cagle, "America Sees Shades of Gay," 24.

16 *The American Heritage College Dictionary*, 3rd ed. (New York: Houghton Mifflin Company, 1993), 50.

17 Leland, "Bisexuality Emerges as a New Sexual Identity," 50.

18 Darling, "Bisexuality," 138.

19 Marjorie Garber, *Vice Versa: Bisexuality and the Eroticism of Everyday Life* (New York: Touchstone, 1995), 140.

20 Lyle Slack, "Keanu's Excellent Adventure," *Maclean's*, 23 January 1995, 54.

21 *Keanu Reeves: A Tear-Out Photo Book* (London: Oliver Books, 1994).

22 "Keanu Reeves: Teen Idol's Excellent Adventure," *Biograph Presents: Hollywood's Hottest Hunks* 1.6 (New York: Biograph Communications, Inc., 1997), 75.

23 "Keanu Reeves: Teen Idol's Excellent Adventure," 70.

24 "Wedding Bells Aren't in Keanu's Future," *Press-Telegram*, 5 October 1995, People section, A2.

25 Lauren David Peden, "In Search of Keanu," *Mademoiselle*, March 1996, 110.

26 Nickson, *Keanu Reeves*, 5.

27 "The 50 Most Beautiful People in the World," *People*, 8 May 1995.

28 "Keanu Reeves: Teen Idol's Excellent Adventure," 74.

29 David Ansen, "Turning Shakespearean Tricks," *Newsweek*, 7 October 1991, 66; John Simon, "Review of *My Own Private Idaho*," *National Review*, 2 December 1991, 61.

30 David Denby, "A Fine Mess," *New York*, 7 October 1991, 80.

31 John Simon, "Polished Thriller, Polish Joke," *National Review*, 11 July 1994, 62.

32 David Denby, "The Boys and the Bus," *New York*, 13 June 1994, 82.

33 Nickson, *Keanu Reeves*, 156.

34 Peter Travers, "Movies Die Hard on a Bus," *Rolling Stone*, 30 June 1994, 80.

35 David Ansen, "Goodbye, Airhead," *Newsweek*, 13 June 1994, 53.

36 Natasha Stoynoff, Karen Brailsford, and Kristina Johnson, "A Most Excellent Enigma," *People*, 11 July 1994, 49.

37 Stanley Kauffmann, "Thrills and Chills," *New Republic*, 4 July 1994, 26.

38 Simon, "Polished Thriller, Polish Joke," 62.

39 Slack, "Keanu's Excellent Adventure," 54.

40 Nickson, *Keanu Reeves*, 2.

41 Tim Allis, "Keanu Sets the Record Straight," *Out*, July–August 1995, 116. The following discussion of narcissism and image construction borrows heavily from a prior work on Reeves in "Gay Male Spectatorship and Keanu Reeves," *Pictures of a Generation on Hold: Selected Papers*, ed. Murray Pomerance and John Sakeris (Toronto: Media Studies Working Group, 1996), 14.

42 Kristine McKenna, "Keanu's Eccentric Adventure," *Los Angeles Times*, 5 June 1994, Calendar section, 3. For more about Professor Prima's course, see "Keanu Reeves in Theory," *New Yorker*, 21 March 1994, 58.

43 Keanu Reeves: A Tear-Out Photo Book, 3.

44 Liz Smith, "Reeves' Weighty Decision," Los Angeles Times, 5 June 1996.

45 Jane Armstrong, Laurel, NJ, "Letters to Editor," Vanity Fair, October 1995.

46 Nickson, Keanu Reeves, 5.

47 Tom Green, "Built for 'Speed'/Keanu Reeves, Catching a Bus to the Big Time/Former Dude Is a Dynamo in Demand," USA Today, 9 June 1994, Life section, 1D; Carrie Rickey, "The Importance of Being Keanu: The Heart-throb of 'Speed' Talks about His Transformation from Airhead to Man of Action," Chicago Tribune, 26 June 1994, Entertainment section, 16.

48 a.fan, 16 February 1996, in [alt.fan.keanu-reeves], retrieved 18 March 1996.

49 a.fan, 20 February 1996, in [alt.fan.keanu-reeves], retrieved 18 March 1996.

50 John H. Richardson, "Yearning for Keanu," Premiere, March 1996, 58–65, 96–97.

51 Dennis Cooper, "Keanu Reeves," Interview, September 1990, 136.

52 Richardson, "Yearning for Keanu," 97.

53 Cooper, "Keanu Reeves," 134.

54 Angela Holden, "Blissed Out, Switched On Perfect Body: What Makes Keanu Reeves Not Just a Movie Star but a Total Babe?" The Independent, 19 September 1994, Living Page, 22.

55 "The Society for Keanu Consciousness," The Society for Keanu Consciousness [http://www.empirenet.com/~rdaelcy/skc/index.html], retrieved 21 August 1997.

56 Tom Shone suggests that "not since Arnold Schwarzenegger agreed to go looking for his brain in Total Recall has an actor submitted to so cruelly masochistic a piece of casting." See "Not a Brain in That Pretty Head," The Sunday Times (London), 11 February 1996. On the other hand, Manohla Dargis is closer to the spirit of the Society for Keanu Consciousness in her assessment of the casting of Reeves: "Keanu Reeves will be skewered for Johnny Mnemonic. . . . It isn't his fault. Not only are the film's numerous failings not due to him, he's one of the few real excuses to see it at all. . . . Johnny's a blank slate, which makes the decision to cast Reeves just about as brilliant as Bertolucci's choice of him as Buddha. . . . Other reasons to meditate on Reeves as Johnny are his strange, sepulchral voice, body language that invokes wrenching figures from Long's great early '80s paintings, and a modified flat-top that could snare him a spot in the pantheon of Chester Gould. Then there's the timing—consistently off the beat, Reeves puts out rhythms that punctuate the film's flatness. If this were a film by Godard it might be Brechtian; as it is, it's simply Keanu." See her review in L.A. Weekly, 26 May 1995, 35.

57 "Keanumandu," The Society for Keanu Consciousness [http://www.empirenet.com/~rdaeley/skc/keanumandu.html], retrieved 21 August 1997.

58 Carrie Rickey, "Call It the Cult of Keanu Reeves—Toronto Actor Is Speeding Away from Adolescence at a Record Clip," The Toronto Star, 13 June 1994, F1.

59 Rickey, "The Importance of Being Keanu," 16.

60 "Keanu Reeves: Teen Idol's Excellent Adventure," 70.

61 "Keanu Reeves: Teen Idol's Excellent Adventure," 71. Nickson (34–35) points out the irony of the suggested name change in light of the fact that "Keanu," as a Hawaiian name, was hardly exotic or un-American to begin with.

62 Holden, "Blissed Out," 22.

63 James Kaplan, "Why Keanu Reeves Won't Sell His Soul," *Premiere*, September 1997, 64–69, 99.

64 Holden, "Blissed Out," 22.

65 "The 50 Most Beautiful People in the World," *People*, 8 May 1995.

66 Caro, in [alt.fan.keanu-reeves], retrieved 4 May 1996.

67 Eileen Daspin, "Big Keanu," *W*, July 1994.

68 Nickson, *Keanu Reeves*, 192.

69 Rickey, "The Importance of Being Keanu," 16.

70 John Simon describes Scott as "a rich bisexual son in the hustler's life for a lark." See his review of the film in *National Review*, 2 December 1991, 61. James Kaplan similarly describes Scott as "the ne'er-do-well bisexual son of Portland's mayor" ("Why Keanu Reeves Won't Sell His Soul," 69).

71 "Questions and Answers," *The Society for Keanu Consciousness* [http://www.empirenet.com/~rdaeley/skc/index.html], retrieved 21 August 1997.

72 Theron [theron@pobox.com], in [alt.fan.keanu-reeves], retrieved 16 February 1996.

73 Such a debate did indeed arise on [alt.fan.keanu-reeves] in February of 1996.

74 David Migcovsky [dmigcov@interlog.com], in [alt.fan.keanu-reeves], retrieved 15 February 1996.

75 Allis, "Keanu Sets the Record Straight," 117.

76 Daspin, "Big Keanu."

77 Ray Hunter [cobraman@bellsouth.net], "Re: Keanu's Sexuality," 12 August 1997, in [alt.fan.keanu-reeves], retrieved 18 August 1997.

78 Theron, [theron@pobox.com], "Re: Keanu's Sexuality," 15 August 1997, in [alt.fan.keanu-reeves], retrieved 18 August 1997.

79 For both sides of this debate in the context of "bisexuality," see Ara Wilson, "Just Add Water: Searching for the Bisexual Politic," *OutLook* 16 (Spring 1992): 22–28; and in the same issue, Carol A. Queen, "Strangers at Home: Bisexuals in the Queer Movement," 23, 29–33.

80 Allis, "Keanu Sets the Record Straight," 116.

81 Michael Shnayerson, "Young and Restless," *Vanity Fair*, August 1995, 146.

82 Teresa deLauretis, *The Practice of Love: Lesbian Sexuality and Perverse Desire* (Bloomington: Indiana University Press, 1994), 129.

83 Judith Butler, *Bodies that Matter: On the Discursive Limits of "Sex"* (New York: Routledge, 1993), 115–16.

84 "Is Keanu Gay?" *KeanuNet* [http://www.users.interport.net/~eperkins.gay.

html], retrieved 17 January 1996. The current address of the website is [http://www.keanunet.com/gay.html].

85 Bob Satuloff, "Male Movie Sexpots: Can Straight Men Take the Heat?" *New York Native*, 9 September 1991, 29.

86 Nickson, *Keanu Reeves*, 26.

87 Cooper, "Keanu Reeves," 134.

88 Cooper, "Keanu Reeves," 134. I observed another instance of gay appropriation at the sing-along gay bar Marie's Crisis Cafe in Greenwich Village in 1998, where patrons sang a rendition of a well-known *Oklahoma* classic, changing the refrain to "They call the wind Keanu."

89 Paul Burston, "My Own Private Keanu," in *What Are You Looking At?* (London: Cassell, 1995), 32.

90 "Queer Planet Idols," *Queer Planet* [http://www.webcom.com/austin/QPlanet/entertainment/idols.html], retrieved 21 August 1997.

91 Allis, "Keanu Sets the Record Straight," 117.

92 Rickey, "The Importance of Being Keanu," 16.

93 John Patrick, "Wishful Rumors: Keanu Reeves, Etc.," in *The Best of the Superstars 1996: The Year in Sex* (Sarasota, FL: STARBooks Press, 1996), 14.

94 Satuloff, "Male Movie Sexpots: Can Straight Men Take the Heat?" 28.

95 Bob Satuloff, "How to Hang Ten In a Closet," *New York Native*, 22 July 1991, 28–29.

96 Burston, "My Own Private Keanu," 34.

97 The following discussion of *Speed* borrows from my previous analysis of the film in "Gay Male Spectatorship and Keanu Reeves," in *Pictures of a Generation on Hold: Selected Papers*, ed. Murray Pomerance and John Sakeris (Toronto: Media Studies Working Group, 1996), 14–18.

98 Burston, "My Own Private Keanu," 35.

99 Michael Bronski, "Underground Like a Wild Potato," *Gay Community News*, 27 October 1991, 16.

100 Belissa Cohen, "LA Deeda," *L. A. Weekly*, 18 October 1991.

101 Bronski, "Underground Like a Wild Potato," 10.

102 Burston, "My Own Private Keanu," 34.

103 John Mandes, " 'Idaho' Stalks Hustlers' Reality With Precision," *Philadelphia Gay News*, 18–24 October 1991, 25.

104 Steve Warren, "Private Idaho Goes Public," *San Francisco Sentinel*, 10 October 1991, 38.

105 Bruce Vilanch, "Wishful Rumoring," *The Advocate*, 7 March 1995, 67.

106 Nickson, *Keanu Reeves*, 26.

107 Brian J. Robb, *River Phoenix: A Short Life* (New York: Harper Collins, 1994), 110.

108 Nickson, *Keanu Reeves*, 111.

109 Critical accounts note the various ways in which the narrative is structured as

a search for the mother. Donald Lyons suggests that "Van Sant has reanimated the tired tropes of the road movie by giving them a wholly new meaning—the road as Whitmanesque/Twainesque ribbon leading to a never-perhaps-attainable unity with the author (mother?) of being." See "Gus Van Sant," *Film Comment* (September–October 1991): 6–12. Harvey R. Greenberg notes that "the 'fucked-up' roadface [which Mike sees in an Idaho landscape before one narcoleptic episode] prefigures the maternal breast engraved on Mike's shattered psyche as an ambivalent source of raw reflection and endless replenishment. In a trance, he falls literally into his mother's arms—the salmon, leaping toward home, another image of her recuperation—before his oneiric idyll crashes around him, and he awakens into the sordid bliss of the climax he's just sold." See his review of the film in *Film Quarterly* 46.1 (Fall 1992): 23–25.

110 Robert Lang, "My Own Private Idaho and the New Queer Road Movies," in *The Road Movie Book*, eds. Steven Cohan and Ina Rae Hark (New York: Routledge, 1997), 343.

111 David Ehrenstein, "Talking Pictures," *The Advocate*, 24 September 1991, 85.

112 Allis, "Keanu Sets the Record Straight," 65.

113 Warren, "Van Sant Won't Gussy Up to His Own Private Art," 39.

114 "Keanu Reeves: Teen Idol's Excellent Adventure," 75.

115 "Keanu Reeves' Hot Secret Dates with Cheers Beauty," *Star*, 21 November 1995, 31.

116 "Johnny Mnemonic Hunk Keanu Blasts Back at Gay Slur," *Star*, 31 June 1995, 15.

117 Dana Kennedy, "Can Gay Stars Shine?" *Entertainment Weekly*, 8 September 1995, 36.

118 Patrick, "Wishful Rumors," 16.

119 Billy Masters, "Filth," *Gay Chicago Magazine*, 8–18 August 1996, 54.

120 Billy Masters, "Filth," *Gay Chicago Magazine*, 20 February–2 March 1997), 48.

121 David Ehrenstein, *Open Secret: Gay Hollywood 1928–1998* (New York: William Morrow and Company, Inc., 1998), 197.

122 Patrick, "Wishful Rumors," 15.

123 Vilanch, "Wishful Rumoring," 67.

124 Ehrenstein, *Open Secret*, 197.

125 Quoted in Patrick, "Wishful Rumors," 17.

126 A. J. Benza, "So . . . Hollywood," *Take One*, 6 June 1997 [http://www.roughcut.com.take1/so_hollywood_97jun1.html], retrieved 10 August 1997.

127 Larry Perovic, "Keanu's Hot Hollywood Adventure," 1995 [www.trashfish.com/cr/keanu.txt], 1995, retrieved 1 August 1997.

128 Henry Jenkins, "'Welcome to Bisexuality, Captain Kirk': Slash and the Fan-Writing Community," *Textual Poachers: Television Fans & Participatory Culture* (New York: Routledge, 1992), 185–222.

129 Constance Penley, "Feminism, Psychoanalysis, and the Study of Popular Culture," in *Cultural Studies*, eds. Lawrence Grossberg, Cary Nelson, and Paula Treichler (New York: Routledge, 1992).

Afterword

1 Peter Galvin, "Selleck Speaks Out," *The Advocate*, 16 September 1997, 30.

Scholarly Works and Government Publications

Altman, Dennis. *The Homosexualization of America, The Americanization of the Homosexual*. New York: St. Martin's Press, 1982.

Babuscio, Jack. "James Dean—A Gay Riddle." *Gay News* 79 (1975): 17–18.

Becker, Howard S. *Outsiders: Studies in the Sociology of Deviance*. London: Free Press of Glencoe, 1963.

Biskind, Peter. *Seeing is Believing*. New York: Random House, 1981.

Burston, Paul. "My Own Private Keanu." In *What Are You Looking At?* London: Cassell, 1995.

Brooks, Peter. "The Melodramatic Imagination." In *Imitations of Life: A Reader on Film & Television Melodrama*, ed. Marcia Landy, 50–67. Detroit: Wayne State University Press, 1991.

Butler, Judith. *Gender Trouble: Feminism and the Subversion of Identity*. New York: Routledge, 1990.

———. *Bodies That Matter: On the Discursive Limits of 'Sex.'* New York: Routledge, 1993.

Cohan, Steven. *Masked Men: Masculinity and the Movies in the Fifties*. Bloomington, IN: Indiana University Press, 1997.

Corber, Robert. *In the Name of National Security: Hitchcock, Homophobia, and the Political Construction of Gender in Postwar America*. Durham, NC: Duke University Press, 1993.

———. *Homosexuality in Cold War America: Resistance and the Crisis of Masculinity.* Durham, NC: Duke University Press, 1997.

Corliss, Richard. "The Legion of Decency." *Film Comment* 4, no. 4 (Summer 1968): 24–61.

Cory, Donald Webster. *The Homosexual in America: A Subjective Approach.* New York: Greenberg, 1951.

Cowie, Elizabeth. *Representing the Woman: Cinema and Psychoanalysis.* Minneapolis: University of Minnesota Press, 1997.

DeAngelis, Michael. "Gay Male Spectatorship and Keanu Reeves." In *Pictures of a Generation on Hold: Selected Papers*, ed. Murray Pomerance and John Sakeris, 11–19. Toronto: Media Studies Working Group, 1996.

de Certeau, Michel. *The Practice of Everyday Life.* Berkeley: University of California Press, 1984.

de Lauretis, Teresa. *The Practice of Love: Lesbian Sexuality and Perverse Desire.* Bloomington, IN: Indiana University Press, 1994.

d'Emilio, John. *Sexual Politics, Sexual Communities.* Chicago: University of Chicago Press, 1983.

———. *Making Trouble: Essays on Gay History, Politics, and the University.* New York: Routledge, 1992.

d'Emilio, John, and Estelle B. Freedman. *Intimate Matters: A History of Sexuality in America.* New York: Harper & Row, 1988.

Desjardins, Mary. "*Meeting Two Queens:* Feminist Film-making, Identity Politics, and the Melodramatic Fantasy." *Film Quarterly* 48, no. 3 (Spring 1995): 26–33.

Dollimore, Jonathan. *Sexual Dissidence: Augustine to Wilde, Freud to Foucault.* New York: Oxford University Press, 1991.

Doty, Alexander. *Making Things Perfectly Queer: Interpreting Mass Culture.* Minneapolis: University of Minnesota Press, 1993.

Dyer, Richard. *Stars.* London: BFI Publishing, 1979.

———. *Heavenly Bodies: Film Stars and Society.* London: BFI Publishing, 1986.

———. *Now You See It: Studies on Lesbian and Gay Film.* London: Routledge, 1990.

———. "*A Star Is Born* and the Construction of Authenticity." In *Stardom: Industry of Desire*, ed. Christine Gledhill, 32–40. New York: Routledge, 1991.

Ehrenreich, Barbara. *The Hearts of Men: American Dreams and the Flight from Commitment.* New York: Anchor Press, 1983.

Ehrenstein, David. *Open Secret: Gay Hollywood, 1928–1998.* New York: William Morrow and Company, Inc., 1998.

Foucault, Michel. *The History of Sexuality, Volume 1: An Introduction.* New York: Vintage Books, 1990.

Fuchs, Cynthia J. "The Buddy Politic." In *Screening the Male: Exploring Masculinities in Hollywood Cinema*, ed. Steven Cohan and Ina Rae Hark, 194–210. New York: Routledge, 1993.

Gamson, Joshua. *Claims to Fame: Celebrity in Contemporary America.* Berkeley: University of California Press, 1994.

Garber, Marjorie. *Vice Versa: Bisexuality and the Eroticism of Everyday Life.* New York: Touchstone, 1995.

Gilbert, James. *A Cycle of Outrage: America's Reaction to the Juvenile Delinquent of the 1950s.* New York: Oxford University Press, 1986.

Gledhill, Christine. "Signs of Melodrama." In *Stardom: Industry of Desire,* ed. Christine Gledhill, 207-29. New York: Routledge, 1991.

Greenberg, David F. *The Construction of Homosexuality.* Chicago: University of Chicago Press, 1988.

Hall, Stuart. "Encoding/Decoding." In *Culture, Media, Language: Working Papers in Cultural Studies,* ed. Stuart Hall, Dorothy Hobson, Andrew Loew, and Paul Willis. London: Hutchinson, 1980.

Harris, Daniel. *The Rise and Fall of Gay Culture.* New York: Hyperion, 1997.

Hofstede, David. *James Dean: A Bio-Bibliography.* Westport, CT: Greenwood Press, 1996.

Jeffords, Susan. *Hard Bodies: Hollywood Masculinity in the Reagan Era.* New Brunswick, NJ: Rutgers University Press, 1994.

Jenkins, Henry. *Textual Poachers: Television Fans and Participatory Culture.* New York: Routledge, 1992.

Johansson, Warren, and William A. Percy. *Outing: Shattering the Conspiracy of Silence.* New York: Harrington Park Press, 1994.

Klinger, Barbara. *Melodrama and Meaning: History, Culture, and the Films of Douglas Sirk.* Bloomington, IN: Indiana University Press, 1994.

Lang, Robert. "My Own Private Idaho and the New Queer Road Movies." In *The Road Movie Book,* eds. Steven Cohan and Ina Rae Hark. New York: Routledge, 330-48.

Laplanche, Jean, and J. P. Pontalis. *The Language of Psychoanalysis,* trans. Donald Nicholson-Smith. New York: W. W. Norton & Company, 1973.

May, Elaine Tyler. *Homeward Bound: American Families in the Cold War Era.* New York: Basic Books, 1988.

Miller, Neil. *Out of the Past: Gay and Lesbian History from 1869 to the Present.* New York: Vintage Books, 1995.

Modleski, Tania. *Feminism without Women: Culture and Criticism in a "Postfeminist" Age.* New York: Routledge, 1991.

Moretti, Franco. *Signs Taken for Wonders.* London: Verso, 1983.

Morin, Edgar. "The Case of James Dean." *Evergreen Review* 5 (1958): 5-12.

Neale, Steve. "Melodrama and Tears." *Screen* 27, no. 6 (November/December 1986): 6-22.

———. "Masculinity as Spectacle: Reflections on Men in Mainstream Cinema." In *Screening the Male: Exploring Masculinities in Hollywood Cinema,* ed. Steven Cohan and Ina Rae Hark, 9-20. New York: Routledge, 1993.

Noriega, Chon. "'SOMETHING'S MISSING HERE!': Homosexuality and Film Reviews during the Production Code Era, 1934–1962." *Cinema Journal* 30, no. 1 (Fall 1990): 20–41.

Nowell-Smith, Geoffrey. "Minnelli and Melodrama." In *Home Is Where the Heart Is: Studies in Melodrama and the Woman's Film*, ed. Christine Gledhill, 70–74. London: BFI Publishing, 1987.

Ovesey, Lionel. "The Homosexual Conflict: An Adaptational Analysis." *Psychiatry* 17 (1954): 243–50.

Penley, Constance. "Feminism, Psychoanalysis, and the Study of Popular Culture." In *Cultural Studies*, ed. Lawrence Grossberg, Cary Nelson, and Paula Treichler. New York: Routledge, 1992.

Rodowick, David. "Madness, Authority and Ideology: The Domestic Melodrama of the 1950s." In *Home Is Where the Heart Is: Studies in Melodrama and the Woman's Film*, ed. Christine Gledhill, 268–80. London: BFI Publishing, 1987.

Russo, Vito. *The Celluloid Closet*, 2d ed. New York: Harper & Row, 1987.

Schlesinger, Arthur. *The Vital Center: The Politics of Freedom*. Boston: Houghton Mifflin Co., 1949.

Sharrett, Christopher. "Myth, Male Fantasy, and Simulacra in Mad Max and The Road Warrior." *Journal of Popular Film and Television* 13, no. 2 (Summer 1985): 81–91.

Signorile, Michelangelo. *Queer in America: Sex, the Media, and the Closets of Power.* New York: Random House, 1993.

———. *Life Outside: The Signorile Report on Gay Men: Sex, Drugs, Muscles, and the Passages of Life*. New York: HarperCollins, 1997.

Sklar, Robert. *Movie-Made America: A Cultural History of the Movies*. New York: Vintage Books, 1975.

Stacey, Jackie. *Star Gazing: Hollywood Cinema and Female Spectatorship*. New York: Routledge, 1994.

Staiger, Janet. *Interpreting Films: Studies in the Historical Reception of American Cinema*. Princeton, NJ: Princeton University Press, 1992.

Stewart, Omer C., Ph.D. "Homosexuality Among the American Indians and Other Native Peoples of the World." *Mattachine Review* 6, no. 1 (January 1960): 9–12.

Suarez, Juan A. *Bike Boys, Drag Queens, and Superstars: Avant-Garde, Mass Culture, and Gay Identities in the 1960s Underground Cinema*. Bloomington, IN: Indiana University Press, 1996.

Tyler, Parker. *Screening the Sexes: Homosexuality in the Movies*. New York: Anchor Books, 1972.

U. S. Congress. Senate. Committee on Expenditures in Executive Departments, Employment of Homosexuals and Other Sex Perverts in Government. 81st Cong., 2nd sess., 1950. Quoted in John d'Emilio, *Sexual Politics, Sexual Communities*.

U. S. Congress. Senate. Subcommittee to Investigate Juvenile Delinquency of the Committee of the Judiciary. 84th Cong., 1st sess., 15 June 1955. Quoted in *Film Culture* 1 (Winter 1955): 14-16.

Watney, Simon. "Hollywood's Homosexual World." *Screen* 23, nos. 3-4 (November-December 1982): 107-22.

Waugh, Thomas. *Hard to Imagine: Gay Male Eroticism in Photography and Film from Their Beginnings to Stonewall.* New York: Columbia University Press, 1996.

Wertham, Fredric. *Seduction of the Innocent.* New York: Rinehart, 1954.

Williams, Linda. "Film Bodies: Gender, Genre, and Excess." *Film Quarterly* (Summer 1991): 2-13.

Wood, Robin. *Hollywood from Vietnam to Reagan.* New York: Columbia University Press, 1986.

Booklength Star Biographies

Alexander, Paul. *Boulevard of Broken Dreams: The Life, Times and Legend of James Dean.* New York: Penguin Books, 1994.

Anger, Kenneth. *Hollywood Babylon II.* New York: E. P. Dutton, Inc., 1984.

Bast, William. *James Dean: A Biography.* New York: Ballantine Books, 1956.

Dalton, David. *James Dean: The Mutant King.* New York: St. Martin's Press, 1974.

Gilmore, John. *The Real James Dean.* New York: Pyramid Books, 1975.

Herndon, Venable. *James Dean: A Short Life.* Garden City, NY: Doubleday, 1974.

Howlett, John. *James Dean: A Biography.* New York: Beaufort Books, 1975.

Keanu Reeves: A Tear-Out Photo Book. London: Oliver Books, 1994.

Marinetti, Ronald. *The James Dean Story: A Myth-Shattering Biography of an Icon.* New York: Birch Lane Press, 1995.

Nickson, Chris. *Keanu Reeves.* New York: St. Martin's Press, 1996.

Oram, James. *Reluctant Star: The Mel Gibson Story.* London: Fontana, 1991.

Perry, Roland. *Lethal Hero.* London: Oliver Books, 1993.

Ragan, David. *Mel Gibson.* New York: Dell, 1985.

Riese, Randall. *The Unabridged James Dean: His Life and Legacy from A to Z.* New York: Random House, 1991.

Robb, Brian J. *River Phoenix: A Short Life.* New York: HarperCollins, 1994.

———. *Keanu Reeves: An Excellent Adventure.* London: Plexus Publishing Limited, 1997.

Sinyard, Neil. *Mel Gibson.* New York: Crescent Books, 1992.

Spoto, Donald. *Rebel: The Life and Legend of James Dean.* New York: HarperCollins, 1996.

Archival Documents

Files on *East of Eden,* Warner Bros. Archives, Cinema-Television Library, University of Southern California, Los Angeles.

Files on *Giant*, Warner Bros. Archives, Cinema-Television Library, University of
    Southern California, Los Angeles.
Files on *Rebel Without a Cause*, Warner Bros. Archives, Cinema-Television Library,
    University of Southern California, Los Angeles.
Hedda Hopper Files, Special Collection, Margaret Herrick Library, Academy of
    Motion Picture Arts and Sciences, Los Angeles.
Personal File of James Dean, Margaret Herrick Library, Academy of Motion Pic-
    ture Arts and Sciences, Los Angeles.
Production Code Files, Special Collection, Margaret Herrick Library, Academy
    of Motion Picture Arts and Sciences, Los Angeles.

Magazine and Newspaper Articles, Film Reviews,
Editorials, and Published Letters

"The 50 Most Beautiful People in the World." *People*, 8 May 1995.
"The 1992 Sissy Awards." *The Advocate*, 30 June 1992, 37–42.
A. D., California. "Readers Write." *Mattachine Review* 3 (May–June 1955): 33–35.
Allis, Tim. "Keanu Sets the Record Straight." *Out*, July–August 1995, 64–65, 116–
    17.
Alpert, Hollis. "It's Dean, Dean, Dean." *Saturday Review*, 13 October 1956, 28–29.
Ansen, David. "Rock Tycoon." *Newsweek*, 31 July 1978, 40–47.
———. "The Incredible Hunks." *Newsweek*, 23 May 1983, 48–51.
———. "Urban Rambo." *Newsweek*, 16 March 1987, 72.
———. "Gibson and Glover Return." *Newsweek*, 17 July 1989, 68.
———. "Turning Shakespearean Tricks." *Newsweek*, 7 October 1991, 66.
———. "Goodbye, Mr. Gibson." *Newsweek*, 30 August 1993, 52.
———. "Goodbye, Airhead." *Newsweek*, 13 June 1994, 52–53.
Archer, Eugene. "Generation Without a Cause." *Film Culture* 2, no. 1 (1956): 18–
    21.
Archerd, Army. "Just for Variety." *Daily Variety*, 29 May 1996, 4.
Armstrong, Jane, Laurel, New Jersey. "Letters to Editor." *Vanity Fair*, October
    1995.
Ashenden, Larry. "Did Jimmy Dean Leave a Son?" *On the QT*, July 1957, 18–20,
    65.
Astrachan, Sam. "The New Lost Generation." *New Republic*, 4 February 1957, 17–
    18.
Attwood, William. "Why Does He Work So Hard?" *Look*, 4 March 1958, 71–75.
Bast, William. "There Was a Boy . . ." *Photoplay*, September 1955, 39–40, 98–100;
    Photoplay, October 1955, 49–51, 103–106; *Photoplay*, November 1955, 52, 107–
    10.
Bean, Robin. "Dean—Ten Years After." *Films and Filming* 12, no. 1 (October 1965):
    12–15.

Benson, Sheila. "Action on a Full Tank in 'Warrior.'" *Los Angeles Times*, 20 May 1982, 7–8.

Blythe, Nell. "Jimmy Dean Fights Back from the Grave." *Movie Life*, June 1956, 23–26, 67–69.

———. "The Untold Story of the Love Jimmy Lost." *Movie Life*, January 1957, 48–50, 64.

Bower, Helen. "Oscars Will Go to East of Eden." *Detroit Free Press*, 11 March 1955, 11.

Boynton, Robert S. "Going Both Ways." *Vogue*, June 1995, 132, 143.

Bronski, Michael. "Underground Like a Wild Potato." *Gay Community News*, 27 October 1991, 10, 16.

Bush, Larry. "The State of the Gay Union." *The Advocate*, 21 January 1982, 22–29, 74.

Cagle, Jess. "America Sees Shades of Gay." *Entertainment Weekly*, 8 September 1995, 20–31.

Callo, Jim. "Up from Down Under: Heartthrob Mel Gibson Lives Dangerously—But Only in the Movies." *People*, 14 February 1983, 99–102.

Cameron, Lou. "The Triumph and Tragedy of James Dean." In *James Dean Revealed!*, ed. David Dalton, 14–45. New York: Delta Books, 1991.

Canby, Vincent. "Post-Nuclear 'Road Warrior.'" *The New York Times*, 29 April 1982, C24.

Capen, Jeanne Balch. "The Strange Revival of James Dean." *The American Weekly*, 29 July 1956, 4, 6.

Carter, Lynne. "I Was A Friend of Jimmy Dean." *Rave*, January 1957, 30–35.

———. "I Learned About LOVE From Jimmy Dean." *Rave*, April 1957, 24, 27.

Cohen, Belissa. "LA Deeda." *L. A. Weekly*, 18 October 1991.

Cohen, Jeff, and Norman Solomon. "Why the Movie Industry Likes to Play It Straight." *The Seattle Times*, 16 October 1993, A13.

Cole, Clayton. "The Dean Myth." *Films and Filming* 3, no. 4 (1957): 17.

Condon, Mary Anne, Chicago. "Readers Inc." *Photoplay*, April 1957, 34.

Cooper, Dennis. "Keanu Reeves." *Interview*, September 1990, 132–37.

Corliss, Richard. "Apocalypse . . . Pow!" *Time*, 10 May 1982, 115.

Crowther, Bosley. "The Screen: 'East of Eden' Has Debut." *The New York Times*, 10 March 1955, 33.

———. "The Screen: Delinquency." *The New York Times*, 27 October 1955, 28.

———. "The Screen: Large Subject." *The New York Times*, 11 October 1956, 51.

Curtis, Quentin. "A Premise that Promises Too Much." *The Independent*, 2 October 1994, 27.

Dalton, David, ed. *James Dean Revealed!* New York: Delta Books, 1991.

Darcy, Elizabeth. "Mel Gibson: Superstar . . . Super Dad!" *McCall's*, January 1985, 79, 114.

Dargis, Manohla. Review of *Johnny Mnemonic*. *L. A. Weekly*, 26 May 1995, 35.

Darling, Lynn. "Bisexuality." *Harper's Bazaar,* June 1995, 136–138, 170, 172.

Daspin, Eileen. "Big Keanu." *W,* July 1994.

"Dean of the One-Shotters." *Time,* 3 September 1956, 54–55.

"Death Premonition By Dean Recalled." *Los Angeles Times,* 2 October 1955.

DeKolbe, Robert. "James Dean Speaks from the Grave." In *James Dean Revealed!,* ed. David Dalton, 138–43. New York: Delta Books, 1991.

Denby, David. "A Fine Mess." *New York,* 7 October 1991, 79–80.

———. "The Boys and the Bus." *New York,* 13 June 1994, 82.

DeNiro, Madison, Vancouver. "Letters to the Editor." *The Advocate,* 1 April 1997, 6, 8.

"Department of Fleeting Fame." *Los Angeles Mirror,* 26 January 1961.

Eady, Brenda. "Unforgettable Faces of Our Time." *People,* 31 April 1993.

"East of Eden." *Variety,* 16 February 1955.

Ehrenstein, David. "Talking Pictures." *The Advocate,* 24 September 1991, 85.

Emerson, Ken. "The Village People: America's Male Ideal." *Rolling Stone,* 5 October 1978, 26–30.

Fox, David. "Gay Film Fest Loses Out on Four Films." *Los Angeles Times,* 9 July 1991.

Frutkin, Alan. "Gibson Straight Up." *The Advocate,* 4 March 1997, 43–44.

Galvin, Peter. "Selleck Speaks Out." *The Advocate,* 16 September 1997, 30.

"Gays: A Major Force in the Marketplace." *Business Week,* 3 September 1979, 118–120.

"Gays on the March." *Time,* 8 September 1975, 32–43.

"The Gay World's Leather Fringe: Do Homosexual Males Consciously Seek Danger?" *Time,* 24 March 1980, 74–75.

Gelman, David. "'Gays' and the Press." *Newsweek,* 20 October 1975, 93–94.

"Giant." *Variety,* 10 October 1956, 6.

Gilmore, John. "I Had Sex With James Dean!" *The Hollywood Star Reporter,* 1980, 15–20.

Goldstein, Richard. "S&M: The Dark Side of Gay Liberation." *Village Voice,* 7 July 1975, 10–13.

"Gossip in Gotham." *New York Journal-American,* 11 August 1995, 11.

Green, Michelle. "The Dish from Down Under." *People,* 4 February 1985, 70–76.

Green, Tom. "Built for 'Speed'/Keanu Reeves, Catching a Bus to the Big Time/ Former Dude Is a Dynamo in Demand." *USA Today,* 9 June 1994, Life section, 1D.

Greenberg, Harvey R. Review of *My Own Private Idaho. Film Quarterly* 46, no. 1 (Fall 1992): 23–25.

Harron, Mary. "Picture that Majors on Motion." *The Independent,* 9 October 1994, Sunday Review section, 21.

Haskell, Molly. "J. C. Enterprises, Inc." *Saturday Review,* 30 October 1971, 65–67, 82.

Hatch, Robert. Review of *Giant*. *The Nation*, 20 October 1956, 334.

Highwater, Jamake. "Dancing in the Seventies." *Horizon*, May 1977, 30–33.

Holden, Angela. "Blissed Out, Switched On Perfect Body: What Makes Keanu Reeves Not Just a Movie Star but a Total Babe?" *The Independent*, 19 September 1994, 22.

"Hollywood Can Wait." *Newsweek*, 31 May 1982, 67.

"The Homosexual: Newly Visible, Newly Understood." *Time*, 31 October 1969, 56, 61–67.

Hopper, Hedda. "Keep Your Eye on James Dean." *Chicago Tribune*, 27 March 1995, Magazine section, 40.

"How Gay Is Gay?" *Time*, 23 April 1979, 72–78.

Hunt, Evelyn. "To James Dean." *Photoplay*, January 1956, 50–51.

———. "So Little Time (To James Dean)." *Photoplay*, June 1956, 32.

"In Memory of James Dean." *The Fairmount News*, Special Edition, 7 October 1955.

"Interview with Mel Gibson." *Playboy*, July 1995, 51–56, 68, 136–42.

Ireland, Doug. "The New Homophobia: Open Season on Gays." *The Nation*, 15 September 1979, 207–210.

Jahr, Cliff. "James Dean Was Dylan and Maybe Garbo Too." *Village Voice*, 6 November 1975, 124.

"James Dean's Fans Still Write to Him." *Los Angeles Mirror*, 30 September 1960, Part II, 2.

"Johnny Mnemonic Hunk Keanu Reeves Blasts Back at Gay Slur." *Star*, 31 June 1995, 15.

Johnson, Harry. "And a Red too. . . ." *One* 1, no. 9 (September 1953): 2–3.

Kaplan, James. "Why Keanu Reeves Won't Sell His Soul." *Premiere*, September 1997, 64–69, 99.

Kass, Robert. Review of *East of Eden*. *Catholic World*, April 1955, 60–61.

Kauffmann, Stanley. "Thrills and Chills." *New Republic*, 4 July 1994, 26.

"Kazan's Steinbeck." *Newsweek*, 7 March 1955, 90–91.

"Keanu Reeves' Hot Secret Dates with Cheers Beauty." *Star*, 21 November 1995, 31.

"Keanu Reeves in Theory." *New Yorker*, 21 March 1994, 58.

"Keanu Reeves: Teen Idol's Excellent Adventure." In *Biograph Presents: Hollywood's Hottest Hunks*, vol.1, no. 6 (New York: Biograph Communications, Inc., 1997), 68–81.

Kennedy, Dana. "Can Gay Stars Shine?" *Entertainment Weekly*, 8 September 1995, 32–36.

Klawans, Stuart. "Faster, Copycat! Kill! Kill!" *Village Voice*, 11 July 1989, 72.

Knight, Arthur. Review of *Rebel Without a Cause*. *Saturday Review*, November 1955, 29.

Korman, Seymour. "The Last Hours of James Dean." *Chicago Tribune*, 6 February 1956.

Kornbluth, Jesse. "Merchandising Disco for the Masses." *The New York Times*, 18 February 1979, Sunday Magazine section, 18, 21–24, 44–45.

Krell, Arthur B. "We Need a Great Literature." *One* 2, no. 5 (May 1954): 19–23.

Kriebel, Charles. "Editor's Update." *After Dark*, May 1980, 10.

———. "Editor's Update." *After Dark*, July 1980, 8.

La Valley, Al. "Out of the Closet and on to the Screen." *American Film* 7, no. 10 (1982): 57–81.

Leland, John. "Bisexuality Emerges as a New Sexual Identity." *Newsweek*, 17 July 1995, 44–50.

Leonard, George B., Jr. "The American Male: Why Is He Afraid to be Different?" *Look*, 18 February 1958, 95–105.

Loder, Kurt. "The Heroes of Thunderdome: On the Road with Mad Max." *Rolling Stone*, 29 August 1985, 40–44, 74.

Lombardi, John. "Selling Gays to the Masses." *Village Voice*, 30 June 1975, 10–11.

Lundgren, Mark. "Macho Mel Gibson Is a Big Sissy." *The San Francisco Chronicle*, 15 June 1992, People section, D3.

Lyons, Donald. "Gus Van Sant." *Film Comment*, September–October 1991, 6–12.

Mandes, John. "'Idaho' Stalks Hustlers' Reality With Precision." *Philadelphia Gay News*, 18–24 October 1991, 4, 25.

"A Man to Whom the Angels Flock." *Fortune*, June 1977, 44.

Marlowe, Derek. "Soliloquy on James Dean's Forty-Fifth Birthday." *New York*, 8 November 1976, 41–46.

Masters, Billy. "Filth." *Gay Chicago Magazine*, 8–18 August 1996, 54–55.

———. "Filth." *Gay Chicago Magazine*, 20 February–2 March 1997, 48–49.

Maychick, Diana. "Mel Gibson Unbuttoned." *Mademoiselle*, March 1987, 232–34.

McCarten, John. "Steinbeck, Lay that Bible Down." *New Yorker*, March 1955, 140–41.

———. "Southwestern Primitives." *New Yorker*, 20 October 1956, 178–79.

McKenna, Kristine. "Keanu's Eccentric Adventure." *Los Angeles Times*, 5 June 1994, Calendar section, 3.

McVey, Douglas. "Rebel Without a Cause." *Films and Filming*, August 1977, 16–24.

Mead, Taylor. "The Movies Are a Revolution." *Film Culture* 29 (Summer 1964): 9.

"Mel Gibson: From Macho Man to Family Man." *Ladies' Home Journal*, August 1987, 72–74.

Michener, Charles. "'Shane' in Black Leather." *Newsweek*, 31 May 1982, 67, 70.

Miller, Peter. "Touches of Misogyny, Homophobia, and a Visit to a Film Set." *New York Native*, 28 May 1990, 24.

Mills, Joseph. "Can You Forgive Them?" *Gay Times*, March 1994, 36–40.

Mishkin, Leo. "'Rebel' Has Share of Merit: Mainly a Monument to Dean." *The Morning Telegraph*, 27 October 1955, 3.

Moskin, Robert J. "The American Male: Why Do Women Dominate Him?" *Look*, 4 February 1958, 77–80.

Montgomery, Clifton. "Taxis, Tokens, and Quick Takes at the Movies." *The Advocate*, 21 January 1982, 45, 47.

———. "Film Ticket." *The Advocate*, 8 July 1982, 45.

"Moody New Star." *Life*, 7 March 1955, 125–28.

Moore, Richard. "Lone Wolf." *Modern Screen*, August 1955, 28–29, 75.

"A Moving Performance." *Newsweek*, 7 November 1955, 117.

"The New Pictures." *Time*, 22 October 1956, 108, 110.

Nielsen, Evelyn Washburn. "The Truth About James Dean." *Chicago Tribune*, 9 September 1956, Sunday Magazine section, 22–23, 48–49.

O'Toole, Lawrence. "Gay Style." *Maclean's*, 18 February 1980, 41–47.

Parsons, Louella. "Hollywood is Talking About . . ." *Los Angeles Examiner*, 15 May 1955, sec. 5, 9.

Patrick, John. "Wishful Rumors: Keanu Reeves, Etc." In *The Best of the Superstars 1996: The Year in Sex*. Sarasota, FL: STARBooks Press, 1996.

Peden, Lauren David. "In Search of Keanu." *Mademoiselle*, March 1996, 108, 110.

Pedersen, Lyn. "The Importance of Being Different." *One* 2, no. 3 (March 1954): 4–6.

Phipps, Courtland. Review of *Rebel Without a Cause*. *Films in Review* 6, no. 9 (1955): 467–68.

———. Review of *Giant*. *Films in Review* 7, no. 9 (1956): 466–67.

P. R., Texas. "Readers Write." *Mattachine Review* 4 (July–August 1955): 34–35.

Queen, Carol A. "Strangers at Home: Bisexuals in the Queer Movement." *Outlook* 16 (Spring 1992): 23, 29–33.

Radcliffe, E. B. "A Best Ten Study of Pride and Envy." *The Cincinnati Enquirer*, 15 April 1955.

Raleigh, Joel. "The Girl James Dean Was Going to Marry!" *Lowdown*, May 1957, 16–17, 62–64.

Rau, Neil. "The Fight Was for Blood —and They Got it." *Los Angeles Examiner*, 22 May 1955, 15.

"Readers Inc." Letter from Evelyn Hunt to the editor. *Photoplay*, June 1956, 32; *Photoplay*, January 1957, 8; *Photoplay*, April 1957, 34.

"'Rebel Without a Cause' at Astor." *New York Post*, 27 October 1955, 41.

Richardson, John H. "Yearning for Keanu." *Premiere*, March 1996, 58–65, 96–97.

Rickey, Carrie. "The Importance of Being Keanu: The Heartthrob of 'Speed' Talks about His Transformation from Airhead to Man of Action." *Chicago Tribune*, 26 June 1994, Arts section, 16.

———. "Call It the Cult of Keanu: Toronto Actor is Speeding Away from Adolescence at a Record Clip." *The Toronto Star*, 13 June 1994, Entertainment section, p. F4.

Rodriguez, Rene. "Hollywood Is Catching Up with Gay Movies." *Austin-American Statesman*, 18 August 1994, E5.

Rogow, Lee. "Essay for Elia." *Saturday Review*, 19 March 1955, 25.

Roller, Alfred C. "The James Dean Myth Blows Up." *World Telegram and Sun Saturday Magazine*, 3 November 1956.

Russo, Vito. "The Celluloid Closet: Silver Screen Sin." *After Dark*, August–September 1981, 40–42.

———. "A Critic Gets 'Bad,' Mad, and Just Plain Fed Up With Bigots and Spineless Gays." *The Advocate*, 4 June 1990, 60.

Ryan, James, and G. Luther Whitington. "Homophobia in Hollywood." *The Advocate*, 26 March 1991, 32–41.

Sarris, Andrew. *East of Eden. Film Culture* 1, no. 3 (1955): 24.

———. *Giant. Film Culture* 2, no. 4 (1956): 23–24.

Satuloff, Bob. "Male Movie Sexpots: Can Straight Men Take the Heat?" *New York Native*, 9 September 1991, 28–29.

———. "Homophobia Goes to the Movies." *Christopher Street*, 25 May 1992, 13–17.

Schaeffer, Sam. "James Dean's Black Madonna." *Whisper*, February 1956, 12–16.

———. "James Dean—The Ghost Driver of Polonio Pass." *Whisper*, December 1957, 8–11, 57.

Scheuer, Philip K. "James Dean Cheats Car Death in Bit of Film Irony." *Los Angeles Times*, 30 October 1955, Part IV, 2.

Schnayerson, Michael. "Young and Restless." *Vanity Fair*, August 1995, 94–100, 146–48.

Schwartz, Tony. "Stigwood's Midas Touch." *Newsweek*, 23 January 1978, 40, 50.

Scullin, George. "James Dean: The Legend and the Facts." *Look*, 16 October 1956, 120–28.

Shapiro, Susan. "Sex Onscreen: Explicit, Yes; Erotic, Rarely." *After Dark*, July 1980, 41, 46.

Shone, Tom. "Not a Brain in That Pretty Head." *The Sunday Times* (London), 11 February 1996.

Simon, John. Review of *My Own Private Idaho. National Review*, 2 December 1991, 61.

———. "Polished Thriller, Polish Joke." *National Review*, 11 July 1994, 62.

Skolsky, Sidney. "Demon Dean." *Photoplay*, July 1995, 38, 77–78.

Slack, Lyle. "Keanu's Excellent Adventure." *Maclean's*, 23 January 1995, 52–57.

"The Slow Fade." *Crawdaddy*, March 1978, 49–56.

Smith, Liz. "Reeves Weighty Decision." *Los Angeles Times*, 5 June 1996.

Stabiner, Karen. "Tapping the Homosexual Market." *The New York Times*, 2 May 1982, sec. 6, 34, 36, 74, 76, 78, 80–82, 84–85.

"Stars That Won't Dim." *Newsweek*, 18 June 1956, 22.

"The Stigwood Style: Cashing in on Splash." *Business Week*, 24 July 1978, 53–54.

Stoynoff, Natasha, Karen Brailsford, and Kristina Johnson. "A Most Excellent Enigma." *People*, 11 July 1994, 49.

"Supermogul in the Land of Opportunity." *Forbes*, 10 July 1978, 42.

Swaim, Marlene, St. Louis. "Readers Inc." *Photoplay*, January 1957, 8.

Teel, James D. "The Puritans Have Landed." *After Dark*, March 1981, 22–23.

Travers, Peter. "Movies Die Hard on a Bus." *Rolling Stone*, 30 June 1994, 79–80.

Tusher, Bill. "The Girls in James Dean's Life." *TV and Movie Screen*, 1955, 20, 68–69.

Vilanch, Bruce. "Wishful Rumoring." *The Advocate*, 7 March 1995, 67.

Villard, Bob. "Road Warriors." *Cinefantastique* 12 (May-June 1982): 6.

Von Wiedenman, Donald. "NBC to Air 'Portrait' of Dean." *The Advocate*, 25 February 1976, 33, 37–38.

Warren, James. "Bashing Back: Gay and Lesbian Weekly Names Mel Gibson Its Sissy of the Year." *Chicago Tribune*, 25 June 1992, Tempo section, 2.

Warren, Steve. "Van Sant Won't Gussy Up to His Own Private Art." *San Francisco Sentinel*, 10 October 1991, 39.

———. "Private Idaho Goes Public." *San Francisco Sentinel*, 10 October 1991, 38.

"Wedding Bells Aren't in Keanu's Future." *Press-Telegram*, 5 October 1995, People section, A2.

Widem, Allen M. "Film 'Trial' Opens at Loew's Poli; 'Rebel Without a Cause' at Strand." *The Hartford Times*, 2 November 1955, 38.

Wilson, Ara. "Just Add Water: Searching for the Bisexual Politic." *Outlook* 16 (Spring 1992): 22–28.

Wynn, J. C. Review of *Rebel Without a Cause*. *Presbyterian Life*, 26 November 1955, 42.

Yakir, Dan. "Those Gallipoli Boys." *After Dark*, November 1981, 46, 48.

Yant, Monica. "Man Without a Homosexual Face." *Los Angeles Times*, 5 September 1993, Calendar section, 28.

Zissner, William K. "Rebel Without a Cause." *New York Herald Tribune*, 27 October 1955, 19.

Electronic Documents

amethyst. [amethyst@nc5.infi.net]. "Cunanan role offered to Keanu Reeves—your opinions?" 1 August 1997. In [alt.fan.keanu_reeves.moderated]. Retrieved 12 August 1997.

Benza, A. J. "So . . . Hollywood." *Take One*. 6 June 1997. [http://www.roughcut.com.take1/so_Hollywood_97jun1.html]. Retrieved 1 August 1997.

Bgrinc. [bgrinc@ral.mindspring.com]. "Re: Cunanan role offered to Keanu Reeves—your opinions?" 1 August 1997. In [alt.fan.keanu_reeves.moderated]. Retrieved 12 August 1997.

"'Braveheart'—An Exercise in Dishonesty." GLAAD Reports. July/August 1995. [http://www.glaad.org:80/glaad/9507/dishonest-history.html]. Retrieved 14 February 1997.

Francois, Charles B. [cbf@akula.com]. "Re: Hamlet Was Gay." In [rec.arts.movies.current_films]. Retrieved 20 January 1997.

Hunter, Ray. [cobraman@bellsouth.net]. "Re: Keanu's Sexuality." 12 August 1997. In [alt.fan.keanu-reeves]. Retrieved 18 August 1997.

"Is Keanu Gay??" *KeanuNet.* [http://www.users.interport.net/~eperkins.gay.html]. Retrieved 17 January 1996. The current address of the Web site is [http://www.keanunet.com/gay.html].

"Keanumandu." *The Society for Keanu Consciousness.* [http://www.empirenet.com/~rdaeley/skc/keanumandu.html]. Retrieved 21 August 1997.

Kielwasser, Al. "Braveheart." GLAAD *Reports.* July 1995. [http://www.glaad:org80/glaad/9507/braveheart.html]. Retrieved 14 February 1997.

kimbo. [rgreen@juno.com]. "Re: Cunanan role offered to Keanu Reeves—your opinions?" 5 August 1997. In [alt.fan.keanu-reeves.moderated]. Retrieved 12 August 1997.

"Los Angeles 'Braveheart' Demonstration Coverage." GLAAD *Reports.* July–August 1995. [http://www.glaad.org:80/glaad/9507/braveheart-demo.html]. Retrieved 14 February 1997.

Migcovsky, David. [dmigcov@interlog.com]. In [alt.fan.keanu-reeves]. 15 February 1996.

Mysti96501. [mysti96501@aol.com]. "Re: Cunanan role offered to Keanu Reeves—your opinions?" 5 August 1997. In [alt.fan.keanu-reeves.moderated]. Retrieved 12 August 1997.

"Queer Planet Idols." *Queer Planet.* [http://www.webcom.com/austin/QPlanet/entertainment/idols.html]. 21 August 1997.

"Questions and Answers." *The Society for Keanu Consciousness.* [http://www.empirenet.com/~rdaeley/skc/questions.html]. Retrieved 21 August 1997.

Perovic, Larry. "Keanu's Hot Hollywood Adventure." [www.trashfish.com/cr/keanu.txt]. Retrieved 1 August 1997.

[root@nwsbf02.news.aol.com]. "Re: Mel Gibson's Anti-Gay History." In [soc.motss]. 4 February 1996.

Skeen, Michael. [ms007b@uhura.cc.rochester.edu]. "Response to Mel Gibson." In [alt.journalism.gay_press]. 1 April 1996.

"The Society for Keanu Consciousness." *The Society for Keanu Consciousness.* [http://www.empirenet.com/~rdaeley/skc/index.html]. 21 August 1997.

Theron. [theron@pobox.com]. In [alt.fan.keanu-reeves]. 16 February 1996.

———. [theron@pobox.com]. "Re: Keanu's Sexuality." 15 August 1997. In [alt.fan.keanu-reeves]. Retrieved 18 August 1997.

Wockner, Rex. "Mel Gibson's Anti-Gay History." *Cyber Queer* Lounge, ed. Tom Hicks. [http://www.cyberzine.org/html.GLAIDS/Wockner/gibson.html]. Retrieved 26 November 1996.

Michael DeAngelis is Assistant Professor and
Director of the Undergraduate Program in the
School of New Learning at DePaul University.

Library of Congress Cataloging-in-
Publication Data
DeAngelis, Michael.
Gay fandom and crossover stardom : James Dean,
Mel Gibson, and Keanu Reeves.
p. cm.
Includes bibliographical references and index.
ISBN 0-8223-2728-7 (alk. paper)
ISBN 0-8223-2738-4 (pbk. : alk. paper)
1. Motion pictures and gay men.   2. Dean,
James, 1931–1955—Criticism and interpretation.
3. Gibson, Mel—Criticism and interpretation.
4. Reeves, Keanu—Criticism and interpretation.
I. Title.
PN1995.9.H55 D43   2001
791.43'086'642—dc21   2001023153